ANT EGG SOUP

NATACHA DU PONT DE BIE

ANT EGG SOUP
The Adventures of a Food
Tourist in Laos

SCEPTRE

First published in Great Britain in 2004 by Hodder and Stoughton
A division of Hodder Headline

A Sceptre Book

1 3 5 7 9 10 8 6 4 2

A CIP catalogue record for this title is
available from the British Library

Trade Paperback ISBN 0340 83253 3
Hardback ISBN 0340 82567 7

Typeset in Sabon
by Palimpest Book Production Limited, Polmont, Stirlingshire

Printed and bound by
Mackays of Chatham Ltd, Chatham, Kent

Hodder and Stoughton
A division of Hodder Headline
338 Euston Road
London NW1 3BH

To Giles Healy, for bringing me back down to earth with wit and style and for putting up with me and this book with extraordinary tolerance and patience. An enlightened nonconformist, he's a man like no other and I dedicate this book to him with all my love.

I would also like to dedicate it to the memory of Alan Davidson.

A word about Lao recipes

Laotian people have their own individual recipes and cuisine – this book is most definitely not an attempt to write a definitive Lao cookbook. I just happened to be passing by, a tourist with an inquisitive nature and an empty stomach writing down what I enjoyed. The recipes that appear in this book are the ones that I observed Laotians cooking at home or in simple cafés that were, in reality, extensions of the home kitchen. The food was fresh and rural and the recipes bound to a traditional methodology that I found repeated all over the country. I was very struck by the generosity of spirit in which these recipes were given, and I'd like to thank all the wonderful, open-hearted Laotians who helped me collect them along the way.

A note on naming

This book is a true account of my travels in Laos in 2000. However, Laos is a small Communist state with a vigorous gossip system. As a result I have changed some people's names and the places where selected events occurred to protect certain people against a misinterpretation of their views or actions.

A contribution from the profits of this book will be donated to the charity GAPE by the author. The charity does valuable work on a village level, producing and distributing Lao language videos and books on conservation, promoting ethnic issues within local government, implementing non-formal education projects in remote areas, promoting sustainable use of forest foods and initiating many projects to conserve and protect rare wildlife. Donations, however small, will be gratefully received.

The Global Association for People and the Environment (GAPE) is a non-profit non-governmental organisation (NGO) set up in late 1999. Our mission is:

1) to assist people in developing their own potential in an ecologically senstive and socially just manner;
2) to implement and coordinate community development and environmental conservation programmes in various countries worldwide; and
3) to facilitate people-centred learning through supporting community-based education programmes, and an emphasis on ecological issues.

'Assisting people in an environmentally friendly way, protecting the environment in a people friendly way' is GAPE's motto, and it clearly illustrates our philosophy. On the one hand, we are committed to supporting disadvantaged people in non-industrialised countries in ways that improve their lives, but on the other hand, we are well aware that simple charity and short-sighted development that either directly or indirectly leads to environmental degradation and does not consider long-term sustainability issues is unlikely to lead to real quality-of-life advancements for local people. This is especially true in the poorest countries in the world, like Laos, because there it is generally the poorest and most disadvantaged, including ethnic minorities and people living in remote areas, who are the most reliant on a clean and healthy environment for their livelihoods, and who are the most likely to suffer if development is done in a way that leads to ecological degradation and destruction.

At present GAPE is operating the 'Remote Village Education Support Project' in Pathoumphone District, Champasak Province, southern Laos. If you would like to support GAPE's work in Laos, donations would be greatly appreciated. Please also check our website for more information – *www.gapeinternational.org*

Please send donations by cheque or money order to:

The Global Association for People and the Environment (GAPE),
576 Dalmation Drive,
Parksville, B.C.,
Canada, V9P 1Y4

CONTENTS

CHINA

LAO PEOPLE'S DEMOCRATIC REPUBLIC

MYANMAR

Muang Sing

Phongsali
PHONGSALI

HANOI

BOKEO
Houei
Xay

Luang
Nam Tha

Udomxai
Pakmong

Xieng Khoung

UDOMXAI

Muang Noi

Nong Khiaw

•Sam Neua

Packbeng

LUANG
PRABANG

HUA PHAN

Luang
Prabang

Plain of
Jars

XIENG
KHOUNG

Sayboury •

•Kasi

Phonsavan

South
China
Sea

Vang
Vieng

VIENTIANE

SAYBOURY

•Phone
Hong

Paksan

BOLIK-
HAMSAI

VIETNAM

VIENTIANE

THAILAND

Mekong River

Thakhek
KHAMMUAN

Savannakhet •

SAVANNAKHET

Pacific
Ocean

South
China
Sea

SALAVAN
Salavan

SEKONG

Ubon
Ratchathani

Bolaven
Plateau

•Sekong

Indian
Ocean

Pakse
Champasak

Paksong

Attopeu

CHAMPASAK ATTOPEU

Islands

• BANGKOK

CAMBODIA

— — My path
—·—·— National boundaries
– – – Province boundaries
——— Rivers

JMC

INTRODUCTION
How I Became a Food Tourist

I'm not a chef and I'm not a journalist, I'm just a greedy romantic who was transported by an idea and went to discover more. I adore food in every way: looking at it, smelling it, tasting it, reading about it and talking about it. As long as it tastes good I'll tuck into anything from tinned baked beans to saffron-scented sea urchins. I love discovering new tastes and ideas; it fills me with joy and excitement. And I love travelling, so I've combined the two and become a sort of 'food tourist'.

While others are lying comatose on the beach or cycling up mountains revelling in the agony as their lungs become pods of pain, I'll be down at the local market, elbow-deep in produce, grilling people on where to find the best indigenous restaurants and cafés. Like a mad person, I'll get up at six in the morning to photograph exotic fruit displays whilst snacking on local fast-food delights, or watch women walking to market with bowls of live fish on their heads. And I'll trek for hours, and I mean hours (or even days if it's a really good lead), in search of a good lunch.

I started young. I was born in Paris in 1967. It was the gastronomic capital of the world – how could I not be affected? My mother, my sister Rebecca and I lived outside Paris in the village of Mountainville and my first memories are of the kitchen.

I remember sitting in my high chair amidst a whirl of aromas, surveying the chopping of herbs and the steaming pots whilst being fed little titbits to keep me happy, watching impassively as my mother skinned a rabbit and then longing for the lumps of dark chocolate she added to the rabbit casserole. The memory is blurry and vague, but the aromas are fixed potently in my mind. I still have evocative dreams of eating in France, outside in the warm evening shadow, stars just sprinkling the mauve sky, the smell of fresh hay, listening to the waves of chirping cicadas.

My mother is a fantastic, imaginative cook, and having lived in both Italy and France she had received an excellent culinary training as a young woman. When we were growing up she used to test her recipes on us. While other children were fed burgers and tinned spaghetti hoops, we were served Lebanese lemon chicken, sautéed lambs brains or rose-scented compote. Supper was often arranged on fig leaves (we had a tree in our garden), given a weird and wonderful theme or colour coordinated, according to her whim.

In the early seventies we returned to London when my father decided to take a trip around the world with a woman with buck-teeth. My parents became embroiled in a messy divorce and the money flowed in sporadically. Life was always a bit chaotic when it came to making ends meet, which meant my mother had to use her imaginative resources.

She has always been a bit of a faddist. She flings herself whole-heartedly into new ventures with wild enthusiasm because for her, frankly, that's the fun of it. But she's like a flambé. After the first flash of fire she tends to fizzle out a bit. She has had dozens of jobs over the years. There was the chocolate making scheme, which unfortunately took place in the heatwave of 1976 and died a sticky death in the back seat of our car. There was the time she decided that writing a Mills & Boon romantic novel would provide the answer to all our financial worries. She got their starter pack to learn the 'formula', and for a few months buried herself in sheaves of paper at the kitchen table; it was not to be, however: Romeo ended up gay and Juliet joined an ashram. Then there was the natural, home-made cosmetics business, the antique kitchen equipment stall and the stuffed toy debacle, not forgetting the vibrating PVC cushions. The list goes on. But one thing has remained constant throughout her many projects – cooking. The kitchen has always been crammed with piles of cookery books, and she keeps bursting files of recipes just waiting to be whipped up into brilliant volumes of culinary delight.

While we were growing up, whenever my mother could manage it we went abroad to interesting places 'to expand our horizons'. It began with a trip to Marrakesh in 1972; in between my wailing and dancing with the Berber women, I followed the perfumed aromas to the kitchens where the staff fed me with spun honey pastries. I remember the smoky-frankincense scent of the women, the restaurants open to the sky.

Then we went to Asia and I fell into a state of rapt wonderment, stunned by the alien smells, the humidity and the incredible lushness of the vegetation. We were on a rather tight budget and used to steal breakfast rolls and fruit to eat for lunch, but of course we always went out for dinner. In Hong Kong we followed tips from locals and managed to find dozens of tiny, fantastic restaurants hidden in the warren of buildings and unnamed streets. A month later we were in sleepy Bali. There were about three hotels and only one brick building in the capital (the surfers hadn't arrived yet). The landscape was greener than anything I had experienced so far, sparkling with moisture which created little rainbows in unexpected places.

From there we continued to Thailand, where my mother decided she would start a new business importing snakeskin briefcases and belts, so while she went to discuss business with traders, we went off in search of prostitutes and transvestites with methodical determination. We found them in hotel magazines, zoned in on their hot spots and went to look for them like birdwatchers. For some reason we were fascinated by them, particularly the ladyboys. They stood around like exotic birds and we shared their gossip and street snacks. My mother was particularly horrified by this hobby, which we dreamt up all on our own. She finally put a stop to it when (passing by the venereal disease clinic in the car park) we dragged her to the famous basement bar of the M— Hotel, in search of one of our new-found friends. We all stood at the bar for a naïve and awkward five minutes while ladies of the night signed the thumbs up to my mother for bringing such choice white specimens (I was thirteen) to their establishment, and then fled just as the golf ball and snake show was beginning to get under way. 'Never again!' she hissed through her teeth as she dragged us out. Back in England, the snakeskin business never really took off.

As usual the money ran out, and my mother went to work for an Arab businessman as his PA. He lived in a huge suite at the Hilton Hotel while his wife and several children squeezed into a tiny flat near the British Museum. I remember he insisted on eating the same lemon chicken dish for lunch every single day, which his wife cooked in the morning and brought to his office. She introduced us to the joys of Lebanese cooking, which I love still. Tabbouleh, a Lebanese burghul wheat salad made with parsley and mint, is my comfort food; I can eat it by the kilo.

When I was nineteen we made our last big expedition 'as a family' – a marathon trip to India. We ate our way around Rajasthan, Goa, Delhi and Bombay, collecting recipes from street stalls and sampling home cooking with people we met along the way. My mother adores a bit of luxury, though, so we didn't always rough it. We had a system of spending ten days in cheap rooms eating at tiny cafés; then we'd splash out, all squeeze into one room at a fabulous palace hotel and feast in their dining room. On the second day of that tour, Rebecca and I insisted on buying two (dirt cheap) Edwardian green glass chandeliers which we then had to carry everywhere for the next eight weeks. Everyone thought we were crazy. Whether we were trekking through the desert or squirming through the heaving crowds of a wedding procession, those chandeliers came tinkling behind. They bounced along on the roofs of buses, clonked up the muddy stairs of guest houses and teetered on the balconies of palaces as we admired the views.

We had a great time: three women against the world. We travelled widely, and everywhere we went we picked up recipes. For me, as a result, food and place have always been inextricably joined. The smell and taste of food transports me. My most memorable meals have always been, not just about the food, but about where I was and the people I was eating it with. Like that time when I ate fresh lobster with my boyfriend on a cold pebble beach in Norfolk. It was boiled in an old oil drum by a fisherman, who cracked open the shell and handed it to us, hot, with a knob of butter. I was in love and it tasted like ambrosia. Or coming back from a long winter walk in Italy with friends: drinking rough wine and making *pane Toscano*, toast with squashed cannellini beans scented with rosemary and the greenest of green, thick, virgin olive oil while everyone waited, ravenous, around a fire. We devoured it like fiends and it tasted of Tuscan air and earth. A good meal spent with good people revitalises all my senses and invigorates me.

So that's how I became a food tourist. I'm simply following in my mother's footsteps.

A couple of years ago I planned to go to Vietnam purely because I was familiar with the food and was interested in learning more about it. I bought all the South-east Asian guidebooks and, ignoring all the travel information as usual, went straight to the 'Food and Where to Eat' sections. Then something happened to change my destination. I read a sentence in the Lonely Planet guide stating that there was only one book in print on Lao cuisine written in the English language. For someone like me that was just too tempting. Where exactly was Laos? Why had I never heard of Laotian food? I knew absolutely nothing about it, and when I asked around no one else did either. There was a whole cuisine out there that I could discover from scratch.

This was like a food-tourist equivalent of a whodunnit: a real treasure hunt. I had to find out more.

I dashed down to the Books for Cooks bookshop on the trail of the mysterious volume. It took us an hour to trace it. The lone cookbook was called *Traditional Recipes of Laos* and was printed by Prospect Books, a tiny publisher of culinary academia and rare recipes. I placed my order and within a week I had it in my hand, a slim, cream paperback, exquisitely illustrated with delicate pen-and-ink drawings. It was quite a find because it contained the recipes of the late King of Laos's chef, Phia Sing – the recipes of the royal court of Laos!

The book was fascinating. The forward included essays on Lao eating habits, culinary equipment and 'unusual ingredients – illustrated and explained'. The recipes had intriguing titles, like 'Deer prepared as a salad', 'Pickled fish roe cooked in banana leaf packets', and 'Sour wild chicken soup'.

From what I could glean, the staple foods of Laos were 'sticky rice', a form of rice that sticks together and is eaten with the hand; freshwater fish; wild meat from the jungle; and a huge variety of salad vegetables and leaves. Unlike some Thai and Chinese food, the dishes in the book were not swamped with coconut gravy and shiny sauces. Rather, the real flavour of produce was highlighted and refined with the use of fresh herbs, roots and light stocks. It sounded fresh and delicious. I wanted to know more.

As I relayed my excitement to the ladies at Books for Cooks, I discovered the even more exciting news that the owner of Prospect Books was Alan Davidson, the ex-ambassador to Laos. A prodigious academic, he started the publishing company when he retired from the diplomatic service in 1975, initiated the annual Oxford Symposium of Food History and is now considered one of the world's foremost authorities on food and the culture of eating, with a particular specialisation in fish. Recently, he won the prestigious Erasmus Prize for his exceptional contribution to European culture.

I couldn't wait to meet him, but naturally I was a little apprehensive about approaching such an illustrious figure when I knocked on his door in Chelsea a few weeks later. He had just arrived home from his office and greeted me wearing a floral-patterned sun hat and carrying a bright orange patent-plastic shopping bag full of papers. A silver Buddhist medallion glinted at the neckline of his canary-yellow shirt and I noticed he wore a watch on both wrists. Aged about seventy-five, with thick grey hair and an impish expression, my immediate impression was that of an absent-minded professor, but, as I was to discover very quickly, his delightfully eccentric appearance camouflaged a razor-sharp mind. He remembered every word I ever said to him and sometimes he lost patience with my occasionally dreamy approach to life. As I got to know him over the coming months, I was moved by his generosity of spirit and thoughtful kindness towards me, and to this day hold his friendship in deep regard.

We sat down to tea in his living room and, in his distinctive cultured drawl, he began to tell me the extraordinary story behind the book.

The King's chef had handwritten his precious recipes in two small exercise books which, on his deathbed in 1967, he gave to the Crown Prince for safe keeping. In 1974, Alan happened to be chatting to His Royal Highness when he mentioned his difficulty in finding written sources of Lao fish recipes for a book he was writing on fish species, and the story came out. He borrowed the books and photocopied them before giving them back.

This chance encounter with the Prince and the notebooks became an act of preservation. Soon after this conversation, the Communist Party – the Pathet Lao – took over the country, dissolved the monarchy and the original books were lost for ever.

Alan Davidson published a translation of the notebooks in 1981, giving the proceeds to Laotian political refugees fleeing from the country's re-education camps. He thus ensured that the only record ever written of royal Lao cuisine is available today.

I wanted to know more about Lao food and grilled Alan many times in an attempt to find out what made it unique. He was extremely kind and helpful towards me, but, even though he had lived there, written a book cataloguing Lao fish species and edited Phia's recipe book, he would not be drawn into any detail unless I referred specifically to fish. He would skirt around the question in a frustrating manner. As a food academic, he considered it presumptuous for a foreigner to sum up another nation's cuisine. Instead, he encouraged me to go and find out for myself.

Like many people, I knew very little about Laos. I started to read anything I could find on the place, which wasn't much. I discovered that Laos is one of the few one-party Communist states left in the world. It's a landlocked country, squashed in between five others: Thailand, Myanmar (Burma), China, Vietnam and Cambodia. It's a nation with a lot of borders and a turbulent past. Its early history is defined by clan-based *muang* (settlements) that divided and reformed in various incarnations until 1353 when the great king, Fã Ngum, to this day a much celebrated national hero, founded Lan Xan Hom Khao, the land of 'a Million Elephants and a White Parasol', when he united the *muang* in a series of triumphant battles.

The borders of this violently formed nation have contracted rather dramatically since the mid-fourteenth century, but Fã Ngums's lasting legacy was the creation of the nation state now known as Laos and the conversion of the people to Buddhism.

Since the glorious era of Fã Ngum, the country has had a chequered history. Laos has been occupied or attacked by the Vietnamese, Burmese, Siamese, Chinese, French, Japanese and (secretly) the Americans. It's hardly surprising that when the Communists took over in 1975 they closed the country to outsiders for fifteen years.

In contemporary Laos, it is the French and the Americans who have left the most visible legacy, albeit chiefly crumbling architecture and unexploded bombs. By the time the French began to sneak in during the 1880s, the country had been a vassal of Siam for a hundred years. In an empire-building frenzy, France seized territory from Siam and set the present-day borders for the province they named 'Laos' at the Franco–Siamese Treaty of 1907.

Unfortunately, the French saw Laos only as a hinterland whose economic potential was there for plunder. They invested in the country, used Vietnamese labour, and took the profits back to France. It was a policy of exploitation that could never benefit the Laotians in the long term. They did set up an Indigenous Consultative Assembly which included the Laotian elite, but it was a sham – a national government without a treasury, with a foreign-dominated civil service, no army and no communications network. They stayed until 1945 when the Japanese invaded briefly, causing them to flee.

In the same year Laos was declared an Independent State. However, there followed another period of turmoil as the French tried to come back and were kicked out again. Laos struggled to regain its independence, but others had their eye on it as a strategic pawn in the South-east Asian politics of the Indo-China and Vietnam Wars.

As a result, the country split into three political movements: the Communist Pathet Lao, backed by Vietnam; the Royalist movement backed by the military and American aid; and the Neutralist Royal movement led by Prince Savanna Phouma, who tried to mediate between the two. From 1945 to 1974, Laos had four governments and three coalitions, all of which collapsed, with three attempted coups in between. Meanwhile, America was meddling behind the scenes and bombing parts of Laos to oblivion in search of Vietnamese.

In 1975, the Vietnam War ended and the Americans left abruptly, taking their aid with them. The Communist Pathet Lao took over, and on 2 December 1975 the Lao People's Democratic Republic (Lao PDR) was formed.

The next fifteen years saw a period of Stalinist austerity that drove an estimated three hundred and fifty thousand Laotians over the borders. At least thirty thousand people were sent to prison camps for 're-education', including the King, Queen and Crown Prince who died of starvation in a detention cave. Laos lost almost all of its educated and skilled elite, the currency spiralled out of control and the economy nosedived. Eventually, the government was forced to liberalise its policies for foreign investment and privatisation. In 1990 it opened its doors to limited tourism.

Today, Laos is still a desperately poor country, heavily dependent on foreign aid and hampered by an archaic infrastructure. There are no trains, the roads are awful, the aeroplanes lethal, communications terrible and electricity sporadic, to say the least. But after years of near seclusion, Laos has remained unsullied by polluting industrialisation and has not been infiltrated by modern Western culture.

If the country had managed to maintain its unique identity in the face of the rush and clamour of encroaching globalisation, then surely its cuisine had too. I had to go there.

So I found myself sitting on the banks of the Mekong drinking Lao beer with *Traditional Recipes of Laos* wedged into the rucksack at my feet, ready to start my favourite hobby – recipe collecting.

ONE

Distracted by a Three-Legged Chicken

It was low season in Vientiane and the capital reminded me of a windswept ghost town from a fifties cowboy film: low-storey wooden buildings and verandaed shops lining wind-blown streets. The city was in the middle of a massive construction project and everything was covered with beige dust. The roads were terrible, the pavements even worse. Storm drain covers had disintegrated or fallen in leaving ragged paths of snapped concrete; cavernous holes pronged with twisted, rusty metal rods gaped open like mouths waiting to snare the unsuspecting. The hotels were empty and the place was seemingly deserted. Occasionally a lone figure would scuttle into the powdery sunlight, blinking, only to swiftly disappear again. It didn't look very promising.

The first thing I do when I go on a culinary walkabout is ask everyone I meet where the best place to eat is, and, thanks to the recommendation of the man who stamped my passport, I was sitting in one of the best little restaurants in town, Nang Kham Bang, about to lift a forkful of water-buffalo *laap* to my lips.

Laap, the national dish of Laos, breaks every rule of cautious travel eating. Firstly, it is made from raw meat. Secondly, it contains unpasteurised fermented fish. And thirdly, it's a salad.

A couple of hours earlier I had disembarked at Wattay International Airport in Vientiane with trepidation. I was setting out on a tour of a landlocked country with a notoriously difficult mountainous terrain where 80 per cent of the population are subsistence farmers living in remote villages without electricity, phones or even a rudimentary road system in close proximity, and I didn't know a single native resident. But I can't think of a better way to experience a country and its people than through their cuisine, and I had high hopes for Laos.

I'd never been to a one-party Communist state before, and I'd been warned to bring an envelope bulging with passport photos to staple to the reams of forms I would have to fill in to enter the country. I thought we might be frogmarched from the plane by officious uniformed drones to wait for hours in a grim airport office while my background was scrutinised for insurgent capitalist activity on an ancient and bulky computer. Contrary to my expectations, we wandered haphazardly across the tarmac to a small informal room crowded with smiling, laughing people falling over themselves to welcome us, and there was just one badly photocopied carbon-form to fill in with an old biro. A computer would have seemed positively avant-garde. Deng, the man who stamped my passport, was eager to practise his English. I noticed a lunch basket lying tantalisingly by his elbow on the desk, so I got right down to business.

'I am dying to try real local Lao food. Where would you suggest is the best place to eat in Vientiane?' I asked. 'Somewhere where *you* would go and eat, not an expensive hotel.'

He was fine-boned with the slightly protruding eyes of the myopic. They bulged with excitement at my interest in his beloved native cuisine. 'Oh, you want to eat Lao food! It is the best! You lucky, your flight got in early just in time for lunch. What you want to try first? Maybe you want to eat *laap*?'

'Yes.'

He paused and gave me a devilish look, '*Laap* raw?'

'Definitely.' What was I letting myself in for? I was in a country where refrigeration was virtually non-existent.

'Me, I think the best *laap* at Nam Kham Bang. Hey, Phengsy!' He called over to a young woman helping an old lady lift three vast net bags of what looked like chicken feed on to a trolley. 'She my sister, she bring me lunch today.' He glanced at his basket on the desk and yelled. 'This lady want to try raw *laap*. I send her to Kham Bang, what you think?'

Phengsy came over to us. 'Yes, yes, she very good cook.'

'*Saep li li* (very delicious),' agreed the airport porter trundling past with an ostentatiously boxed television destined for some nouveau riche Lao family.

Behind me, an elegant Lao woman joined in: '*Absolument.*' She spoke fluent English with a French accent and wore an expensive silk suit tailored to her plump body. 'Whenever I come to visit my relatives I stop there for old times' sake.' She laughed merrily. 'She's a good friend.'

'Yes, she make food for my cousin's wedding,' added someone else beside me.

'And my cousin's,' said another.

Everyone seemed to know everyone else and I was reminded that Laos has the lowest population density in South-east Asia, just five million people in a country the size of Great Britain. Within moments, the whole passport office was clamorous with people recommending Kham Bang, her cooking and the joys of Lao food. I was in my element – this was better than anything I could have hoped for. I'd only been in the country two minutes and I'd already started a vigorous discussion on the local cuisine. By the time I left the airport half an hour later, I had a notebook bursting with recommended restaurants and cafés all around the country.

Phengsy, a willing translator for the price of a free lunch, offered to take me straight to Kham Bang's as it was her day off, and soon we were sitting at a Formica table in a grubby room decorated with a four-foot-long promotional plastic wristwatch and several photographs of a fat baby boy being admired by cooing relatives. The café may have looked like a greasy spoon, but the modest interior belied a house of culinary delights.

13

So there I was with a forkful of food at my lips that most tourists would not go within fifty feet of; but I have never been one for that kind of lily-livered behaviour.

My first taste of real Lao food, and it was like nothing I had eaten before. It was delicious: fiery hot, with strips of tasty dried buffalo hide, raw steak tangy with lime juice and refreshed with mint. Every mouthful was a sensation of different flavours and it tasted even better when I scooped it into the edible leaves provided beside it. It was served with a light buffalo broth, which I spooned in between bites, and a basket of Lao sticky rice completed the meal. I could have eaten bowls of the stuff.

'Do you think she might show me how to make it? It's fantastic,' I asked, tucking in with vigour.

'Maybe. I ask her for you.'

Phengsy had a broad smile and had completed a BA in Australia. Her father had died in the 'French war', and shortly afterwards her mother had also passed away in an inadequate Lao hospital, leaving her to be brought up by relatives. She had worked hard and managed to gain a scholarship to an Australian University to study engineering, which enabled her to get a job as a road engineer at TEST (the card read Technology Engineering & Strategy). She did a bit of translating on the side for precious American dollars, and she enthused about Kham Bang's food: 'She very good cook. Her *laap* is made in the Vientiane style using only meat and herbs, no aubergine like in Luang Prabang. I see if she here.'

She went into the kitchen at the back of the room while I studied the poster of the airbrushed Martini cocktail on the wall, and returned with Kham Bang.

'*Sabaii dii* (greetings)', she said and put her hands together in a *nop* to welcome me. She had a wavy bob pulled back behind her ears and a beautiful girlish face. She loved what she did and glowed with the rare contentment of it, which was immensely appealing.

She sat down and we conversed with the help of Phengsy. When she spoke her voice was unexpectedly deep and gravelly. She told me she had been cooking there since she was fourteen.

'Yes,' said Phengsy, 'she learnt from her mother. When people have wedding or big party, they call and she brings her food to their house, everyone know she the best.'

Her *laap*, in particular, was legendary and I asked her about it. The name comes from the words *sok laap* which mean 'lucky'. It is a celebratory dish that is made on special occasions such as welcoming a guest or a family party.

'Like you have roast beef on Sunday with all the members of the family.'

Laap is essentially a salad made from raw meat or fish which is cured in lime juice and mixed with chopped herbs and roasted rice powder. Everyone has their own recipe for *laap*, and during my stay I was to eat it raw, cooked, made with deer, duck, just with offal, with and without lime, with galangal, with different herbs, with raw aubergines; the list goes on and on. In England, I have even eaten it with Laotian friends who made it with wild salmon – fabulous. In the past it was, without doubt, a raw dish, but the more modern habit of cooking the meat has caught on in some kitchens in Laos. But the most vital ingredient, according to Kham Bang, is *paa-dek*.

'*Laap* without *paa-dek* is not *laap*!' Kham Bang burst out in English, with a throaty laugh that reverberated around the room.

Paa-dek is a condiment made of highly pungent fermented fish chunks, and it is a national essential in Laos. It is lumpy and opaque, in contrast to the clear liquid fish sauce, *nam pa*. It is made by fermenting raw freshwater fish pieces in salt water with rice dust and rice husks; a few months in an earthenware jar in the hot sun usually does it. Most Westerners baulk at the idea of rotten fish but Laotians find it equally repellent that we eat fermented milk with lines of blue mould in it in the form of cheese; once you think of that analogy you may find it easier to swallow.

Paa-dek is one of the most ancient elements of Lao cooking, originating in a far distant past when the aboriginal people of the area first found a way of preserving the bountiful supply of small fish that swells the rivers of Laos in the rainy season. As I was to discover, when *paa-dek* is used within a dish the heady bouquet retreats and it transforms into an intricate and subtle under-flavour of great sophistication. Used simply with sticky rice it converts a staple grain into a meal; add chilli and one's appetite is stimulated with a zest for more. You can make it into soup, sauce or stew, steam it, grill it and bake it, and each time its metamorphic qualities surprise my palate. It is no wonder that *paa-dek* is so dear to the heart of the Laotians; just half a teaspoon inexplicably lifts a dish from the mundane to the refined.

It is usually kept in a jar outside the house (for obvious odorous reasons) and used in almost every dish. You can buy a Thai version in Asian supermarkets, and it really is essential if you want to cook authentic Lao. If you haven't had *paa-dek* you really haven't tasted true Lao cuisine, though anchovy sauce makes a good alternative if you really can't find it.

Kham Bang got up.

'Oh, she make *laap* with you. Wait five minutes while she prepare and then come,' said Phengsy.

A few minutes later we followed her to the kitchen. It was only eight foot square, and such a clutter of gas stoves, charcoal burners, pots, woks and condiment bottles that I was amazed that she found space to cook. Miraculously, a little area had been cleared around a chopping board. Kham Bang had already chopped the buffalo meat and placed it in a steel bowl beside the board. She began to explain the recipe.

'She say that you must chop the meat with a cleaver or big knife, to make mince. You must not buy all ready or use a blender as the texture will be wrong.' She picked some up in her hands to make the point. It was exceedingly finely chopped.

'This time she will cook it but you can make raw. In Lao many cook depending on the taste of the person.'

Ingredient measurements in Lao recipes are often adapted to the taste of the diner rather than the chef, and I was constantly asked for my own preferences. I found this to be true throughout my travels. If I said I liked chilli, more was used; if I admitted to a fondness for sour flavours I was given lime to squeeze in my soup. A proto-recipe could morph into many things with the addition of the supplementary seasonings added at the table.

Kham Bang took the meat and tossed it in a hot wok with a teaspoon of oil. When it was cooked she emptied it into a bowl, and combined it with some chopped cooked liver, lime juice, a dash of fish sauce and a chopped chilli, and then smelt it.

'The smell of the food in Laos is even more important than the taste. Smell first, taste second,' said Kham Bang.

Next, she lifted the lid from a bowl by her side, took out a small ladle of *nam paa-dek* (the liquid surrounding the fish chunks in *paa-dek*) and wafted it under my nose for the first time. I was amazed. I had expected it to have that faint whiff of bile like that grey fermented shrimp paste so popular in South-east Asia. Instead it smelt like cheese, rich, deep and complex, like that pungent French cheese, Epoisses. I have to admit it takes a bit of getting used to, but I put it in my recipes all the time now and I haven't had any complaints yet.

She poured the liquid on the meat and mixed it around with a heaped tablespoon of roasted rice powder she had prepared earlier. Finally she added a good handful of chopped spring onions (green part only), a tablespoon of sliced fried shallots and a large pinch of sliced water-buffalo hide. Buffalo skin is a delicacy in Laos and it is sold dried in strips in the market. For *laap* it is prepared by soaking it in water until soft, then boiling it until tender and slicing it into paper-thin slices. To finish the dish, Kham Bang tore up some small-leaved, fragrant mint and Asian coriander, mixed them into the salad, tasted it and squeezed on another half-lime, then transferred it on to a plate. She ladled some soup into another bowl from a ten-litre stockpot of bones bubbling behind us, and we all sat down to eat.

'And always serve *laap* with soup – *laap paa* (fish) serve with fish soup; chicken, serve with chicken soup, beef *laap* serve with beef soup.'

It tasted quite different from the raw version I had eaten half an hour earlier. The flavour of the meat was more predominant and the aroma less subtle, but still it was extremely good. We chatted as we ate and I discovered that I had arrived just in time for a huge festival that started the next week.

'The Boun Ok Phansa,' said Phengsy. '*Boun* means "festival". We are celebrating the monks coming out of their three-month retreat.'

The festival coincides with the end of the monsoon season – *phansa* comes from the Pali word *vassa* meaning 'rain', *ok phansa* 'the going out of the rains'. For the last three months the monks had been on retreat within the temples, meditating and studying and unable to travel. In Laos, every unmarried male is expected to become a monk for at least three months of his life (often this stretches to many years), and they usually do this in the Lent season. After the ceremonies they are allowed to roam the country again or go home to their families. The people welcome their return to society with prayers and special gifts of food.

'Gifts of food?'

'Yes, we make food for the monks and give donations to the temple,' she said. 'We start very early make food then dress in our best clothes and carry it to the monks. It start at six-thirty. You can come with me.'

On the day of the festival I woke at four in the morning to the scent of mouth-watering cookery. Like most of the women of Vientiane, the ladies in my guest house were already busy making elaborate dishes for the early morning festival. I'd experienced only dusty torpor since my arrival and was beginning to wonder if anything ever happened in this town. I was ready for some action.

By six, the mist that veiled the streets was lifting. Vientiane was transformed. Crowds of people emerged from nowhere, dressed in gorgeous silks and treasured jewels. They carried elaborately tooled silver bowls of mysterious content which caught the rays of the ascending sun and flashed against the innumerable gilded temples secreted amongst the modern blocks. Glitterball flecks of light danced across the concrete roof tops and the avenues filled with families carrying offerings to the many *wats*.

Wats are Buddhist temple compounds that contain several buildings, the most important of which is the *sim*, an ordination hall that houses the statues of the Buddha. Other buildings within the walls include the *that* or *stupa*, a solid spherical building ascending to a point (to symbolise a furled lotus bud) that contain relics of the Buddha and sometimes of wealthy individuals interred within them; the *haw tai*, the library where religious texts are stored; the *salla long tham*, a covered open-air meeting place; *kuti*, monastic quarters; and the *haw kawng*, a drum tower or open hut used to call monks to prayer.

Previously that morning, the monks had gathered in the *sim* to attend confession. They had asked their superiors to point out the faults and sins they might have committed during Lent and begged for forgiveness. Now the ceremonies involving lay people were beginning, with prayers followed by the acceptance of the five Precepts – to abstain from false speech, sexual misconduct, killing living beings, taking things not given and reject intoxicating substances.

The devotees place offerings in alms bowls, bring a special morning meal to the monks, perform ablutions transferring 'merits' to the dead and listen to readings of the *Jatakas* (lives of Buddha). By doing these things the people gain 'merit' with which they hope to improve their luck and future incarnations.

Gaining merit, as I was to find out, is central to the Lao psyche – the more you care for others (not just monks), the more merit you gain, so acts of kindness and charity are bound into the social fabric of everyday life. Already I had observed the characteristic generosity of the Laotian spirit in the open friendliness of the people and the way everyone fed me with such pleasure and goodwill. The sharing of food is seen as a gesture of courtesy, and friends and even passers-by are invited to join meals in progress. The Laotians say it is their practice to prepare extra dishes for just this sort of chance encounter. Tourists are no exception and are commonly welcomed as one of the family.

I met Phengsy outside Wat Ong Teu Mahawihan (Temple of the Heavenly Buddha). As the official residence of the deputy patriarch of the Lao monastic order it is one of the most important temples in Laos and monks come from all over the country to study Darma Buddhist teachings there. An original sixteenth-century bronze Buddha weighing several tonnes is housed in the *sim*, and I wanted to see it.

The temple had obviously just been restored and painted and it positively glowed with newly gilded carvings. A tent had been erected in the courtyard to cover a row of elderly monks sitting behind a long trestle table. Their wooden begging bowls bound with saffron macramé were lined up in front of them, and before those a row of white trays spray-stencilled with bright flowers which were rapidly filling with gifts: money, biscuits, sweets, fruit, crackers, flowers, balls of sticky rice. By now people were pouring into the *wat* and queuing up in a long line to donate from the silver bowls I had admired earlier. The most impoverished brought their gifts in plastic buckets.

As she donated her biscuits Phengsy explained, 'These dry foods are for prisoners, orphans, the poor and the sick, but the best food is for the ancestors, come see.'

On the columned veranda in front of the *sim*, three bossy women were organising the food displays on twelve round bamboo trays covered with pastel-coloured paper doilies. They almost snatched the bowls from donators and fussed over each tray. I wrote the contents in my notebook:

Ceremonial tray of festival food
1. *a bowl of laap, the national dish*
2. *a bowl of sticky rice, some red grains*
3. *enamel bowl containing a tangerine, a piece of cake in plastic, 2 finger biscuits.*
4. *a bowl of soup with aubergine*
5. *a bowl of pearl semolina, pale green, milky looking*
6. *a bowl of pork and rattan stew*
7. *plate of 7 loose cigarettes*

8. *a bowl of bits of grilled chicken*
9. *a bowl of apple slices*
10. *a plate containing red paper packet of joss sticks, 2 thin yellow candles, two 5000 kip notes wrapped with a piece of squared notepaper (with a prayer hand-written on it) tied with an elastic band and a chain of chrysanthemums*

'You see, there should be ten dishes in each tray, like: soup, *laap*, chilli sauce, meat, vegetable, fish, steamed banana leaf, pickle, sweet dessert, prayers – very traditional.' The last plate contained things symbolic to the spirits of one's ancestors who, according to Phengsy, 'smell the food and then the spirit comes down to earth to bring good luck to you.' The handwritten prayers would be recited later by the monks.

Other tables contained more good things to eat like chicken soup, fried beans, baby bananas and steamed vegetables sprinkled with sesame. Though the foods on each table varied deliciously, they all contained a bowl of *laap*, and alongside each table stood a large woven basket of sticky rice.

'The food must be very good, your best cooking. Then when the spirit of your grandma come down she thinks, how tasty! I must send my granddaughter good luck. Also, if you give good food to the monk today then hopefully it will come back to me one day when I am poor.'

'What happens to the food after the ceremony?'

'Oh, the monks eat it.'

Lucky old monks. I was standing before a feast fit for a king. Cooks all over Laos had put their greatest efforts into these dishes and I wasn't allowed to touch them.

'Come, we pay our respects to the Buddha,' said Phengsy, stepping over the bowls.

Outside the inner sanctum door a young monk was sitting at a low, gold-clothed table with a donation box. He was surrounded by more golden donations wrapped in yellow cellophane and larger items such as daybeds and tiered umbrellas with white tassles. As I passed him he pulled out a video camera and started to film the proceedings. I removed my shoes and went inside to find the sixteenth-century Buddha.

The radiant twenty-foot golden statue shone at the back of the *sim* on a platform of glittering mosaic mirror-tiles. He was sitting in the pose in which the Buddha reached enlightenment (legs crossed, right hand resting on his knee, left hand in his lap, palm upward) with a look of ecstasy and contemplation on his bright bronze face. A fluorescent pink lotus on a five-foot disc of fibre optics spun behind his head, shooting whirls of trippy, multicoloured light from its centre, like something you'd find decorating a rave.

We stayed there, mesmerised by the illuminations, for some time. When we finally tore ourselves away at eight-thirty, all the food had gone. The streets were barren again in the white morning light and the *wats* were filled with rows of the devoted listening to repetitive prayers miked out to loudspeakers across the town. Starving, we went in search of breakfast.

The next day Vientiane was in carnival mode and the air crackled with the thrill of it.

The crowd smelt of coconut hair oil and seemed impossibly youthful. People pushed past me, bent on having a good time. They swarmed out of the side streets to the main road along the river like rice pouring from a cut sack, and then, as if at some secret signal, the mob obediently split in two – the right side going in one direction, the left side in the other – and filtered through strategically placed rows of earnest young volunteers who body-searched every individual to preempt any trouble. I was in a Communist country and this was the day of Boun Souang Heua, the Boat Race Festival.

The boys swaggered past, preening their new Elvis haircuts; the girls held parasols and giggled in groups. Rickety funfair rides made of tin had been unfolded in monastery courtyards and hundreds of makeshift stalls, staked down with umbrellas, had mushroomed in the capital overnight; they sold balloons and cheap imported toys the colour of fruit pastilles. Street traders vied for space with tombola stands offering golden prizes of cooking oil and Plussz Vitamin C tablets; but mostly there were food stalls.

Nearly all of them sold the same thing – bamboo tubes full of sticky rice infused with coconut, and barbecued chicken pieces flattened between split sticks. Naturally, everyone marinated their chicken to their own recipe and sometimes you found a piece of steamed yam buried in your rice; but that was what you ate at festivals. It was fast and easily devoured on the trot, so why deviate? After passing the tenth stall, I could resist no longer and pounced.

It was perfect fast food. The chicken was salty-lemony-sweet and so tasty I tore every last morsel from the bone. But it was the sticky rice that really got my attention. This was not ordinary rice – it smelt heavenly and tasted so fresh, and nutty, and moreish.

Sticky rice is so central to Lao cuisine that it has become a distinguishing attribute of the Lao identity, in contrast to the 'plain' rice eaten by its neighbours, an attribute that has become even more marked for Laotians living in exile. The saying goes, 'Laos – sticky rice. Thailand – steamed rice,' and Laotians are such connoisseurs of their rice that most people can distinguish its age, and even specify where it was cultivated, just by smelling it.

All meals are eaten with sticky rice, which is also known in the West as 'glutinous'. It is not the white, puffy mass of gloop that the name might imply from your memory of Chinese takeaways. Sticky rice is steamed until slightly translucent and each grain sticks to the next while holding its form. It is served from beautifully woven baskets and the Laotians use it to mop up food in the same way as Westerners use bread. The rice is rolled into a ball in the hand and with a pinch of a meat, fish or vegetable dish, it is dipped into chilli or other sauces and eaten.

RICE STEAMER

I realised why everyone was selling the same bamboo tubes (*kao lam*) – they were filled with *kao daw* (new rice, or 'novice' rice, to translate correctly), something I had never tried before.

Novice rice is harvested in October and only a small amount is produced, due to the weather restrictions. It is considered the best. Farmers jealously guard it and keep it for the family, or sell it at this festival. It is very rare to find it in the morning market. The next rice crop is harvested in November/December and is called *kao kang* (middle rice). It smells good and is also prized, but not as greatly as the first batch. Finally, *kao pee* (annual rice) is late growing, and the type most plentiful and easily available at the market. This is used as everyday grain and sold globally. Laotians consider it to have no fragrance. The rice we buy in our supermarkets is like floor sweepings to a Laotian nose.

To make *kao lam*, new rice is soaked in fresh coconut water and stuffed into bamboo tubes. These are then laid on an open fire until the rice has baked in the coconut juices. The burnt outer shell is cut away to leave a tube of the soft inner bamboo skin packed with cooked rice, ready to be sold. You peel away the skin and eat it like a popsicle. I tried several more versions in the interests of quality control and I have to agree with the Laotians that *kao daw* is the best rice in the world. I have never eaten rice as good since and yearn to have it again.

I continued with the surge to the river until I was stopped in my tracks by a smell; it was as complex and ripe as an old cheese. Maybe it was a *paa-dek* vendor?

When I smell something new I have to investigate in the hope that the whiff might lead me to a hidden culinary surprise. I stuffed down my third tube of rice and followed my nose.

The odour emanated from a tent at a funfair within the walls of a temple *wat*. A hand-painted sign written in Lao hung above it and a long queue had formed outside. I could not read the words on the sign but the pictures were clear, even though they looked like they had been painted by a drunk child. Inside that tent lay, not food, but a fire-breathing dragon and a three-legged chicken, and you could see them for 500 kip (5p). I had to join the queue, however long.

After a half-hour wait in the sweltering heat I got inside the small tent and nearly passed out in the steamy fug. Slung from a pole in the ceiling hung a wire cage containing the chicken. It had glossy black and copper feathers and a useless third leg hanging from its bottom. It looked pretty perky considering it was swinging in space, surrounded by sweaty people. The iguana, however, did not look so happy. Tragically, the reptile was tied with an elastic band to the top of the cage. Everyone was prodding it and pulling at its comb, lifting up its tail. It looked at me despondently, and as people touched its head it closed its eyes in resignation. On either side of this heartbreaking duo, hanging from nylon string, were two glass cases. One contained a desiccated turtle and the other, a lizard skeleton in mid-run.

The chicken defecated for the hundredth time, judging from the pile of *guano* behind it, and the acrid smell that had led me to this sorry site almost made me retch, accentuated as it was by the ninety-degree heat bouncing off the tent walls. I made my exit from the chamber of horrors feeling guilty to have been party to a charade of such cruelty.

Outside, the crowd was much wilder now. Hip young studs zoomed between the girls on flimsy mopeds and people flung down their elasticated plastic bags of fluorescent-coloured slushy drinks and danced in the streets to the booming speakers pumping out Lao pop tunes.

The annual boat race is a big event in Laos and thousands of people travel to Vientiane for the celebration and the Buddhist ceremonies that precede it. It is held immediately after the three-month Buddhist Lent period of abstinence. The monks come out of retreat, couples are once again allowed to get married and Laos has a big party. Teams of fifty members compete in wooden longboats, rowing against each other for a prized trophy. Each boat represents a *ban* (a village or borough), and they train all year for the big day. Everyone talks about the boat race with great excitement, and it is commemorated on stamps, money and calendars. I was looking forward to seeing it.

I got to the river to find one canoe half full of lime-green-clad men buffooning around and the crowd walking away from the water to celebrate in earnest in town. No wonder everyone was in such a good mood. I had missed the boat race. Why? Because of a three-legged chicken and a lizard tied up in an elastic band. I felt it was divine retribution.

Disappointed and tired, I decided to go back to my hotel through the multitudinous hoards of merrymakers. I passed the government marquee of military men wearing identical mirrored sunglasses, wove through the girls selling paper lotuses, and nearly lost an eye to a boy holding a boiled egg on a stick. It was so crowded I trod on someone every time I moved. It was hot and almost everyone was drinking lurid, flavoured ice drinks served in a plastic bag with a straw. When they finished them they flung them to the ground, and the straws kept getting into my sandals. I reached my guest house with relief.

The next day Vientiane looked like it had caught a skin disease. The entire town was littered with plastic bags that were almost ethereally thin and pale pink like skin flakes – a vile dandruff shed on the landscape. Once, not so long ago, people wrapped their goods in banana leaves that melted away when they were thrown down in the earth. Old habits die hard and plastic bags waft in tatters all over the pristine landscape of Laos. An army of road sweepers was clearing up the mess.

But the litter couldn't dampen my spirits. I was travelling with a loose plan, based on local advice, within a broad time frame (five months in this case). I wanted to tell everyone about the fabulous cuisine I had just begun to discover. And the new day was already bringing me fresh delights: below the balcony, the breakfast stall holders were wheeling their carts of savoury soups to the morning market, trailed by hungry admirers.

Laotians love to eat. I came across people eating all the time; in fact sometimes it seemed as though they never stopped eating. In this country, food and fun appear inexorably joined, and central to the enormous number of joyous festivities that seemingly take place every day in Lao life. They celebrate life with an appetite that provokes grudging admiration from their neighbours; and it shows in the food. It is fresh, honest and bountifully given. The dishes I had seen so far were unaffected and traditional, yet full of new sensations, aromas and unexpected combinations. I had so much more to explore.

Vandara's Cooked Chicken *Laap*
(cooked pork/ raw fish/cooked fish)

When I make *laap* it is always a big hit. You need a good bunch of mint to really set it off, and you can experiment with your own balance of flavours. Some people remove the liver element, I like lots of lime juice, others like more *paa-dek* or fish sauce – it's up to you.

I've listed a choice of recipes here so you can see how it varies. *Laap* salad looks like chopped mince combined with green herbs served on a bed of lettuce; the Luang Prabang fish *laap* is almost a mousse and is spooned from the dish. In Laos, *laap* is always served with a light soup.

I have given a recipe for sour bamboo fish soup, but you could make your own stock soup depending on the main element used (see stock recipes on p. 326)

Chicken *laap*

For this recipe you must include the tastier dark meat as breast is really too bland and dry. Cook the meat first by lightly grilling or steaming it. Alternatively, use raw meat – it will marinate in the lime juice. You can cut out the liver if you prefer.

675 g (1 ½ lb) chicken meat
4 tablespoons Asian coriander, finely chopped
1 tablespoon spring onion, finely chopped
2 red chillis (optional)
5 cm (2 inch) piece galangal, peeled and finely sliced
3 stalks lemon grass, finely chopped
2 tablespoons fish sauce or *paa-dek* water (see p. 332)
2 tablespoons lime juice (or more to taste)

29

1 banana flower bud, finely sliced, or half a small white
   cabbage (optional)
2 tablespoons roasted rice powder (see p. 331)
225 g (1/2 lb) chicken liver, cooked (optional)
1 large handful mint leaves, roughly torn

Take the chicken meat and slice it up (without lung) into slivers using a heavy knife or cleaver (you can buy cleavers in Asian shops and kitchen stores). Do not use a blender as the meat will tear and go gooey. Cut it up again and again until you have a very fine mince. Put the chopped meat into a large bowl.

Do the same to the cooked lung if you are using it and set aside in another bowl.

Add the finely chopped coriander, spring onion, chillis and galangal to the bowl of minced chicken. Add the lemon grass, fish sauce or *paa-dek* and lime juice and mix to your taste.

Now add the chopped lung, banana flower/cabbage and the rice powder. (If you add these ingredients earlier they soak up all the lime and fish sauce and spoil the dish.)

Mix in the mint, add more lime if you wish and serve with a plate of salad and raw vegetables.

Cooked pork *laap*
Instead of chicken use 900 g (2 lb) of pork haunch or rump, including fat, and lung instead of liver. Cut the pork into 5 cm (2 inch) pieces and gently cook it through in a wok. (Vandara used an electric rice steamer to cook the meat.) Do the same with the lung. Continue as recipe p. 29.

Fish *laap*
Use 675 g (1 1/2 lb) raw wild salmon (farmed is too fatty and will collapse when chopped) or try cooked coley fillet instead. Omit the liver in this recipe. Continue as recipe p. 29.

Khamtoune's Sour Bamboo Fish Soup

In Laos they usually use a sour herb called *som fai/som pon* in bamboo soup, but it is hard to find here so my friend Khamtoune ingeniously adds rhubarb instead.

2 litres (3 $\frac{1}{2}$ pints) water with 2 fish stock cubes
fish heads, tails and bones
2 handfuls pickled bamboo shoots, sliced into 5 cm
    (2 inch) pieces (available in jars at Asian stores)
2 stalks rhubarb, chopped into 2.5 cm (1 inch) pieces
1 handful lemon basil
3 spring onions, green tops only

Before you start making the *laap*, get the fish stock simmering with the fish heads, tails and bones for about 20 minutes so that it is reduced to a fuller flavour. Remove the bones and pick off any cooked fish and return it to the stock. Set aside about four ladles of this fish stock in a separate bowl to cool for use in the *laap*.

Keep the soup at a simmer and add the pickled bamboo. Cook for another 5 minutes and then add the rhubarb. When the rhubarb has softened, add the lemon basil and the spring onion tops. Serve immediately with the *laap*.

Festival Barbecued Chicken

6 poussins, flattened spatchcock style
4 teaspoons brown caster sugar
4 tablespoons fish sauce
4 large cloves garlic, peeled

3 stalks lemon grass, sliced finely

1 bird's-eye chilli (optional)

1 tablespoon vegetable oil

8–10 tablespoons light soy sauce, or 6 tablespoons dark
soy mixed with 2 tablespoons water

Dissolve the sugar in the fish sauce by stirring vigorously.

Pound the garlic, lemon grass and chilli in a pestle and mortar for about 5 minutes until smoothish (add a little of the fish sauce/sugar if it is too dry to pound). Mix in the fish/sugar liquid and the oil. Rub all over the chicken, getting into every crevice. Leave for 1–6 hours.

Meanwhile, put the light soy sauce in a bowl. When ready to barbecue, place the chicken in the soy sauce and slop it around. Add more if there is not enough to bathe it thoroughly.

Barbecue on a charcoal grill or under an oven grill. The result is extremely tasty. Serve one poussin per guest with sticky rice, chilli *jaew* (p. 104) and *soop pak* (seasonal mixed greens – p. 196).

TWO

MULBERRY LEAF TEMPURA

Mr Thannongsi Sorangkhoun lifted his mournful eyes up to the heavens.

'When I think, I think first in Bulgarian.'

He was wearing a pressed, checked shirt and American chinos and held himself regally, as is correct for a proprietor of a large mulberry farm. He was about fifty with a mop of dyed matt-black hair and deep smile lines canaliculated over his face. He had grand philanthropic ideas and was responsible for the welfare of many people. It showed in the anxiousness in his eyes.

'But here nobody speaks Bulgarian, I cannot talk it to anyone. I miss it so much . . .' He trailed off, sighing heavily. Then a thought flashed across his face.

'Can you speak Bulgarian?'

'Er . . . no, I'm afraid I can't.'

Early that morning I had caught the bus from Vientiane to Vang Vieng on the recommendation of Somsanouk Mixay, the editor of the Vientiane *Times*, a weekly government newspaper printed in English. He enthused about mulberry leaf tea, the latest health craze in Vientiane, and suggested I visit his friend who owned an idyllic organic mulberry farm on the way to Luang Prabang. Intrigued, I took up the invitation.

As I left the capital, construction machines had blocked the traffic and our bus had had to detour past fissures and cavities. I noticed a car that had turned a corner and disappeared down into a void: six soldiers were pulling it out. This made me a little nervous, as did the metre-long cracks on both front window-panes of our vehicle. You never knew what sort of bus would turn up in Laos. Sometimes it would be an ancient lorry or pickup truck; at other times an enormous coach, like a juggernaut, would ease itself into the bus station crushing a thousand tin cans in its path; or you might be pleasantly surprised and find yourself being pushed on to a reconditioned minibus with tinted windows and padded seats. This one, at least, had solid sides to cushion the blows if we rolled off the road.

Luckily the journey was quick and smooth and I was dumped in the dust by a decaying sign that read 'Suanmone Phoudindaeng (Red Earth Hill Mulberry Garden) Organic Farm – Wwoofs welcome.' What were Wwoofs? I staggered down the track with my bag.

It was almost dark when I found the farmhouse buried in the bushes, but Mr Thannongsi Sorangkhoun (known locally as Mr T.) must have seen me coming because he stepped out of the shrubbery to welcome me, followed by a brown and white spotted mongrel whose head was far too big for its body and whose face seemed to grin at you.

Now we were sitting at a round concrete table underneath the stilts of the house and it was all feeling rather surreal.

'Bulgarian is a beautiful language,' he continued, looking through me. 'I miss the poetry . . . the music.'

The Bulgarian connection had me gripped. He turned out to be quadrilingual: he spoke Bulgarian, Lao, French and English, in that order. By chance, he'd been catapulted out of his normal life by the peculiar conditions of the 'American (Vietnam) War' and had spent his formative years being educated in the Eastern European Communist block.

'I went for eight years to Bulgaria, when I was twelve. The government sent us outside the country to avoid the US bombing. My parents were farmers from this area and we were five children. We had no future if we didn't move to big town and get education. We had no money. Our Communist friends help us to study. I was lucky. I was chosen to study abroad.'

Eight years in Bulgaria. I don't know why I was so surprised – the Americans shot out of Laos, taking their aid with them, as soon as the country was no longer of any strategic use in the Vietnam conflict. Russia and its allies filled the void.

As I travelled through Laos, I came across people who had been to agricultural college in Uzbekistan, done teacher training in Gdańsk or learnt fish farming techniques in the Ukraine. They had long since returned home but all of them had in common a wistful air of exotic remembrances past.

'It must have been such a culture shock to leave your village and go to a city in Europe.'

He giggled. 'Oh yes, but we don't have choice. It was the best our Leader could do for us in the situation. I was living in school in the week and adopted by a Bulgarian family on the weekends. After one or two months I speak Bulgarian because nobody speak Lao.' He laughed cheerily and then added with pride, 'I go to the University of Sofia and get a BA in Biology. Then when I came back in 1970 I had to learn to speak Lao again as I had very few words.' He looked down at the table, a little embarrassed.

'I worked with the Pathet Lao in the Liberation in Sam Neua [the headquarters of the Communist offensive] for five year. Then after the Liberation I was an officer for the Department of Forestry, then six year ago I moved back here to start my own organic mulberry farm to make silk.'

'Why the mulberry leaf tea, then?' I asked.

'I have to find other ways to make money. Maybe, we will open a restaurant next year and build some bungalows by the river. But it is silk that we want to make. I started the farm because I wanted to revive the silk industry in my area. It is important to me because, before, when I was young, our mother made money for us to go to school by making one metre a day

35

of silk material. Vang Vieng used to be famous for its silk. But since I come here and plant mulberry tree we haven't made enough money.'

He fiddled with his fingers fretfully.

'We only have two hectares [20,000 square metres], I need more trees, I'm trying to make a collective with the local farmers and I'm working with the school, we train the children and they grow trees too.'

His face had become even more furrowed but suddenly lit up.

'Ah, here is my wife, Koo. She is working very hard on getting good silk quality.'

Koo wore a tight, white headscarf and had a handsome, compassionate face. Though she didn't say a word, her gracious look conveyed 'Welcome' as strongly as if she had said it out loud. She sat down with a bottle and some glasses.

While we had been talking there had been a few new arrivals. A couple of girls were bustling about at the back of the house where a cooker stood attached to a five-foot-high gas cylinder. Several people milled about in between the comforting mess of concrete tables, looms, tin cans of flowers, buckets, silkworm paraphernalia, farm implements, dogs, puppies, turkeys and chickens. The Sorangkhouns' daughter and her school friend skittered in and out of the house and a number of locals stopped in curiosity on their way back from the river down the lane. At one table a French-Canadian couple from Quebec sat reading the required travellers' paperbacks *The Alchemist* and *An Introduction to Buddhism*. They were the 'wwoofs' I'd seen on the sign. WWOOF, I discovered, stood for 'Willing Workers On Organic Farms', a scheme started in Australia which links organic farms to backpackers who want to learn about a culture by working within it. They're employed on the farm for six hours a day in return for free food and accommodation. These two were very laid-back and in their early twenties, both in washed-out black clothes. He had a full beard and sported a cowboy hat; she wore beads.

'Yes, and now the tea become famous,' he continued, 'more and more people drink it. You see tomorrow, Natacha, we pick the leaves for tea every morning at six-thirty, then dry and hand roll, all organic.' He yawned. 'But now we eat.'

Koo had brought us a flask of home-made mulberry wine. She poured us two glasses and slipped away to the cooker. The wine was deep red and heady, sweet like sherry but with a tang. It went down very easily.

'Mmm, this wine is fantastic,' I said, finishing mine a little too quickly.

'Go on, go on,' encouraged Mr T., pouring me another large glass, 'it's good for you. We make everything from mulberry – silk, tea, liqueur; you can use on your skin for eczema. All organic! Like the wine!' He laughed.

Mr T. beckoned to the others and poured wine lavishly into everyone's glasses as they came and sat at the table. 'Everyone likes it. I teach local people how to make. Also from other fruit, fallen from trees, costs less than beer.'

'How do you make it?'

'Well, it very simple. We collect the berries, crush them and put them in a big glass jar,' he said merrily. We were tossing it back by now.

'Then add sugar. Three part berry to one part sugar. Add water a little. Leave closed for two weeks but covered with a cloth so air can get in but insects can't. After that time filter out berry through a cloth and squeeze. Take mulberry juice and add more sugar to how much you like. Then I let it bubble, filter again and put in clay jar with grass stopper. Leave for two months, quiet. Then you can drink,' he added, draining his glass with a grin.

Koo returned with a tantalising plate of dark battered things. 'What's that?' I asked.

'Mulberry leaf tempura!' he exclaimed.

They looked gorgeous. Bottle-green and spade-shaped with a raggedy edge, the leaves were encased in a glistening, diaphanous jacket of batter. We pounced on them while Koo looked on, laughing. They were crisp, salty and delicious. I can't say that that I remember a distinct flavour of mulberry leaf, but the texture and lightness of the snack beat potato crisps any day. We got through three huge platters of them, and since my visit I believe they have become a famous delicacy in the area.

'Wow, I love these mulberry leaves, the batter is fabulous,' I said as the Canadian boy pinched the last one before I could reach it. 'How do you make it?'

He translated my question to his wife in Lao and she left the table with a funny look on her face. A moment later she returned with a glowing yellow box of 'Hime Brand Tempura Batter Mix – ingredients: wheat flour, corn starch, sodium bicarbonate, sodium acid pyro-phosphate, burnt alum, egg yolk powder'.

So much for home cooking. My images of hand-beaten rice flour and whipped country eggs flew into the night. Koo explained through her husband that the secret was to use iced water in the batter mix and that she would, of course, usually make her own but had run out of flour. They did taste good, though, even with the sodium acid pyro-phosphate. Maybe it was the wine, which continued to flow.

We finished the mulberry wine and so moved on to his star fruit variety – slightly cloudy yellow, very fruity, more like a juice; and then the pineapple. It was almost fizzy, but strangely it had no smell, though it tasted like those cubed sweets I bought as a child.

Our light supper consisted of pumpkin soup flavoured with fresh coconut milk, a French-influenced Lao salad and sticky rice. Everyone became very jovial and even though we were talking in three languages, English, French and Lao, we all seemed to understand each other perfectly. Whenever I travel, I read as much as I can about my destination beforehand so I waste less time eating bad food. I take relevant travel books with me and I *always* carry a phrase book. I'm a terrible linguist, but I try to learn even a few words of the local language or dialect, even if I do usually end up with phrase book in hand, gesticulating insanely. I've had many intimate conversations that way, and in Laos I did fine.

Over the soup, Mr T. told me that he was a member of PADETC, an environmental fair trade organisation that aimed to improve communities' self-sufficiency.

At the farm they helped train adults in practical silkworm rearing and organic farming. They were involved in developmental programmes at the local school and promoted Lao culture throughout the region. There seemed to be an endless stream of schemes in the pipeline from training documentaries to eco-trekking and a plan to produce children's story books aimed at popularising the mulberry tree.

However, though the PADETC scheme is registered with the Department of Education it is not a government organisation. Their literature proclaims that they run a programme designed to promote the idea that people should 'have more say in the state-controlled media – TV, radio and newspapers . . . to train government officials on objective reporting, interviewing and presentation without taking any side for the audience . . .' This was old-style socialism at the grass roots level; people helping each other equally for the good of the community as a whole. Over the next few days I met dozens of people who had been assisted by Mr T.

Koo was just as active. The teenage girl, who I'd assumed was their daughter, was an orphan they'd taken in three years before. In fact, over the years they'd brought up twenty (twenty!) orphans as well as their own daughter, who now had children of her own.

'Oh yes, but my wife she is most charitable,' he said, looking at her affectionately. 'One day I come home and she took two orphans without my knowledge. Another time, when my daughter was born, she found a child in the village whose mother had no milk, so she shared her milk with our first daughter and the girls grew up together like sisters.' He put his arm around his foster daughter.

'I just bought her a bicycle so she can go to school faster,' he added.

Even the grinning dog had been rescued. She'd been left behind by some French backpackers who'd realised they couldn't take her over the border to Thailand.

I had arrived at night and kept them up, but we'd had a wonderful evening and I was so pleased that I had decided to stay a few days. I'd never been to a place where everyone seemed so joyful. When I lay on the hard, platform bed that night, my sides ached from laughing so much.

There was mosquito netting on the window, but I noticed, with foreboding, a mosquito flying about my head. I began to make my usual elaborate precautions: spray, portable net, long-sleeved top, cotton trousers, etc. Whenever I go abroad, mosquitoes for miles around break open the champagne and invite all their friends around for a party on me. They like me so much that if I'm with other people, they don't get bitten at all. I can spray on enough DEET repellent to punch a hole in the ozone layer, but still they come, and to make things worse, my bites become huge purple welts that itch maddeningly and unrelentingly for four whole days. I am mosquito nectar.

For extra security I gave my body another drenching of a new, natural repellent I'd found in the market, 'No Mos!', and then realised it contained eucalyptus oil. It felt like I'd just rubbed hot chilli all over my body, so I lay in the dark, miserably waiting for the burning/freezing to subside, and then fell into heavy sleep. I woke in the night and went downstairs to the bathroom with my torch.

I shouldn't have done it. In the morning the tops of my thighs looked like pink bubblewrap. I awoke to find twenty-three bites just below my left buttock and seventeen below my right. It's an area of skin that's easy to miss. They must have feasted as I squatted to pee. That and the fruit wine hangover made me feel a little delicate as I got up at six to watch the mulberry leaves being picked. The cockerels were particularly piercing.

The Canadians were already there when I came down the ladder. They waved hello, got up slowly and pottered off to work.

Under the proud eye of Mr T., I went out into clear sunshine to inspect the tea picking.

'The leaves have to be collected from young trees in the early morning so that they are fresh. This is the best time,' he explained.

The trees looked more like bushes, as their stems were still so thin and bendy. They are pruned twice a year to keep them at a manageable size and last for about fifteen years of production. We followed three girls in their early teens who languidly collected a few leaves from each plant and placed them in a basket before moving on down the row. In the distance, the Canadian boy was not very hard at work doing something very slowly to the mulberry bushes.

We followed the girls for about five minutes.

'You see! All organic! We make compost from weeds and kitchen waste, we even make pesticide from mulberry! We mix leaf with water and a little sugar and it ferments, the liquid makes pesticide and we spray it on the leaves. We can also use it as fertilizer liquid.' His enthusiasm was infectious. 'Let's go and have some tea!' And he bounced off down the grove.

We returned to the house where four plastic-covered tables had been placed next to two portable wood-burning stoves. The Canadian girl was ineptly painting the name of the farm in wobbly writing on a new sign. Mr T. disappeared and returned with a state-of-the-art Bodum clear glass infusion teapot. He poured the pale green tea and watched me closely as I drank it. It was very mild, slightly astringent, with an aniseed aftertaste.

'It is very good for you,' he beamed, handing me a leaflet.

Mulberry leaf tea, it seemed, had miraculous qualities. The leaflet read:

1. It prevents diabetes
2. It reduces cholesterol in the blood
3. It reduces high blood pressure
4. It helps lose weight
5. It reduces asthmatic conditions
6. It rejuvenates your strength
7. It prevents brittleness of the bones due to its high calcium content
8. It contains vitamin A to improve your eyesight
9. It contains vitamin B_1 and B_2
10. It has all the needed 18 amino acids
11. It has low caffeine – only 0.01%
12. It helps prevent cancer.

When I got back to London I looked it up and found that it contains GABA (gamma-aminobutyric acid) which helps control blood pressure and has even shown positive results in patients suffering from depression and premenstrual syndrome. Other ingredients include phytosterol, which reduces cholesterol in the bloodstream, and Deoxynomycin, which balances high or low blood sugar problems. Considering heart disease and diabetes seem to be the fastest growing health problems in the West, not to mention the endless new forms of depression like SAD syndrome, a cup every morning may well be the next craze in Europe.

The girls were back and had begun sorting out their newly picked leaves, rinsing them in a bucket of water and then stacking them into neat piles according to size. The mulberry leaves were larger than the ones we'd eaten the night before, about the dimension of my hand outstretched. One girl would take a bunch of them, still glossy from the morning dew, rinse them in a bucket and then cut out the pale central vein of each one with a big knife. She then chopped the leaves into strips and pushed them along the table to her friend. The strips were blanched for a second in a wok of scalding water before being scooped out with a bamboo strainer and dumped in another bucket of cold water.

'We wash in cold water to keep the tea green,' explained Mr T.

The third girl then took a few handfuls, rolled them between her palms and threw them in a dry, shallow wok placed on a stove on her left. They had to be stirred and rolled constantly for forty minutes to an hour, until completely dry. It was a long process.

The tea wasn't actually rolled on the naked thighs of virgins but I felt as though it might as well have been.

It takes six to eight kilos of leaves to make one kilo of tea and the girls were at it all day long, bright-eyed and chatty. As night fell, they stuffed the tea into hundreds of little transparent bags, twisting the tops into cellophane flowers with Oriental precision. They finished at nine and had produced two kilos. In a good month they produce twenty-five kilos. I shipped some home and it never ceases to amaze me how much work goes into a cup as I drink it.

Mr T. is looking for markets abroad to export the tea to, but it's hard. He is a lone cultivator on a tiny farm in the wilds of a small country with no infrastructure. He may be passionate about his organic produce, but with his limited resources it is almost impossible to advertise and sell it overseas, let alone get it 'certified' organic. Over the following months I met several organic food producers with the same problem.

I hung around for a few days living the good life and then borrowed a bicycle to ride into Vang Vieng and visit the famous caves in the vicinity. Koo packed a basket of sticky rice and bananas for me to fend off the hunger pangs until I returned for supper.

I'd heard a lot about Vang Vieng and had been avoiding it because it had become renowned as a backpacker drug centre. In the last two years the number of guest houses in this tiny town had grown from three to thirty-five to cater for the new arrivals. On the way to the farm the bus had stopped there and my first impressions had not been good. It was overrun with tourists sitting at cafés eating processed cheese pancakes and drinking banana shakes.

A thin American girl was sitting on her bag at the bus station, enthusiastically explaining the joys of the town to newcomers.

'Wow! It's great here. I'm doing a drug tour of South-east Asia. Cambodia, Thailand, Vietnam, but Laos is the best!' She looked very young in her dusty T-shirt and grubby sarong. 'We wanted to try opium, man, and it's awesome. I just zoned out, ended up spending *every* evening in an opium den. Just awesome. But this place has had it! You know, too many tourists. We're off to Muang Sing now.' Her face was full of the ecstasy of it. 'There they sell weed for fifty cents a bag!'

I was repeatedly told the place had been 'ruined' by the very people who were ruining it. I estimated that there were at least fifty foreigners there that day, the majority looking for drugs, with more arriving every hour. Since 1999, tourism in the town has increased by 100 per cent each year. It certainly brings in the cash – the place has been transformed from a tiny backwater in to a town full of shiny new concrete houses.

I shot through on my bike and aimed towards the river and the caves beyond.

When I reached the bank, I joined a group of three fit-looking trekkers, Karl, Max and Greta. They were waiting for the canoe to ferry them across. I told them I was going to Phoukham cave to see a reclining Buddha. Mr T. had recommended it as the best and I suggested they visit it, but they were very sniffy and had their own agenda.

'Why don't we share the boat?'

They looked at each other with sour faces. 'What, with your bicycle?'

'Yes, they'll just lay it across, it'll be fine.'

'I think it's dangerous.'

The water was only about four foot deep. I would have carried the bike across but it was a bit too heavy to lift above my head.

'I think you need your own boat,' she said abrasively.

'Fine,' I said, turning away with annoyance.

So I waited until the boat arrived; watched them haggle over the fare (the price of a second-class stamp), and gazed at the boat as it floated off, deposited them on the other bank, and then came back for me. At last, I set off alone along the bone-bouncing track.

It was an overcast day but bright enough for sunglasses. After half a mile I had to stop – I had never seen a landscape like this before. The countryside before me was flat and vivid green, covered with new rice fields and bisected by brilliant-red earth tracks. The knee-high rice stalks were still tender, and they undulated in shimmering ripples in the wind. Behind the verdant fields lay dark green jungle, bursting and spurting with creepers that were entangled in the trees and bushes and bearded every branch. A few wisps of smoke rose mysteriously from the inner depths.

But it was the monolithic karst mountains that were really striking, searing out of the smooth landscape, scattered like forgotten tombstones. The word 'karst' refers to a terrain formed on carbonate limestone where the groundwater has dissolved the rock to form caves and sinkholes. Colossal obelisks of blackened limestone thrust vigorously out of the ground, dark and masculine. They inspired awe and menace.

They were magnificent.

These karst formations were shaggy between the black crevices and some were so high that their peaks were obscured by cloud. I got back on my bike and rode on for another five kilometres, following obscure signs which I hoped were leading me in the right direction. Hundreds of yellow dragonflies followed me, dancing and skitting above my head. I hadn't seen another soul on my journey so far.

At last I reached a lone bamboo kiosk a hundred yards away from the jutting karst. It was starting to drizzle. Two six-year-old girls, one wearing a *sin* skirt as a dress, the other in a T-shirt emblazoned 'Prozac', gave me a ticket for 3,000 kip (the price of the *Evening Standard*). They followed me as I wheeled my bike over a wobbly log laid across an opaque blue pond, and pointed upwards.

Far in the distance, high up the searing, jagged rock face, was a little black hole – the entrance to Phoukham cave. Gritting my teeth, I started my ascent. This was not a journey for the old and infirm or even the slightly unfit. The path cut between sharp, eroded limestone at what seemed like a ninety-degree angle. The rain was heavier now, and where it wasn't pointy it was slippy. Being naturally clumsy I was a little afraid, but the views were spectacular and I loved it.

The unspoilt natural landscape of Laos is one of the most exceptional things about the country. In England we have this irritating habit of labelling and sanitising our natural sites. You can't walk through a forest without bumping into a wooden stake painted with a red arrow to 'guide' you, or visit a ruin without tripping over a poster showing how it would have looked in 100 BC, badly drawn Romans and all. If the Phoukham cave had been in Devon, it would have had properly cut and gritted steps leading to it, with a metal handrail. There would have been plenty of signs bleating about the dangers of the climb and advising those with a weak heart to take the alternative chairlift. I felt lucky to be risking my life on this unblemished rock.

After two hundred metres I reached the cave and clambered in, wet with rain and sweat. Inside, it opened out into a grotto the size of the Royal Opera House, lit with shafts of light from a big, inaccessible opening lower down. I was totally alone in the dripping cavern and it felt a little eerie.

Far below me, on a protruding flat rock, lay the golden reclining Buddha. The life-size statue slept on a gilt bed covered with a canopy held up with four red-ribboned poles. A few yards away a fifteen-foot-high stalagmite rose from the ground like a huge penis. I went down to investigate.

The big penis had been left unadorned, but the shrine was covered in ropes of floral offerings and sticks of incense. The Buddha reclined with his head in one hand, his almond eyes half open and serene. It no longer felt eerie, dwarfed as I was by the chasm. Instead I felt protected and secure like I'd reached a sanctuary. I lay down on a nearby rock and spent the next hour meditating upon the feeling in total peace, whilst eating my fragrant rice and bananas. Then some noisy people arrived and I left.

The sun had come out and so had the tourists. The climb down was really perilous so I reached the bottom with relief, red-faced and shattered. The pool looked very inviting. A number of Laotian teenagers had appeared and were diving off a tree that hung high over the water. They swam fully clothed, leaping off the branch with abandon.

I stripped off my sweaty attire to reveal my swimsuit, tied my sarong around my chest and dived in. The water was delicious and the teenagers were delighted when I joined in their diving competition. We swam about and swung from a rope hanging from a branch. Whenever I stopped swimming, foot-long fish wiggled up from the depths and kissed my toes. It was heavenly. I got out as discreetly as possible but the two food-shack ladies kept pointing to my rice-pudding whiteness, exclaiming with awe '*Ngaam, ngaam* (Beautiful, beautiful)'.

'How ironic,' I thought, looking down at my lumpen, waxen body as I struggled to cover myself with my wet sarong. They, on the other hand, were absolutely stunning and would have claimed gasps of admiration on any European street.

In Laos, fair skin is seen as the pinnacle of beauty and as I practically glow in the dark (in fact I do on moonlit nights) I got a lot of compliments. Even my florid face was seen as attractive, and was often compared to an apple. It was never going to go to my head as the people around me were so obviously so much more beautiful that it just seemed ridiculous.

I got back on my bicycle, mosquito bites itching. About halfway back I bumped into the people who wouldn't let me put my bike on their boat. They were covered from head to foot in mud.

They stopped me and whined, 'How much further is Phoukham cave?'

'God, what happened to you?' I asked.

'We went to the first cave and had to crawl, not on our knees and hands,' said Karl with wide eyes, 'but on our stomachs!'

'Through a tiny hole. And it was very dark,' added Greta miserably.

They looked bedraggled. I enticed them to carry on with tempting stories of my swim and cycled on.

Before I crossed the river again I decided to take a rest and took a last look back. In the late afternoon, the black wall of limestone karst, deep purple and bruised, rose up behind the quickly shadowing fields, smoky cloud obscuring the furthest away in a pale blue mist. The river bank was frilly with ruffles of wild bamboo and banana plants dripping with moisture.

I sat on a log washed up on the shore and got my book out. The water was shallow at this point, slowed by the sun-bleached shingle which created a natural basin; beyond, islands of rocks with grassy bushes sprouted in the swifter flow. A fisherman was using one of the islands as a base from which to cast his nets.

Several other people were already there. An old woman was washing, wearing her looped *sin* skirt, scrubbing every bit of her body with frothless washing powder. In Laos, washing powder is cheap and made in China. It comes in chains of six-inch-square plastic packets so you can buy an ounce at a time, has hardly any fragrance and doubtful cleansing ability, but villagers use it as body soap, shampoo and clothes cleaner. This lady was taking particular care over her elbows.

I lost interest in my book and watched a young family arrive on a tractor which they parked in the river – father in orange towel, mother in black bra and *sinn*, four-year-old boy wearing red wellies with 'Tweenies' (they're bloody everywhere, I thought) scrawled on the side, and a fat baby clinging to her brother's tatty shorts. They all got out to help lower an empty oil drum into the water. My Day-Glo white skin and red hair pulled the usual straggly following of leaping kids, who gathered around me shouting, '*Falang, falang!*'

Falang is the Lao word for any non-Asian person and it is not considered a derogatory term. It probably derives from the French colonial period – a corruption of '*français*' which was mispronounced '*falangsais*' and then shortened to '*falang*'. As a tourist you are still an unusual phenomenon in Laos (particularly in the rural areas), so people will shout '*falang!*' to get your attention, or groups of kids will scream '*falang!*' around the village to whip up a crowd to come and see you. Sometimes, from miles away, you hear a little peeping '*falang*' as a little dot of a child has spied you from afar.

These kids were particularly amazed at the number of words in the book lying beside me. One little girl with droopy eyes and a ponytail came and sat next to me in a T-shirt that was so old it was almost transparent. She told me her name was Santovan and stared at me, mesmerised. While their mothers beat clothes in the gravel, the children played and splashed about, boys passed by with bundles of sticks and teenagers filled petrol cans with the night water supply. Santovan learnt my name and danced about me singing it.

Dusk was falling when everyone stopped what they were doing for a moment to look to the south-west. In the remote distance I saw an ominous black mass hovering over the river. It seemed to wheel and arc in the air and sometimes bits would curl off, only to join up again somewhere else.

Something was swarming.

As I watched, it got bigger and bigger and then started to flow into the jungle on the other side. The odd thing was that no one seemed very concerned about it; everyone was smiling and getting on with their business. After much persistent miming I discovered that the dark cloud was made up of fruit bats going out for their supper. There must have been millions, making wonderful patterns in the twilight. I gaped at them for a full five minutes before they disappeared.

Darkness was enveloping the landscape. The tractor family were driving back up the path, following their precariously wobbly water drum. Santovan turned out to belong to the fisherman, who waded across to us with a net full of fish. I took the fake hibiscus flower out of my hair and gave it to her as a leaving present. She made a little noise of shock and widened her eyes, then skipped to her father to show him. He beamed at me, then scooped her up in his arms and carried her off by piggyback.

A wonderful sense of well-being settled upon me as I contemplated the tranquillity of this place after the dust of Vientiane. Tomorrow I would travel to the dreamily named city of Luang Prabang, renowned as the gastronomic capital of Laos. It was here that Phia Sing had cooked meals for the King in the Royal Palace, and I'd been led to believe his traditional dishes were still the everyday fare among the people of the town.

I wheeled my bike back to the mulberry plantation in the twilight with a growing sense of excitement. The house, buried in the tight green groves, glowed invitingly in the darkness and the night air smelt of sweet sap.

Organic Café Mulberry Leaf Tempura, plus some other vegetables

Since I visited the Mulberry farm, Mr T. has opened a restaurant, 'The Organic Café', at his house (his daughter has opened another one in Vang Vieng village), and their mulberry leaf tempura and healthy Lao recipes have become famous in the area.

You cannot say that tempura is truly Lao, but Laotian people often eat battered vegetables, bananas and yam as snacks so I'm putting a recipe in. You need a wok or deep pan to fry them in and the batter adheres better to the vegetables if you dry them well in a paper towel to remove excess moisture. The water must be cold; I use fizzy water to give a lighter batter.

20 young mulberry leaves
10 long beans
10 carrot slices
10 pumpkin slices cut into long pieces
10 small asparagus spears
10 long slices fresh tofu
other vegetables to your liking
500 ml (1 pint) vegetable oil

TEMPURA PASTE FOR FRYING.
1 egg
100 ml (4 fl. oz) coconut milk
100 ml (4 fl. oz) ice-cold water (fizzy if you prefer)
150 g (6 oz) wheat flour
1 teaspoon salt
soy sauce and chilli sauce for dipping

Just before serving, beat the egg thoroughly in a bowl, add the coconut milk and the iced water and sift in the flour and salt. Stir gently, then dip the pieces of vegetable one at a time into the batter and fry in hot oil – 180ºC (350ºF) – until lightly browned. Remove with a slotted spoon on to paper towels to drain any excess oil. Then place on a platter and serve instantly to your guests with dipping bowls of soy and chilli sauce.

Pumpkin Soup

4 shallots, seared black then peeled and roughtly sliced
450 g (1 lb) pumpkin, peeled, deseeded and sliced into
   thin wedges
400 ml ($^{3}/_{4}$ pint) chicken stock
400 ml ($^{3}/_{4}$ pint) fresh coconut milk, or 1 tin coconut milk
$^{1}/_{2}$ teaspoon salt
2 dessertspoons fish sauce
black pepper
4 spring onions, green part only, chopped

Skewer the shallots and sear them on an open flame until they are blackened all over, peel them and slice them roughly. (I like to leave part of the blackened skin on to flavour the soup but you can remove it all if you wish.) Peel and deseed the pumpkin and then slice into wedges about $^{1}/_{2}$ cm ($^{1}/_{4}$ inch) thick.

Meanwhile, bring the chicken stock to the boil. Add the pumpkin and shallots. Bring back to a low simmer and add the coconut milk and salt. Simmer until the pumpkin is tender (but not sloppy), which should take about 10 minutes.

Stir in the fish sauce and black pepper to taste and serve with the chopped spring onion sprinkled on top.

THREE

THE ENCHANTMENT OF LUANG PRABANG

Even with a hangover, everything they say about the enchant-
ment of Luang Prabang is true. The gauzy tranquillity of the
place puts a languid drift into your step and causes you to forget
to breathe. As the silvery haze that envelops the town softens
your vision, a diaphanous cloak of dreamy carelessness descends
upon you, and you just have to give in to it.

Encircled by mountains and embraced by a serpentine loop of
water, this sacred city of kings seems to levitate on a cloud of
vapour in the dawn light. The river gleams, smooth and silver,
reflecting the gilded curlicues of the temples and the crumbling
colonnades of antique French villas. Lush palms line the river
bank, and the wooden balustrades of the Lao houses are
entwined with flowers.

Legend has it that the site was originally chosen for settlement because the land was so remarkably beautiful. The myth
tells of two hermit sorcerers, Russi Tong and Russi Tava, who
were wandering along the Mekong when they came upon a
wondrous area of land at the junction of the Mekong and Nam
Khan rivers. The whole place was enveloped in millions of
flame trees with bright red flowers, giving the land an astonish-
ingly lovely appearance. Enchanted by this spectacle the two
sorcerers conjured up the fifteen *nagas* (local water snake spirits), disguised as dignitaries, to create a new city that they
named Sieng Dong, Sieng Tong (flaming city beside the River
Tong).

The day before, I had arrived in Luang Prabang in the late evening as darkness fell. I was staying at the Vanvisa guest house, a small place owned by Madame Vandara, an entrepreneurial Laotian lady whose fame as a fabulous cook had led me to her. However, the evening I arrived she was out of town so I unwisely spent my first night at her guest house testing copious amounts of the local rice liquor, *lao-lao*. This really was unwise, as *lao-lao* is generally made in home-made stills and the alcohol content can be anything from 25 per cent to 90 per cent proof (usually nearer the latter). It is the national drink and it is brought out at *any* excuse for celebration, the idea being to slug it back in shot glasses until you are defiantly drunk. Since you never know how strong it is, this is not difficult. If you're offered *lao-lao*, it is rude to refuse.

I awoke with a truly terrifying hangover, dying of thirst and hardly able to see from the pain in my head. I lay in bed for a few minutes, horribly mesmerised by the khaki ceiling fan whirring above me, and then wrapped a sarong around my naked body and staggered downstairs in search of water. I lurched into the dining room by mistake and came face to face with the whole of Vandara's family and guests sitting formally at breakfast with horrified expressions on their faces. I froze and they burst out laughing.

Vandara got up from the table, smiling brightly. She was in her forties, with sweet elfin looks, bright eyes and a habit of wrinkling up her nose when she didn't like something. She was immaculately dressed in a crisp, white blouse and traditional woven skirt, with a Hermès-style scarf and a navy handbag to match.

'Come, come, sit down. You must be Natacha. Come and have some breakfast.' She had a natural relaxed charm and I liked her immediately.

Like many Laotians who remained after the revolution, Vandara was a true Communist who still proudly believed in the village-socialism of her youth, but nowadays lived with a little profit on the side. She had spent her childhood travelling around the country with her supply teacher parents, avoiding the bombs, and then became a teacher herself. When the government took the desperate measure of opening up to free enterprise and tourism, Vandara grabbed the opportunity and started her guest house. She soon became known for making traditional meals for the guests, which is how I discovered her.

She ushered me into the main room, which was a welcoming clutter of weighty carved furniture crammed between piles of magazines, antique textiles, musical instruments and a curious collection of moth-eaten stuffed animals. The enormous dining table reflected the confusion, spread as it was with a jumble of native foods and French colonial throwbacks – pots of coffee, sweet condensed milk, plates of bananas, rice balls, green tea, last-night's-leftover-greens, little baguettes, honey, chilli sauce, sticky rice in baskets, butter and Vandara's home-made papaya jam.

The French didn't leave much behind them of any practical use (a railway system would have been handy, or even a few good roads), but they did leave a legacy of patisseries and pretty buildings. When I first arrived in the capital Vientiane, I was surprised to find French bistros and street vendors selling pâté baguettes and croissants on every other corner. Even Lao restaurants sold steak, potato *'frites'* and onion soup, but it was French food with a Laotian twist. The pâté is made from wild forest deer, the steak is eaten almost raw and pounded with fish sauce, and baguettes are filled with chilli ketchup and raw carrot.

I mentally thanked France for introducing the hearty Lao coffee as I slugged it back against my hangover and slammed myself awake by eating volcanically hot chilli sauce.

After breakfast I felt a little more human, and we got on to the subject of food. Vandara knew of Phia Sing's cookery book and was thrilled to look at my copy; she was also fascinated by my

English reference books on South-east Asian plants, fish and vegetables. We went through them page by page, clarifying the names in our respective languages, discussing their flavours, uses and nutritional merit.

'Oh yes, and in Luang Prabang we are lucky, everything is natural, unlike your country.' She knew all about GM crops and mad cow disease, and reviled the modern production methods that are tampering with our natural foods. As well as being an expert cook, Vandara had done a degree in chemistry and avidly read science magazines.

'It's terrible.' She wrinkled her nose in distaste at the thought. 'Here in Laos almost all food is naturally organic, but I worry, it is not for long. Organic, it taste better, try this "water morning glory", you see.'

She took a forkful of greens from the bowl on the table and fed some to me.

'What you think?'

The plant has pointed leaves and long jointed stalks that stay firm when cooked.

'Delicious.' It tasted like young spinach tips with the added crunch of the stems.

'Full of iron and vitamin A. I steam this time, but you can eat the shoots raw.'

She popped some into her mouth.

'Tomorrow, we go to market and you see how big and beautiful everything is. You stay here Natacha – you will get healthy.'

The next morning I felt full of energy.

I had read in a guidebook that Lao markets started at five in the morning and were completely over by eight, so I dutifully set my alarm and was walking by the river by five-thirty. The roads were swathed in mist and empty except for a few monks sweeping the dust from the temple grounds with grass brooms. I was walking through the wonderful anachronism that is

Luang Prabang. War, poverty and an extreme isolationist government policy have saved it from the rush of modernisation and it is deemed so unspoilt that UNESCO has now designated the entire town as a world heritage site.

I dipped into the back streets towards the market and found myself in an elegant residential district of winding lanes, coconut groves and duck ponds. I was right in the middle of town but it felt like a village. Luang Prabang is in fact split up into several *bans*, the word for 'village' – districts based on exactly that, a village with a headman in control of each one.

In this area the houses were an odd assortment of colonial, Lao and modern styles. Dilapidated French stucco villas with grandiose entrances, arcades and sweeping stairways stood beside Lao-French houses built in the traditional stilted style but with tiled roofs and wide blue-shuttered windows; French-Lao buildings with indigenous fretwork below the roof gables to let in a free flow of air nestled next to modern concrete structures clad in crazy paving and sporting the latest satellite dish.

UNESCO is just in time to save the old buildings and restrict the construction of new ones, but while tourists like myself dote on the crumbling architecture, most Laotians dream of new concrete houses with modern conveniences. Who can blame them? Given a choice between living in subsiding ruins or simple homes of wood and woven bamboo, who wouldn't want the Lao equivalent of a Barratt home? Only later do they find that their hastily built concrete box is damp and cold in the wet season, and corrugated iron roofs deafen you in a monsoon shower. By then they have no choice left as the cost of building a new timber house has become prohibitively expensive due to the international demand for tropical hardwoods.

I wandered around, crossing wobbly boards laid over storm ditches and pausing to breathe in the scent of cooking rice mixed with incense. The house were built amongst verdant, flowered knolls pecked by ducks and chickens, lotus-covered ponds and thickets of dancing bamboo. It was such a peaceful place I gave myself up to it and just floated along to the distant rhythm of temple chanting.

The city gradually awoke. Some people were obviously very wealthy: the blare of the ubiquitous satellite television began to squeak through the shutters, and rare, fancy 4x4 cars stood proudly outside the doorways of crumbling mansions. Many of the grand decaying houses I was passing had once belonged (and I suppose still do) to members of the immense royal family who fled or 'disappeared' after the Revolution. Once, the whole of the Upper Peninsula was reserved for royalty and aristocracy. Now there was a new hierarchy here, people who put their glittering trucks before the renovation of their historic houses.

At length I arrived at the market to find it deserted. I was too early, as usual.

Every town and village in Laos has a daily market that begins gradually at first light (about six-thirty). Sometimes this consists of a handful of old stalls selling three cabbages, a few bunches of soft, boiled peanuts and a couple of still radiant songbirds shot at daybreak. Others, like this one, are huge: a pungent, steaming, seething mass.

Big markets are usually divided into three parts: a covered abattoir, run by women wildly hacking up water buffalo and surrounded by piles of steaming livers and other offal; a covered dry goods market with hot-food vendors jostling for space with rice sellers and stalls overflowing with shampoo and biscuits; and an outside or partially covered area, where fresh produce is laid out on bags or tables.

I waited, and as the darkness lifted I could see people coming from the hills around with bundles on their heads. A tannoy started up, playing tinny music intermingled with the morning news, and soon it was buzzing. Women arrived, unfolded a bit of sacking on a trestle table and spread out their goods in symmetrical piles arranged to arrest you in mid stride: flat bean pods with a delicate gradation from darkest jade through chartreuse to palest green; tiny aubergines the size of peas; hollow bamboo stuffed with straw at each end to trap the savoured grubs inside; heaps of cabbages and lettuces picked that morning; dishes of curries to be popped in a little plastic bag and taken away; rats? cats? and God-knows-what barbecued to the point of incineration on sticks; tomatoes whose heady aroma hit you at ten paces; plucked chickens in cellophane bags; steamed rice wrapped in banana leaf rolls; bitter jungle flowers that taste good steamed; bowls of live fish, squirming; pyramids of big, pappy apples; hillocks of tiny water shrimp; stacks of rough, home-made cigarettes and cigars; mounds of cassava cakes dried as a snack; live frogs sold in bunches with their legs sewn to clusters of twigs; weird and unidentifiable mushrooms; stalls of maze, chillies, wild watercress, sweet potatoes, nuts, oranges, green papaya, bananas, tamarind, garlic, ginger, lemon grass, spring onions, mint, coriander, basil, purple beans, eggs, bean curd, crabs, quails, turnips, cucumbers . . .

PLUCKED CHICKENS STUFFED INTO PLASTIC BAGS

I'd arranged to meet Vandara for a tour and spotted her in the butchery area. I negotiated my way through, occasionally being splatted by blood as women wielded their cleavers with vigour. The tables were divided into different types of meat, and some people simply specialised in offal. One trestle was just stomachs and livers, the one next to it a mountain of pig feet, and the next furry black lungs slung casually over each other like a pile of coats at a party. Vandara was selecting a chicken from a row of plucked specimens whose feet were sticking up in the air for inspection. Chickens in Laos run wild and free and seem to have developed extraordinarily large feet and thunder-thighs as a consequence. Vandara grabbed a really big pair, as Laotians think they're the best part of the bird.

'Ah, Natacha, *Sabaii dii.*'

We moved on, but I stopped Vandara when I noticed a stall selling little hillocks of white grubs on shiny green leaves.

'What are those?' I asked Vandara, moving closer.

'Red ant larvae.'

They were laid out in neat piles like discarded Egyptian sarcophagi. They were an opaque white and looked like dainty alabaster carvings of their adult siblings. Laotians love them for their taste and they're an important source of protein and fat for tribal people. I supposed that someone must have dug them out of the ground and then spent hours picking over them to remove the sand and grit. I said as much to Vandara.

'Oh no!' she exclaimed, laughing at my idiocy, 'they're very clean, they build their nests in trees. They make a ball of leaves, hang it from a branch and live inside.'

'How do you eat them?'

'Usually we make ant egg soup, or sometimes omelettes. They taste good.' She rummaged around in the little snowy mounds, picking a few up with her thumb and forefinger and smelling them. 'Paah! These are old!'

There were lots of dead ants curled up in desiccated balls between them. She dropped them and swept off, to my great disappointment. I'd never thought of eating ant eggs, let alone making an omelette with them.

I'll try anything as long as it is edible. Anything, that is, except big, fat beetles. I have a phobia about their horrid, juicy abdomens (the best bit, apparently) which stems from my irrational loathing of the underneath parts of cockroaches. Turn a cockroach over in my presence and I'll leave the room. I don't know where this came from, but it's very bothersome as I have to deal with cockroaches constantly when I'm travelling.

These were not fat beetles, and I was intrigued to know what ant eggs tasted like. I skulked behind, scanning the market to see if there were any more stalls selling them, but there were none to be seen.

We walked through the dry goods area passing thousands of little things wrapped in tiny plastic bags (to be thrown on the ground later) and out into the sunshine of the vegetable market. I'd already had a good trawl through when I'd arrived, but it was an education to look again with Vandara at my side. She was right – the produce was exemplary, enough to make even the top French provincial vegetable market look tired and inadequate.

Outside, some women had just arrived and were selling vivid green knots of limp wet weed with threadlike strands as fine as mermaid hair. This was the famous river algae of Luang Prabang. It is gathered from the rocks when the river is low in the dry season and has even more miraculous qualities than Mr T.'s mulberry tea. It is supposedly one of the most nutritious foods for its weight in the world, and it was for this reason that the obscure Lao delicacy found itself launched into space and orbiting the earth as a tasty meal for Soviet astronauts. Why swallow pills when this is so delicious and it has all the nutrition you need in one small and almost weightless portion?

Laotians make it into a crisp fried snack, *kai pen* (algae sheets), served in the form of paper-thin green squares to be dipped in chilli sauce and eaten with drinks. In this form it looks a bit like the Japanese seaweed, *nori*, but that always leaves a metallic taste in my mouth. This has a much milder spinach flavour and salty tanginess. I couldn't eat enough of it.

Laotians make *kai pen* using a similar method to handmade paper. The algae is gathered, washed and combed to rid it of impurities and sand, and then dipped in tamarind juice which sticks it together. The strands are laid side by side on a framed woven bamboo mat, like those they use to make paper, and then beaten down flat. This results in a sheet of green algae, on to which are then scattered razor-thin slices of spring onions, galangal, tomatoes, garlic and a sprinkling of sesame seeds, until the finished article looks like a Jackson Pollock painting. They are left to dry in the sun and two hours later are ready to fry or grill. (Now, with the wonders of the Internet, you can order this by post at a reasonable price – see suppliers on p. 335).

THE FAMOUS RIVER ALGAE OF LUANG PRABANG

We parted company for the day, but, as I was leaving, Vandara rushed back to me clutching a piece of wood.

'You see this. This is special wood. Called *sa-khan*.'

It didn't look very impressive, just a bit of old stick, but it turned out to be the woody stem of a small forest vine, *piper boehmeriaefolium*.

'We use this to make the *or lam* stew, special to Luang Prabang. Tonight, we go to my friend, Mrs Khanthaly Misaiphon's restaurant. You try.'

The Pak Houay Mixay Restaurant lay in a quiet street off the Mekong River road and was shaded by trees strung with coloured fairy lights. Paper stars swung in the breeze above a picket-fenced veranda enclosing a few check-clothed tables scattered amongst pots of lavish flowers. As we entered the gate I noticed a sink had been plumbed to the inside of the fence, with soap and a towel hanging beside it – this was a good sign.

As much of Lao food is eaten with the hands – balled-up sticky rice taken with a pinch of food – Laotians always wash their hands before and after they eat. If you want to eat genuine Lao food in a restaurant, look for a bowl of water on a stand by the door (or a plumbed basin in more wealthy establishments). Another useful sign to look for is a group of Communist officials having a party. There is a great deal of bureaucracy in Laos, which means lots of department administrators travelling around the country. These important people need to eat; and when being formally entertained in the evening, they tend to eschew French and Chinese restaurants for the comfort of reasonably priced proper home cooking, a celebratory dish of *laap*, and, of course, lots of *lao-lao*.

There was a group of fifteen of these officials inside, already drunk, so I felt even more reassured that this was going to be good. Several of them were blocking the doorway, admiring a four-foot fish tank with 'DO NOT TOUCH' written in English in marker pen on the glass. It was crammed full with one large and torpid ornamental fish. The fish swam forward two inches in the space available to it, then turned around, straightened up and swam two inches the other way, round and round. I saw these fish all over the place, white and uninteresting looking. They were supposed to be 'lucky and come from the Amazon'. It didn't look very lucky to me.

We found a table on the veranda and were joined by the owner, Mrs Misaiphon. Bejewelled, and with a white badger-stripe in her hair, she had a big laugh and a crunchy voice, and she laid her expensive patent leather handbag on the table like a trophy. She had once run a successful jewellery store, but gave it to her sister when she got bored sitting in the shop all day. Her family thought she was mad to start a restaurant in her middle age, but now that it was so successful they all worked for her in rotation.

Beers arrived and Mrs Misaiphon gave an almost imperceptible sign to one of her nephew waiters, at which her crew snapped to attention. A Lucullan feast of Luang Prabang specialities began to arrive at the table – river weed soup, *laap*, Luang Prabang chicken stew, beef *or lam* stew, watercress salad, venison sausages, *jaew bong* (buffalo skin chilli sauce) and the usual complement of sticky rice. In Laos, the whole menu is presented at the same time so you can appreciate all the variety at one glance. In this way you can eat what you like, in whatever quantity you prefer, whenever you choose. From the Asian point of view, a Western meal where food is served to you dictatorially one dish at a time must seem very strange. You are supposed to finish everything on your plate even if you don't like it, and you have no idea what is coming next, not to mention the added inconvenience that you're not allowed to burp or eat with your hands and everyone rudely talks while they're eating. The Lao way seems positively libertarian by comparison.

Everything was delicious, but I particularly liked the chicken stew, which was flavoured with seared aubergines and dill, and, like many Lao dishes I tried, tasted smoky. Laotians often sear their ingredients before they cook or pound them, and it gives a distinctive flavour that was a new and exciting revelation to me. The *or lam* was like nothing I had eaten before as the special wood gave it a distinctive spicy tang. The watercress salad was also interesting as the cress was crisp and fiery with small round leaves, a special variety unique to the area, and made with an egg-based dressing that had its origins in the French occupation. All the dishes were representative of Luang Prabang-style cooking, as found in Phia Sing's book; the people of this province are very proud of their particular cuisine.

While we ate, I quizzed Vandara and her friend on the differences between Luang Prabang style and the rest of the food of the Laos.

'It small thing, the way we chop, or use ingredients,' said Vandara.

'*Laap paa* (fish *laap*) in Luang Prabang,' added Mrs Misaiphon, 'here we make like soft, we pound and beat, not chop like in country style.'

'And *or lam*, I never had outside Luang Prabang, it is special to here. They make different in Vientiane, different type of *or*.' *Or* means 'to braise' and refers to a type of slow-cooked stew.

'In fact, I don't think they make *or lam* outside Laos,' said Mrs Misaiphon, picking up a ball of rice daintily from the basket beside her.

'And Luang Prabang food is different, better and more special. We are very fussy, we use only the best thing or we don't bother. In Vientiane, people, they just throw things in, whatever they have. We never do that in Luang Prabang, we must have the right ingredients before we start cooking. Phia Sing's book is Luang Prabang style but royal, very traditional,' said Vandara. 'In Luang Prabang we like to keep our long-established recipes.'

'Yes, still many old recipe the same we use now,' replied Mrs Misaiphon, at which point they both went off into a lively discussion in Lao about which dishes were still used and what was in them, totally forgetting that I could only snatch tantalising phrases from the conversation. Finally, after what seemed like an age, I managed to get them to stop and translate what they had been saying for the last ten minutes.

The translation: 'We prepare fresh, depend on season, it tastes good.' Vandara shrugged her shoulders.

Mrs Misaiphon saw my face and sympathised. 'You come and see,' she said, getting up and beckoning me to follow.

I didn't have to be asked twice. We passed the depressed fish and went down some treacherous stairs to her kitchen. It was in the backyard and looked like it had been built by an insane person in a hurry. Four wildly haphazard brick walls defying gravity were holding up a domed corrugated iron roof open at both ends. The room was lined with a crazy collection of cupboards, plank shelves and cookers ranging from electric rice steamers and clay wood-burning stoves to gas cookers, wok burners and a small convection oven. It was chaotic but scrupulously clean.

Five people were preparing food very fast around a twelve-foot table covered in rose-patterned sticky-back plastic. At its centre stood a score of ceramic bowls full of prechopped ingredients – peeled garlic cloves, yellow and green bird's-eye chillies, lemon grass, onions, shallots, tomatoes, mint, coriander, various basils, dill, ginger, galangal, spring onion, lotus root, fine-chopped beans, spring onions, Chinese chives, banana bud, roasted rice, some large, spongy-looking flowers, and many other unidentifiable things I was dying to examine.

'We use plants from the forest,' explained Mrs Misaiphon, 'like the *sa-khan* wood for *or lam*. You taste.' She fished a sliver of wood from the stew bubbling behind her and I tried it. It was strange and spicy. The taste was faintly metallic with a mere trace of clove. It made the inside of my mouth tingle and zing.

'You see, refreshing, isn't it? Now you know what the jungle tastes like.' She laughed heartily. 'Now drink some water, you be surprise!'

I drank as requested. The plain water suddenly tasted of lemon. I was surprised and said as much. It really was a unique flavour.

'*Ahan Lao!* (Lao food),' she said proudly. 'You see. It taste different, different smell. Difficult to explain as it comes from experience. I have to teach you.'

For some time I watched her relatives fly around the kitchen making food under her expert eye before I remembered Vandara sitting alone upstairs.

I left reluctantly, but, as promised, the next day Mrs Misaiphon showed me how to make the Luang Prabang chicken stew I liked so much. She told me, 'For you this does not have rare ingredients. You can make at home easy with fish or with chicken, of course it will not be real Luang Prabang but good too.' And it is easy. I make it often.

Luang Prabang is not just the gastronomic capital of Laos, it is also a city of temples. Wherever you walk, there is a fine *wat* on hand in which to stroll dreamily – there are thirty-two to choose from. Many are elaborately stencilled with gold designs on a red or black background (three religious colours that secular buildings were barred from displaying) or decorated with mirror mosaic murals depicting religious stories. The temples are breathtakingly beautiful and make the major contribution to the ethereal feel of the place.

I visited nearly all the *wats* of Luang Prabang, but it was only when I climbed the three hundred and thirty-eight steps to the top of the sacred Mount Phusi in the centre of the town that I noticed the ones on the other side of the Mekong. I hired a canoe to get to them.

It would be difficult to find a fairer prospect than the view across the river from Wat Long Khoun. Luang Prabang is still dominated by the luminous gold stupa, That Chom Si, which stands like a beacon atop Mount Phusi. In the past a watchman stood and marked out the Laotian *gnam* hours with a drum from this point. A *gnam* was an ancient term for time based on the sun and the stars that is still used for ceremonial purposes. Most curiously, the Laotian day was divided into sixteen named *gnams* (watches) of one and a half hours each, starting with *tut-tang* – 6 a.m. to 7.30 a.m. For some reason it had never occurred to me that other cultures might split up their day into different segmentations; but why not?

The vista has hardly changed since Delaporte, an adventurous French naval officer, stood here and sketched it a hundred and thirty-five years ago. Beneath the hill the town nuzzles in the palms, embraced by a necklace of sapphire-blue mountains. The red tiled roofs peep between the fronds that frame the river bank, and the canoes idle by on the great Mekong as they have done for centuries.

This was the temple where the kings of Luang Prabang went into retreat for three days and nights before their coronation. From here the future king had a perfect view of the town he was to rule and spent this time in meditation on the responsibilities ahead; Wat Long Khoun (Temple of the Blessed Chant) was originally built in the eighteenth century, extended in the 1930s and then restored and conserved by a joint French–Lao project in 1995 at the cost of 500,000 francs (about 70,000 euros).

I turned from the view to the *wat*'s airy courtyard surrounded by a scatter of squat, timber-framed stucco buildings in pristine condition that looked more like cottages than spiritual houses. Their expert restoration added to the feeling that I had stepped back in time.

Then, from nowhere, a small boy appeared and introduced himself to me.

' *Sabaii dii* (hello). My name is Nam, where you going?'

He wore a Motorhead T-shirt, and while one hand twirled a small machete, the other was permanently held out for kip.

'I guide you, kip, kip.' He looked about nine.

He raced up to the exquisite *sim* hall ahead of me and started to weave between the columns, swinging himself around them with one hand.

I dodged past him to the doorway, which was set back behind a covered portico of six pillars intricately decorated with golden rosettes, with a ceiling strewn with weird animal stencils: monkeys carrying other monkeys, bats, mythical birds, cranes and tigers. The templates of these stencils are sacred, and these were the loveliest I had yet seen.

More remarkable, however, were the life-sized murals of two mustachioed Chinese warriors standing guard on either side of the door. Faded and softened with time, they wore odd costumes of bowler-hat-shaped headgear, bows around the neck and heavily padded green jackets, one of which was slashed and ruched in the Elizabethan style. Both were holding pieces of paper or cloth, and beside each was a painted oval seal filled with Chinese characters. They are said to be representations of the Ho (or Haw) bandits from southern China who pillaged Luang Prabang in 1887, but considering that they caused the King to flee and the French to gain a foothold as 'protectors' of the beleaguered town, it seems an eccentric mural to paint on your temple doorway.

Inside, the paintings of Buddha's life on the surrounding walls were delightful, including picnics by Lao waterfalls and monks sitting around on clouds. Some were risqué – naked women lying about playing music, others ferocious, depicting men in a shipwreck being devoured by fish with big teeth, their blood spurting.

The *wat* also contained a rare *gouti* (meditation hall) – a hundred-foot-long corridor, walled and roofed, for walking meditation. Inside, it was cool and lit by pale green light reflected from the luminosity of the leaves outside the minia-ture windows. I went inside and walked awhile in the footsteps of the kings.

Nam soon had me out of my reverie, however, with demands to show me 'the cave temple'. We walked a few hundred yards and I gave him some cash to let me in.

Wat Tham is a limestone cave, with stairs and balustrades cut from the stone, leading into a deep black hole. It is filled with defunct Buddha statues: broken, rotten and singed by fire. The images are still believed to be potent, so they can't just be thrown away. Instead they are placed here and venerated annually at New Year. There were lots of them: headless, armless, legless and faceless, but strangely compelling. This was the antithesis of the famous Buddha-stuffed Pak Ou caves I'd visited downriver, and as I edged my way in alone with my torch, I preferred this place. A sanctuary for old and broken Buddhas; one felt protec-tive of them, these casualties of calamity.

It would have been perfect except that Nam was waiting impatiently at the entrance, clanging his machete against the wall. As I left he sprang at me for more kip. I gave him a bit extra and told him to go *away*. I wanted to investigate the abandoned villa below the cave on my own. I'd noticed it from the other side, but no one seemed to know who it belonged to.

The house was built in the French colonial-Lao style, white stucco with wide shuttered windows and a two-tiered roof design borrowed from Lao temple architecture. It was still intact outside, but the interior was in a shocking state. I nosed around fantasising about owning it. Wherever I go there always seems to be some romantic wreck in need of urgent restoration that calls my name.

Nam was back again, sniffing loudly and following my every step, leaping to look more closely if I even twitched towards my notebook.

'Where you coming from? Where you going?' he kept asking again and again. And I kept answering in the hope he would leave me alone. He started prodding an indigo butterfly out of the rafters with a big stick. I looked out of one of the rotting picture windows across the Mekong to lovely Luang Prabang and, much to Nam's amusement, fell through the floor. It was time to go.

I couldn't leave Luang Prabang, however, without seeing the Royal Palace where Phia Sing cooked all those delicious meals for the royal family. Now defunct in this Communist state, the palace has become the National Museum – a great, low spread of a building with lots of tiled roofs and an impressive doorway. Built in 1904 by the French colonial administration in the *beaux arts* style with Lao details, it was seen as a symbol of the promised (but never realised) modernisation of Laos by the new protectorate. It replaced a timber, and no doubt more beautiful, building that was demolished to make way for it.

When the Communists took over in 1975, the seventy-year-old King Savang Vatthana supposedly 'gave' the palace to the government. He left his home and lived quietly in a house in Luang Prabang with the (meaningless) title of Adviser to President Souphanouvong until March 1977. Then he was taken away by helicopter to Houaphan along with Queen Khamboui and Crown Prince Say Vongsavang. There they were imprisoned in a cave where they allegedly starved to death.

In the late 1990s, the journalist Christopher Kremmer followed up the story and eventually found an eyewitness, a fellow inmate of the captive royal family. During a secret meeting Kremmer was told that the Crown Prince, in particular, had found the situation of their internment intolerable. One night he stood up from the dinner table and burst out that they were being forced to eat foul and inadequate food. How could the King of Laos be treated in such a way? Their guards cooked their food and this was, to them, a violent insult. To make matters worse, Vong Savang refused to apologise. As a result, the family were humiliated further and then made to cook their derisory rations for themselves. The situation became more severe and the Prince contracted dysentery and then a fever of the brain. He was supposed to have died in 1978. The King and Queen were moved to another camp, in even poorer conditions, where they died shortly afterwards. Sadly, according to the source, they were all buried in unmarked graves without ceremony. Many Laotians believe that royal ghosts haunt the palace.

When I arrived at five past ten in the morning I was immediately accosted by a reedy guard in a khaki short-sleeved shirt and trousers.

'We close! We close! At eleven we have meeting.'

'OK, I'll be out by then.'

'No, we have meeting.'

'Look, I've come to see the palace. I have time.' I strode past him. He let me go but the lady at the desk was equally hostile. I insisted on a ticket and they relented ungraciously and practically frogmarched me to the secured Phra Bang room that opened on to the outside veranda of the palace.

The Phra Bang is a solid gold Buddha image that changed the town's name from 'Flaming City beside the River Tong' in 1560 in the hope that it would bring good fortune. It is the palladium of the kingdom, but I was really more interested in finding the kitchens, so took a cursory glance at the three-foot-high statue (a bit podgy, with two creases of fat on his neck) and turned to find the guard coughing thinly behind me to urge me on. My time was short if I wanted to see the palace.

Once inside I walked across the hall to the international gift room. The girl pushed me straight out again as I had gone into the room in the wrong order and I was not going to be allowed to wander. So started my trot through the palace.

There were some interesting paintings of Lao village life painted in the 1930s by a French artist, Alix de Fautereau, and the throne room glass mosaics were the best of their class, but it was the royal apartments that held my thrall. They were totally barren and drab. In fact the whole palace had been stripped of any soft or luxurious thing; anything that might remind visitors that a real family had once lived a life here. I went into the Queen's bedroom but all that remained was lumpy dark furniture, not a rug or a trinket to be seen. The other rooms were just as spartan.

I wondered what the living Crown Prince Soulivong would think of his former home now. After 'disappearing' the King, Queen and their son (the heir to the throne Vong Savang), Vong's son managed to escape and lives quietly as a 'king-in-waiting', unable to return to his homeland.

It was half past ten, and the guard came back. 'Close eleven, close eleven.'

'I know,' I said, pointing to my watch which showed half past.

He pointed to his own watch that showed (incorrectly) ten-forty. 'Close eleven,' he screeched again.

'Well I still have twenty minutes, then.'

He gave me a bad-tempered look.

'What has happened to all the decorations? The carpets, fabrics, china and paintings?'

'Transferred to the storage area due to unsuitable conditions,' he mumbled under his breath and stomped away past a gilt Louis XIV sofa that had miraculously escaped the purge.

It was such a pity that the authorities had removed everything of personal interest. I looked in vain for the bowler hat in a glass case in the throne room that Alan Davidson, the English ambassador to Laos, had seen when he visited the King in the seventies. When Davidson asked why it was given such pride of place, the King replied that he had bought his 'melon' in Savile Row and was wearing it when he unwittingly got caught up in the Paris riots of 1968. A gendarme accidentally conked him on the head with his truncheon and the hat had saved the king of Laos from a cracked skull. There was still a dent in the hat to prove it. Now it had gone, along with everything else.

I raced on to the dining room. The furniture was carved in that huge and oppressive style that reminded me of the musty French bed-and-breakfast places I had been to as a child. Four vast sideboards lined the walls around a table that sat twelve. Two glass cabinets contained a Western bone china dinner service decorated in cobalt and gold gilt. I could have been in the house of an old maiden aunt in Lyon. Where were the low bamboo tables, the woven platters, sticky rice baskets, the ceramic soup bowls? Had Phia Sing served his wonderful Lao meals at a foreign-style table? Had the royal family been so entranced by the French that they had given up their own Lao manner of dining?

I'd have loved to ask the surviving heir to the throne, Crown Prince Soulivong, who is exiled in France; but the chance of that was impossible as I knew that he never, ever gave interviews.

The guard had returned to linger behind me. I asked, 'Is there another dining room in the palace?'

He looked at me incredulously. 'This only dining room.'

'Well, where is the kitchen? May I see that?' I asked hopefully.

'In outside building.' He looked at me even more incredulously, and then suspiciously. Obviously I was a capitalist spy. What kind of tourist would want to see a kitchen?

'Now storage room.'

'Can I see it?'

'No. We close.'

I finished my tour in the international gift room filled with china chickens from Poland, a plastic model of the Apollo II given by Nixon, and other inappropriate gifts (why don't governments give things of value any more?). I almost gave a whoop of joy as I left the leaden atmosphere. Maybe there *were* ghosts.

I was shoved out into the garden by the guard. He pointed to a plain wooden building behind the palace, so shuttered and barred it was almost sealed. 'There kitchen. Now you go! We close.' Disappointed, I turned away.

As I left I noticed that the gilt pediment above the palace entrance had just been regilded. It depicts the traditional royal symbol of a three-headed elephant, a parasol and seven serpents. The elephant denotes the unification of the three former kingdoms under the Luang Prabang monarchy, the parasol reflects the divine source of the King's authority and symbolises the reverence of the Lao people to the founders of the first kingdom, and the snakes represent the protection of the River Nagas. The pediment flashed in the sun.

Luang Prabang is a town where everything once revolved around the royal family. Much still centres around its missing royal heart, and the regime that removed the King has difficulty in knowing how to present his legacy. By opening the palace, they had unavoidably revived memories of the royal past they had taken such care to repress for the last twenty-five years. The guide pamphlet claims that the King resigned and moved into a house down the road, and conveniently forgets to mention anything else. You can't pull a thin veil of socialism over the past and expect to obscure the truth of history. As one Luang Prabang resident said to me, 'It's like killing the Pope and then organising tours to the Vatican.'

The new push for tourism in Laos has shown up the conflict between the political and economic aims of the government today. The 'National Museum' palace is a case in point: everything about it runs counter to the regime, yet they need to generate income by opening it to sightseers. The results are hopeless curatorial confusion and lack of grace – but it is real.

I didn't get to see the kitchens and the dining room was shockingly French, but I reflected that I had just been romanticising a Lao royal culinary experience – which in fact was alive and well in the food that I was eating. Phia Sing's recipes were being cooked in Luang Prabang every day because his traditional dishes still form the basis of everyday fare among the rich and poor alike, from the *or lam* I was served in restaurants to the country chicken stews I ate in the market and sour soups I sipped in people's homes.

I had to admit that I liked the sense that things were run on their own agenda without acquiescing to formulaic tourist demands. I didn't want to watch twenty teenagers in foil head-dresses doing a traditional dance while I ate a Westernised version of a Lao meal; and I didn't want to return by air-conditioned car to a hermetically sealed hotel room while the those same teenagers zoomed home on their mopeds to their real lives. But lots of people do. My grandparents adored that sort of thing, particularly if it involved a cruise ship and all-you-can-eat buffets. And it is coming to Luang Prabang as fast as the new tourist companies can bus in the rich punters.

Kai Pan Chips

Open your packet of algae from Lotus Foods (see suppliers, p. 336) and unfold the large algae sheet. In Laos, they cut the sheets into 5 cm (2 inch) squares and deep-fry them in peanut oil for a few seconds, though they sometimes grill them on a flame grill and serve them with beer, like potato chips.

To prepare without frying, lightly mist/brush the squares with light oil and bake in a 250ºC (500ºF) oven or under a hot grill for 2 minutes. Whether you fry or grill, you need to keep watch as it burns easily.

It should be crisp and dark green when ready; if it's dark brown you've burnt it. Serve with chilli sauce.

Mrs Misaiphon's Luang Prabang Chicken and Aubergine Stew

1 litre (1 ³/₄ pint) chicken stock flavoured with lemon
    grass (see below)
1 head garlic, finely chopped
1 green bird's-eye chilli, finely chopped
5 shallots, finely chopped
10 small aubergines (golfball-sized green/white ones)
2 chicken breasts, cut into 5 cm (2 inch) pieces
2 tablespoons fish sauce (or to taste)
1 handful each of fresh sweet basil and dill

First get the chicken stock going. Fill a pan with the water and add chicken bones plus a couple of onions, a carrot and a piece of celery. Add a stalk of lemon grass bent and tied in a loose knot to release the flavour. Boil down to reduce the liquid by about half, skimming off the scum every once in a while. Strain when ready to produce a clear light stock.

Fry the chopped garlic, chilli and shallots together until the shallots are soft and translucent. Set aside.

Remove the stalks from the aubergines and sear until they are charcoal-black all over. Remove the worst burnt skin and then steam them until soft. When ready, pound the steamed aubergines in a pestle and mortar together with the fried chilli, garlic and shallots until well mixed, and put to one side.

In a heavy pan, simmer the chicken pieces in the stock for 5 minutes, adding fish sauce to taste. Meanwhile, take the aubergine mixture and quickly toss it in a hot wok with a little oil and then add this to the chicken pot. Raise the heat under the pan and reduce the liquid by half. The result should be a stew, rather than a soup.

Add the basil and dill and serve.

Luang Prabang Salad

This is a delicious salad which is served all over Laos but particularly in Luang Prabang Province. The dressing is cooked in a wok for a few seconds and then poured over the salad.

1 crisp lettuce, such as cos
1 large bunch watercress, the wilder the better
1 bunch mint leaves, stalks removed
1 small handful coriander leaves
1 small handful dill
2 spring onions, roughly chopped
4 small fragrant tomatoes, cut into eighths

6 rounds of cucumber, cut in half
3 hard-boiled eggs, whites only, sliced
1 small handful chopped roasted peanuts

DRESSING
2 cloves garlic, finely sliced
1 spring onion, finely chopped
1 tablespoon fish sauce
1 hard-boiled egg, yolk only
a little sugar
the juice of one lime

Assemble the salad ingredients on a plate to your own design.

Take the sliced garlic, spring onion and fish sauce and place them in a hot wok with a drop of oil. Cook for 10 seconds, stirring constantly, then add the cooked egg yolk and meld it in until it disappears into the sauce.

Add a pinch of sugar and the lime juice and it's ready. Pour over the salad and top with chopped peanuts. Serve immediately or it will wilt.

FOUR

BUTTERFLIES AND OFFAL SALAD

After the sophistication of Luang Prabang cuisine I craved something simpler. I'd heard about an unspoilt village about a hundred kilometres north on the Nam Ou river. It was called Muang Noi and was said to be like Vang Vieng before the back-packers got to it. You had to take a couple of buses and a boat to get there. The bus journey to Nong Khiaw was comparative-ly comfortable as roads in Luang Prabang Province are made of good tarmac; from there I caught a boat to Muang Noi.

Throughout my stay I travelled by every method possible in Laos: bicycle, bus, truck, *tuk-tuk* (motorbike taxi), slow boat, speed boat (not recommended unless you want be forced to wear a helmet that smells of someone else's hair, go deaf for a day afterwards and arrive with a black, bruised bottom) and aero-plane – all of which were packed to exploding point and likely to break down several times. Slow boat was by far the best option of travel, as it gave one a chance to consider the landscape and decelerate to Lao time. The houseboats are no-frills wooden affairs, roofed in tin, run on a tiny outboard motor, and have an open-to-the-river-toilet-hole at one end encased in a cupboard made for people with snake hips.

I lay back on the roof of my slow boat and let out a stress-releasing sigh. The landscape was indeed similar to Vang Vieng, but it was less theatrical and wilder; the mountains looked untouched and the river banks were uncultivated. The sky was azure-blue with fluffy little clouds, and so vivid against the dark bouclé of the mountains that it looked unreal, like a poster in a travel agent's window. I was once more struck by the rural beauty of this country. I didn't see a single sign of humanity in the hour and a half it took to reach the village: no people, no boats, no traffic, no planes flying overhead, just the unadulterated land-scape gliding past.

Muang Noi was just as I had heard, a Lao country village that had yet to receive the inexorable pleasures of electricity and hoards of tourists, though there were at least twenty backpack-ers in town. The houses were all wood, the people friendly and, I noticed, rather cheery. As I walked around to find a place to stay I discovered that this was a village of whistlers – there were tunes warbling from all directions.

It was nearly noon and I was starving for some real rural fare.

I found a room quickly (4,000 kip a night, the equivalent of a packet of crisps) in a promising family house that had a separate kitchen and a plump patriarch. I was shown a simple wood-plank room with two glassless windows overlooking the village street. The bench bed had an inch-thick mattress, ill-fitting sheets that fell off the instant you moved and, heaven, a big blue nylon mosquito net that tucked under the mattress.

Rob, an American medical student, was also staying at the house. He loved *laap* but when I told him it probably included entrails his face fell. The family were fabulous. Mrs Phengsy K—, the mother, had unearthed an English/Lao phrase book, so well-thumbed it had almost faded away, and with it we conversed in detail. She was thirty-eight, had messy hair and a big heart. She had been married for twenty years, and had seven children. One of her sons Bak Ling had been learning English for nine months and was quite good at it, though some of the words he had learnt were surprisingly archaic. He was ten and wanted to study in Vientiane. His name means 'little monkey' and he kept trying to scare us with tales of snakes and tigers. Her two younger daugh-ters played skip-rope continuously, while the other little ones came and went with an enviable freedom denied to English children these days.

Mr K. was a rotund man who smiled easily. Laotians aren't fat and never obese, so it was unusual to meet a man with such a pronounced paunch. As I suspected, he loved food and was the chef of the family. He was genuinely thrilled that I was interested in Lao cooking and invited me to watch him make lunch and then join the family meal.

I couldn't understand what he was going to cook except that it was pork, a family favourite and a typical village dish. Great.

I followed him to the back of the house to the basic kitchen. A sink bowl was set into a table next to a water-storage can. There was a charcoal stove and, unusually for such a backwater, a gas ring attached to a bottle. I looked on in anticipation.

Mr K. lit the gas ring with a match, unhooked a plastic bag hanging from a nail on the wall and took out a lump of white pork fat, skin attached, the size and thickness of a house brick. He dropped it into a shallow wok on the ring and gave his belly a big slap.

The lard fizzed and popped until it became a great curl of golden crackling floating in a lake of liquid fat three inches deep that nearly filled the wok to the brim. Mr K. removed the crackling with some chopsticks and smacked his lips as he put it to one side. He picked up a tiny, two-inch bowl of chopped pork meat and threw it in, letting it sizzle while he went to a dilapidated cupboard and got the main ingredient – a large bowl of pig lung complete with massive arteries. I was certainly in for some country cooking.

He chopped it up roughly and then put it back in the bowl, adding some salt, sugar, monosodium glutamate (MSG), fish sauce and soy, mixing it with his hands. He took a deep inhalation to test the smell and then threw in a few chopped chillies to finalise the lung seasoning. He washed his hands vigorously and then took a plastic bag from the side.

'*Pak*,' he said, smiling. *Pak* means greens of any type, and these were last night's leftovers: some kind of spinach-type plant cooked with shallots and garlic.

One of his daughters arrived in the kitchen with a dead chicken (for later) which she threw casually into one of the many chipped enamel bowls by the sink. She then proceeded to wash a bunch of spring onions, some dill and some coriander.

Meanwhile, Mr K. drained the pork from the wok with a slotted spoon and added some chopped garlic and ginger, stirring for a minute. He threw in the entrails and fried them for five minutes while his daughter washed the chopping board, wiped it on her shorts and then chopped the spring onions, coriander, dill and some lemon grass with a weighty cleaver.

Finally the greens were added to the lung at the last moment, and then removed from the heat and drained. The fresh chopped ingredients were tossed into the dish, Sichuan pepper was shaken on top and lunch was ready.

The rest of the family arrived and we all sat at a round table surrounding the big plate of offal. A large bowl of hot stock soup, reheated from breakfast, was placed beside the dish. Sticky rice, the crackling, chilli sauce and fresh salad vegetables – lettuce, spring onions, herbs from the garden – completed our lunch.

Mr K. quietened the family down and put his hands together, saying, '*Ma yo kin yo* (Come yo! Eat yo!).' The traditional blessing, like grace, said before a meal, relates to the legend of Khun Borom, an origin myth of great antiquity linked to some of man's earliest collective memories of the region. It explains the prehistory of the 'Tai' peoples (not the people of Thailand but the South-east Asian linguistic group of eighty million related speakers) and includes the flood myth found throughout the world.

The invocation concluded and our meal could begin. As the guest I was offered the first portion, then everyone tucked in with alacrity. The food tasted delicious, really good. The meatiness of the lung contrasted with the citrus of the lemon grass, which was cut with chilli, and the fact that it was cooked in dripping made it all the better (like the best chips).

I asked Ling about the Khun Borom story.

'There are many ways to tell the story, but the basic is this,' he said, stuffing his mouth with such a large amount that it was hard to understand him.

'Yes,' he continued, 'Heaven was rule by God, Phya Thene and Earth by three chiefs. Three, named Khun Ket, Khun Kan and Khun Pu Lan Xong.' He said the words slowly for the benefit of my obvious idiocy. 'Men live by hunting and fishing and Phya Thene expected to share in their bounty. He was not given a contribute, and he no like this, so sent down a big flood in revenge. The three lords were clever and built a floating house and went back to heaven to beg forgiveness from Phya Thene.'

Ling stopped to stuff some more food into his mouth. The family were really tucking in now. They ate the lung with balls of sticky rice and salad leaves, and we dipped our spoons into the communal soup bowl to refresh our palate between bites. The crackling was also used as a scoop for the main dish or simply eaten with a great daub of chilli paste. It was hard to understand Ling, as his desire to eat as much as possible in as short a time as he could took over from his story-telling. I looked the story up myself later.

After the flood subsided the world was left in such chaos that Phya Thene sent his son Khun Borom and a cortège of attendants to rule over Earth. One day, while Khun Borom was laying out the rice fields, he came across a gourd plant entwined with a liana vine (sometimes it is said that the plant sprang from the nostrils of a great buffalo sent to help with the rice planting). The plant grew so huge that it blotted out the sun, leaving the world dark and bitterly cold. Khun Borom ordered it to be chopped down, but none of his attendants came forward as the tree would surely crush anyone who cut it when it fell. An elderly couple, Phu Gneu and his wife Gna Gneu, offered their lives to do the job and in return asked that after death they would receive offerings and their spirits would be invoked before every meal. After three months of sawing, the liana fell, crushing the old people in its path, and sunshine returned to the Earth.

Ling managed to swallow and continued. 'Several big, big pumpkins (gourds) immediately sprang from the plant and a big noise could be heard.' Ling had left the table to act out the drama for me. He leapt about, waved his arms, clanged a spoon on his empty plate and made a big noise, much to the amusement of the table. 'Khun Borum pierced the first gourd with a red hot poker.' He stabbed the air dramatically, telling the story first in English, then in Lao. 'Out poured thousands of men! Then he opened the others with a chisel. Bang, bang, bang and more men poured out with all the creatures of the earth.' He raced around us doing comic impressions of animals: an elephant, then a tiger (attacking me) and anything else he could think of. 'Then gold, silver, silk, seeds came out and all many wonderful things.'

The people said to have come out of the first mythical gourd were the 'Kha', blackened with soot from the poker (the word literally means slave and is a disparaging term for the original Austro-Asiatic tribes who entered the area around five thousand years ago). The second race of men, who came from the chiselled gourds, were unblackened, the lighter skinned 'Tai'.

According to the anthropologist Professor Peter Bellwood of the Australian National University, in the prehistoric past, when land bridges connected South-east Asia with Indonesia and Borneo, the whole area was inhabited by hunter-gatherer populations related remotely, in a genetic sense, to the peoples of Australia and New Guinea. The liana tree and gourd myth is all we have left of the first race of men that peopled Laos.

'And the old people that saved Laos from the big tree are remembered before every meal,' said Ling, plomping down in his seat and scooping himself another plate of lung.

I like offal and I think it is a shame that as nations get richer they tend to eschew innards for bland white meat. In the past such waste was unthinkable: we all ate offal and enjoyed it. Now, however, we have forgotten how good those offcuts can be and our delicious old English dishes like 'calf's head with cockscombs, kidneys and crayfish' are virtually unknown today.

But the big flapping arteries, I had to admit, I had some problems with. It wasn't the taste but the texture – they were like rubber bands and I felt as though I was swallowing hosepipe. The rest of the family seemed to revel in their chewiness, knocking each other's forks in a bid to get the really long bits. They gnawed on them, eyes alight, and kept giving me more. It was hard going, but I managed to eat them all and convey that I loved rubbery arteries more than anything I've ever tasted, which went down well.

It was a hearty meal, and after all that chewing I needed a walk.

I waddled out of the village and along a narrow track into the undergrowth of elephant ear plants and hairy bamboo. The family had suggested that I visit a cave nearby that the villagers had used as a refuge when the Americans bombed the area. I walked slowly to the lilting rhythm of cicadas, some birds whose song sounded like distant police sirens, and someone whistling across the mountains. The wood smelt of eucalyptus and was so dense that I couldn't see through the leaves. I crossed scores of little streams pouring out of the roots of enormous trees, and crushed mauve flower petals underfoot that had fallen to the ground from high above.

After about ten minutes I was bashed in the eye by an emerald worm hanging like a jewel from a thread in the canopy, and it was then that I began to notice the butterflies: tiny lilac ones, yellow ones with polka dots and black wing tips, large ebony ones with a blaze of lime across the wing, iridescent ones as blue as lapis lazuli; huge chocolate ones with rows of butter dots, inky-blue ones, shimmering violet in the light, big ginger ones like flying biscuits, gargantuan swallowtails dipping and tumbling, and, my favourite, a velvety brown one smutted with red under-wings which it flashed like naughty knickers. It flaunted itself on leaves as I passed and shivered expectantly on the ground before me, waiting to be viewed, before fluttering away like an exotic sweet wrapper.

The rest of the walk was a lepidopterist's dream. There are over five hundred species of butterfly in Laos (some still practically unknown to science), and it seemed that most of them were following my trail. I walked for an hour, my heart singing with the joy of such a gorgeous spectacle, when I heard rushing water and came to a dappled glade.

A shaggy karst mountain soared above me and hung over the entrance to a deep, uneven hole punched into the limestone. The bottom of the cavern was a depression filled with water which formed a swimming pool that fed into a shingled stream leading out to the main river. It was idyllic and hard to imagine that once dozens of people probably stood here, out of their minds with fear, as bombs exploded all around them.

Now, all was harmony. Butterflies chased each other and skimmed over the surface, the sunshine fell through the trees lighting up pebbles with flecks of crimson, and I could hear the gloop, gloop sound of the water slapping against the cave walls.

I dumped my bag by a cluster of creamy lilies and waded in up to my ankles in the cool water as little fish the colour of the stones darted away from my toes or scuttled over submerged rocks as though they had feet. They looked prehistoric, and I wondered if these were the progeny of the famous *pa kheng*, the 'walking fish' reported to be able to leave its stream to cross roads and fields, and even to climb palm trees on the lookout for a better habitat. It did feel primordial inside the cave with the source of the water bubbling up from underground. I was hot and the pool felt heavenly, so I waded deeper up to my knees.

Then I took a risk. I removed all my clothes, left them on a rock and swam naked.

Luckily, the three men returning from chopping wood in the forest stopped whistling to stare at me *after* I had finished swimming and put my clothes back on. Just.

Back in the village it was suppertime and the K. family had made a celebratory *laap* in Rob's honour and mine. Rob was an intelligent and intrepid traveller but he refused the *laap* because I had mentioned the (sometimes raw) entrail factor. This one was particularly dark grey, but it was due to the amount of roasted rice powder used rather than guts. It was made with chicken, finely sliced banana flower, shallots, cooked aubergine, a little coriander leaf and loads of garlic, all very roughly chopped – country style. It was really tasty but I felt terrible that I'd put Rob off his favourite dish. I did everything to get him to change his mind and was finally successful.

I spent the next couple of days tasting village food and trekking up local waterfalls which gave me a huge appetite to eat it. The everyday food of the village was very simple and revolved around sticky rice and grilled or deep-fried fish. They definitely had a taste for wild foods, which they preferred for its unique flavour. Again and again I heard people proclaiming the wonders of wild meat, leaves and fish. I asked about ant eggs, but though everyone was enthusiastic about their merits, no one (though they did try) was able to find any for me.

Finding and catching wild foods was a favourite game for children, who would go off with a butterfly net to ensnare crickets, crabs or shrimp for supper. Small boys stalked the trees with slings in the hope of catching birds, and their parents set traps in the fields and rivers for frogs, rats and fish. Vegetables were home-grown, gathered from the jungle or bought from the Friday market by those that could afford it.

Breakfast was either soup with herbs and maybe an egg, or rice with dried meat. Lunch was usually the leftovers from the night before with added rice, and dinner was fish with greens, rice and various home-made chilli condiments. It was good plain food, if a little repetitive, but I'm invigorated by the rough and tumble of everyday fare and I ate it greedily. The simplicity of the dishes may not have made for sophisticated recipes – a grilled fish stuffed with a few leaves, tiny steamed crabs with sticky rice, some chillies pounded with seared lemon grass and garlic – but this was real food that represented a real way of life. It had the smell of the soil.

On my last night I went for a beer at the local 'bar-cum-restaurant' – a couple of tables on the veranda of a house with its own electricity generator that powered a single light bulb on a wire. It was buzzing with a dozen *felang* by the time I got there at eight-fifteen. The rest of the village around the bar was pitch-black and closed for the night.

Two huge joints were being passed around, someone had brought a portable stereo and the place was swinging to the rhythms of American soft rock. I ordered a warm (no fridges) Beer Lao and sat down with the realisation that I was the oldest person there by about ten years. Conversation revolved around Harold Robbins and opium.

The bare bulb cast a pool of light around the café, and just on the periphery, almost hidden by the darkness, I noticed three Laotian boys ages about fifteen. Their faces were bright with curiosity and they were visibly straining to take it all in. One was bolder than the others – he had an Elvis quiff and was desperate to join the party. He kept starting to step forward into the light only to jump back nervously.

'There's nothing to do in Laos, it's so boring,' said the girl beside me to her new boyfriend. I almost choked on my beer.

'Yeah,' the other agreed. 'I much preferred Goa, we raved all night in Goa. Spent Christmas on the beach partying.'

'No, man,' said another boy toking on a joint. 'You don't understand. You've got to relax into it in Laos. Just relax. It's cool here.' He passed the dope. 'Here, have this.'

The Laotian teenagers were getting braver. Elvis in particular, was edging closer like a moth to a flame.

'Well, I guess there are some benefits,' she said, taking the joint with a big grin. 'I mean, it's so cheap to get high here.' Blah, blah, blah.

God, I was getting bored of these kinds of conversations, and I started thinking about how early I had to get up to start my ten-hour bus journey to the north-western town of Luang Nam Tha.

Elvis dared to pull up a chair and was welcomed with open arms. A large cup of expensive Mekong whisky was slapped in front of him and his two friends followed quickly behind.

My stay in the village had been enormously enjoyable. I was learning that Laotians are a big-hearted people of great generosity and charm. The easy-going nature of village life in Muang Noi resulted in a level of carefree happiness that seemed revelatory to my jaded old soul. I'm not saying that there weren't problems. It wasn't an idyll – there was poverty, malaria and the general difficulties of everyday community life; but it was a beautiful place to live and the people loved it there. Drugs and the allure of drug money would inevitably change all that.

I slipped into the night with a heavy feeling of doom.

Egg Soup from the Village

$\frac{1}{2}$ litre (1 pint) light chicken stock (or plain water if you prefer)
2 eggs
2 flavourful medium tomatoes cut into eighths
a pinch of salt
3 tablespoons chopped spring onions, green part only
20 whole mint leaves

Bring the stock to the boil in a saucepan or wok and lower to a simmer. When simmering, break two eggs into the pan and stir, agitating the water constantly for 3 minutes. Add the tomato slices and some salt. Cook for a further minute. Pour into a bowl and add the spring onion and the mint. Serve as a refreshing breakfast soup.

Pig Lung Salad

900 g (2 lb) white pork fat, skin attached, approx
    30 x 15 cm (12 x 6 inch) block
1 very small bowl chopped lean pork meat
450 g (1 lb) pig lung and 225g ($\frac{1}{2}$ lb) pig arteries
1 pinch salt
1 pinch monosodium glutamate (optional)
1 teaspoon sugar
1 teaspoon fish sauce
1 teaspoon light soy sauce
7 chillies, roughly chopped
1 small bowl spinach, fried with shallots and garlic
3–7 cloves garlic, peeled and sliced
10 cm (4 inch) piece ginger, peeled and sliced

4 spring onions, chopped

4 tablespoons coriander leaves

4 tablespoons dill, chopped

2 tablespoons lemon grass, chopped

a pinch of Sichuan pepper

Put a wok on to heat and put in the block of pork fat. Wait until the fat has melted (watch out – it will fill the wok) and the skin has turned into golden crackling. Remove the crackling and put to one side.

Put the chopped pork into the fat in the wok and let it sizzle for a while.

Meanwhile, chop up the lung and arteries quite roughly, put in a bowl and add the salt, MSG if using, sugar, soy sauce, fish sauce and the chopped chillies and mix around to coat.

Next take the spinach and fry it separately for a couple of minutes with a handful of chopped shallots and a finely chopped garlic clove. Keep aside.

Now remove the pork from the wok with a slotted spoon and put to one side. Pour out the fat and set aside to use in some other dish. Add to the wok the garlic and ginger and stir for a minute. Next add the lung and arteries and fry for 5 minutes.

At the last moment add the spinach, remove the wok from the heat. Toss the minced pork back in along with the chopped spring onions, coriander, dill and lemon grass, shake on some Sichuan pepper and serve. Mr K. served it alongside a bowl of hot stock soup, sticky rice, the crackling, chilli sauce and fresh salad vegetables – lettuce, spring onions and herbs from the garden.

FIVE

NOODLES IN THE NORTH

Luang Nam Tha is a town of merchants. What they sell and where they sell it I never discovered, but the people who live there are rich. It doesn't look like much at first, but there are deals going on behind closed doors and wads of money changing hands.

It shows in the architecture. The streets sprawl out from the deceptively scrawny central strip into wide lanes of substantial properties, and black gauze satellite dishes speckle the rooflines. The houses are predominantly concrete and built in the 'neo-bourgeois-Thai-style', a hotchpotch of Asian and Western designs affected by wedding-cake plasterwork. Façades of curly balconies held up by Corinthian columns twisted out of all proportion, painted in sugared-almond colours, are all the rage with the Lao nouveau riche.

I found a room at Darasavath guest house, a traditional wooden building with an enamel bowl of water by the entrance and a group of Lao government officials having a dinner party in the restaurant. The owner, Seng Sone Darasavath, was thirty years old, extrovert and canny. She spoke English and Chinese and crocheted hats at great speed in between capably multitasking the business and looking after her excitable toddler, Micky.

She took the time to sit down and introduce herself to me whilst coping with twenty raucous diners and offered to teach me how to make *jaew*, the two sauces she served me with my dinner of chicken and potato curry. The sauces were super-hot, one made with fermented shrimp paste and another with mushrooms.

Jaew is pounded sauce or rough paste, the main ingredient of which is chilli. The varieties are endless, ranging from simple blends of chilli, salt and fresh herb leaves to unctuous condiments whose recipes are handed down through families. *Jaew* is essential to a Lao meal and the secret of a really good one is to sear one or more of the ingredients on a charcoal fire. It is served in a separate bowl and everyone dips food into the communal dish rather than scooping a personal portion on to their plate.

In the north, *jaew*s are so hot that when I first tried one it felt like someone had sneaked up behind me and slapped me on the back with a frying pan. I almost lost my breath, not to mention the roof of my mouth and my tongue. I soon got used to it and my chilli tolerance has gone up a thousandfold for ever. Contrary to most people's belief, they are good for you. They stimulate the production of mucus in the stomach lining which protects it against irritation, they're antiseptic, good for the circulation and excellent at clearing the respiratory system of excess phlegm. Try eating *jaew* next time you have a heavy cold. It works wonders.

Chillies, of course, are not native to Laos but come from Mexico and the Americas. The Portuguese brought chillies to South-east Asia when they arrived in Siam in 1511. Over the centuries, they replaced peppercorns (a native of Malabar, India) as the preferred spice of heat, starting as a subtler flavouring which built up over the years. My friend Khamtoune believes that Lao food has got hotter, even in her lifetime, and came back from Laos recently shocked by the new strength of chilli used in her native Luang Prabang cuisine. She believes it to be the influence of northern Thai cuisine now that there are so many Thai tourists in Laos.

Seng Sone's *jaew* was extremely hot but she was quite impressed by my new-found chilli stamina. She nipped back to my table several times during the evening to tell me of her plans to start another guest house restaurant in the countryside.

'I am waiting for my baby to grow up to be a big boy because it is difficult to take care of him. I have an area outside here, about eleven kilometre. A hill, maybe I build another guest house on it, in countryside. With restaurant,' she added.

The party of people behind us were rising up to propose a toast but were so smashed that they could not actually stand. Several men began to get to their feet, holding on to each other for balance, and then sank back down again in a chain like a Mexican wave at a football match.

Seng Sone was unfazed. She tilted her head to the teetering piles of dishes on the long table behind us and smiled. 'In Lao you make more moneee from food than from guest house.' She dragged out the 'e' of 'money' in a typically Lao way.

The Laotian officials left abruptly at nine (people don't stay up late in provincial Laos) and reeled back to their government-owned hotel to 'go disco'.

Seng Sone rose to clear their table. 'Tomorrow morning, eleven o'clock, I show you how to make *jaew* my way.'

I finished my meal by ten and was still feeling lively; I wanted to see what this disco was like. I followed the clanging music, my way lit by millions of stars.

When I arrived at the Hong Tha Xay Som Boun Hotel, the music was ear-splitting. Coloured flashing lights shone from the windows of the prefab bungalow that was the hottest nightspot of Luang Nam Tha. I was ready to party. I looked inside to find the room completely empty except for a lone DJ at a mixing deck in the corner. A glitterball spun from the centre of the ceiling throwing barbs of light conspicuously over my frame in the doorway. For a moment I fantasised about doing a *Saturday Night Fever* solo, and then turned and fled just in time to see the face of the DJ fall in disappointment.

I spent the next day cooking condiments with Seng Sone and wandering around the town. There was not that much to see but there was the Luang Nam Tha museum, a brand-new single-storey building with a shiny tiled floor. A guard let me in and then went to sit back down on his bed in the corner. He obviously lived there, the full-time protector of a huge safe coated with pearlised plastic made to look like crushed velvet. This is a popular safe casing in Laos, and this one was midnight blue, but I had already come across a fuchsia pink one (travel agent) and a lovely tangerine one (in a bank) on my travels. He ignored me as he studied his English language book.

The objects were set up around the walls, some in glass cases, and some standing alone: slices of tree trunk, three stuffed animal heads on blocks of wood, ancient pottery jars decorated with primitive paintings of elephants, tribal costumes, musical instruments and some prehistoric standing stones with mysterious markings. All the labels were, understandably, in Lao, so maddeningly I could not even read the dates.

The largest section was devoted to the revolution, a motley collection of around thirty rusting weapons: guns, ancient powder horns, rifles, pistols, machine guns and bombs were laid out on three benches. On the floor beside them stood a missile launcher and a machine gun on wheels. The sign beside it was in English (no doubt so that visiting foreigners could feel safe in their beds) and read: 'Locally produced weapons on display here were used during traditionally [sic] for hunting wild animals and later during the revolution. In 1998 the population was requested to hand over weapons of this type to ensure peace and security in the countryside.'

Some of the weapons looked almost nineteenth-century; I imagined that those powder horns must have come in useful during the war. Next to these was a topographical model of the Luang Nam Tha valley, boxed in glass. Painted vivid green, it illustrated the villages and rivers amongst the hilly landscape, but primarily there were lots and lots of little cannon.

Photographs of 'Heroes of the Revolution' lined the walls: men and women with prematurely aged faces and the look of seeing too much death in their eyes. Then, in true Communist style, these were followed by jaunty pictures of officials shaking hands at bridge construction sites, a progressive sewing factory and the local football team.

I thought I had come to the end of the pleasures of Luang Nam Tha when I overheard someone say that there were hot showers at a place called the Boat Landing Guest House six kilometres out of town. When I asked around, I discovered that the guest house styled itself as an eco-tourism lodge, with luxurious wooden bungalows and a restaurant that was gaining a reputation for local specialities. I like roughing it and you have a much better time when you do, but, like my mother, I do love a bit of luxury too. Hot showers! I could not resist. The *tuk-tuk* could not get me there fast enough.

The Boat Landing was located by the river at Ban Kone, meaning 'village Kone', but locals seemed to call it 'old village' as opposed to the 'new' Luang Nam Tha. Here, the houses were timber and the people's lives revolved around the land and the river as opposed to mercantile business. They were growing maize in their gardens, ducks raced around in bustling flocks and the occasional battered tractor juddered by. It looked very appealing.

The guest house bungalows were built, in traditional Lao style, of woven bamboo with some 'international' additions for comfort: hand-embroidered linen, reading lamps, floor cushions to lounge upon, and French windows that opened on to a veranda a few yards from the Nam Tha river. But the pièce de résistance was the solar-powered shower. Hot water. Not only that, but downy cotton towels (my spongy old travel towel had begun to smell like a truffle) and solar-powered lighting so I could read all night if I liked.

My clothes came off in a blur and I sent out everything I had to be laundered. I luxuriated in the hot water, washing each strand of my hair until it squeaked, and then lay about for the next few hours revelling in my room with a view.

That evening, I was the first to arrive at the restaurant. I took off my flip-flops and stepped up to a raised veranda decorated with simple handmade paper lanterns, cane chairs, and tables with homespun indigo tablecloths. Pawn, the owner, was standing behind the reception-cum-bar involved in a telephone conversation. The rest of his immediate family, his wife Joy, his son Liam, his sisters Deuy, Ning and Mee, his mother Oin, and Noi, his best friend, were sitting at a large corner table conspicuously covered with a plastic cloth patterned with pea pods. Pawn's newborn son, nicknamed 'little bear' lay in a bamboo Moses basket that hung from the rafters. Everyone was eating their supper before the guests arrived.

Pawn came over with a cold Beer Lao and a friendly smile that highlighted a set of good white teeth and the high flat cheekbones of the north. He was aged twenty-seven, and had the extremely rare status in Laos of having both completed higher education and travelled abroad. He had a degree in architectural drawing from Vientiane University and had spent time in Thailand. He was young, fit and comfortable with himself, and his huge extended family were there to support him.

He told me how, a few years ago, he and an American friend, Bill Tuffin (an NGO), had come up with the idea of starting a guest house that was sympathetic to the local environment. It had only been open a few months but news of its rare comforts were already spreading by word of mouth and I was lucky to get a room.

As soon as I told him about my interest in food, he took me over to meet the family. His wife, Joy, had beautiful eyes set wide apart, large pouting lips and long thick hair. She was famous for her cooking as she had run a restaurant in Vientiane, but since she had just had the baby, Pawn's mother and sisters were doing the catering. I asked them what I should order for my supper that was most typical of the area.

'You must try *kao soi* noodle, it's the local specialty of Luang Namtha Province.'

'What's that?'

'Oh, you see! People eating in the market in the morning. They make rice noodle and cut with scissors, that's how it got the name. *Kao* mean "rice" and *soi* mean "to cut with scissors". The sauce is made with mince pork.'

I was starving.

He added, laughing, 'It look like Lao spaghetti Bolognese.' Spaghetti is a staple of hotels' 'international restaurant' menus all over Asia.

'We make the sauce with fermented soy beans, the Lao way, and spoon on top. My mother, she make you some now.'

'Can I watch?'

He asked his mother. She smiled and said something to her daughter, Deuy, as she tapped her watch.

'Yes, quick, before we get too busy.'

I followed the two women into the extremely small kitchen.

Deuy, whose high eyebrows made her look constantly surprised, peeled two whole heads of garlic (about fifteen very small cloves) and four shallots with concentration. She pounded them together and fried them in a little oil until a fragrant smell arose, then she added some salt. Her mother, meanwhile, chopped pork with a cleaver and then she introduced me to a jar of fermented soya bean paste by jamming my nose right into it. The paste had an earthy aroma resonant of soy sauce but it was much richer and, at the same time, piquant. She added a large lump to the wok. A heaped teaspoon of hot chilli powder was also added and everything was cooked for a few minutes before adding the pork. A swoon-inducing smell arose that made my mouth water. The meat was cooked for about ten minutes on a medium heat and then she poured in half a cup of stock and stirred the sauce.

Fresh, soft rice noodles were taken from a basket on the side and refreshed with boiling water and put in a bowl. The sauce was spooned on top and chopped spring onions sprinkled to finish.

I was sent to a table and served the dish with a plate of steamed green beans, water spinach and slices of lime to squeeze on top. Three people stood in front of my table waiting for my reaction to the dish. Luckily it tasted fabulous – savoury, tangy and sour all at once. It did look rather like spaghetti Bolognese, but I liked it better and said as much, to the pleasure of my hosts.

I retired to my room a happy woman and lay down on my bed. Soft! My bed was soft. After weeks of sleeping on my tummy on rock-hard bench beds my pelvic bones had become permanently bruised. Getting to sleep was not a problem.

I woke to a view of fishermen casting hand-nets from sliver-thin canoes. It was so quiet that all I could hear was the sound of crickets and frogs. No tannoy blasting out the day's news or fighting dogs or cockerels at dawn. I had slept well, I was clean and I had just been taught how to cook the local speciality – what could be a better way to start the day?

I rented a bike from the guest house and crossed to the other side of the river to Ban Phoung, a Tai Dam (Black Tai minority) village, followed by a group of schoolgirls on bikes holding zingy coloured parasols.

It was an attractive community of thatched huts that melded into the ochre trees and contrasted with the emerald rice fields beyond. Each house had little bowls of herbs growing by the door and there were herb gardens on stilted troughs all over the village. Salad gardens covered the river bed which was edged with ramshackle pig and cow shacks. A couple of little shop-houses sold things like seeds, toothbrushes, washing powder, soft drinks and eggs. By now I had a whole tribe of kids following me shouting '*falang*'. They were all under six and wore hand-me-down clothes in various states of disintegration.

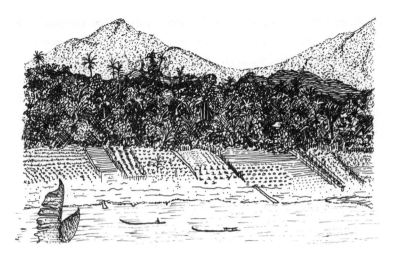

SALAD GARDENS ON THE BANKS OF THE MEKONG

I was always coming across these gangs in Laos. Children looked after themselves, roaming widely under the communal eyes of several relatives scattered throughout a village. Very small children cared for really tiny ones with competent ease, and little people were potty trained practically before they could walk. I often saw kids up trees, swimming in rivers, punting canoes, spearing fish, abseiling across rope bridges – all things sadly lost to our modern urban children.

This lot were very friendly and they yanked me towards a house where a woman, wearing a T-shirt printed with (I am not joking) 'Make your woman orgasm', was pulling silk from a boiling pot of water. We all clustered round her to watch as she threw in more cocoons.

When placed in hot water the filaments of silkworm cocoons are loosened, and the seracin, a waxy substance that gives the raw fibres a coarse texture, is dissolved – it is the high seracin content of South-east Asian silk that gives it its charac-teristic irregularity. The filament in a native Lao cocoon is between four hundred and eight hundred metres long, and from three to twelve filaments are twisted together to form a single thread.

It was amazing to survey the process at first hand. I don't know how she found the ends of the filaments, but she managed to catch the cocoons with a chopstick as they bobbed about in the boiling water and unravel the silk, all in one deft move. She then artfully drew the filaments together and pulled them through a tiny guide hole in a flat stick that lay horizontally above the pot to form the thread. She pulled the thread into a basket and it seemed to go on for ever. I thought of Mr T.'s mother making one metre a day to pay to send them to school.

Obviously there was a by-product of this wondrous process and it was now being proffered to me. A handful of hot silk-worm larvae, straight from the pot. How could I refuse?

I chewed them and found them slightly sticky to the tooth. '*Saep lye lye* (really delicious),' I said, as everyone nodded in agreement. 'They taste a bit like sweetcorn kernels.' This was a little harder to get across.

They were sweet with a faint nutty flavour and did sort of burst in your mouth. They reminded me of my ant egg quest. These weren't ant eggs but they were close. I'd have them again any day. They are full of energy-giving fats and proteins, and very tasty.

Back at the Boat Landing, I lay on my veranda with a book for the rest of the afternoon. A young American girl had moved into the next cabin. She was educated and wealthy, though she wore the usual raggedy tie-dyed backpacker's uniform. As she passed she stopped to quiz me about my travels.

'Where are you going next, then?'

'Muang Sing.'

'Oh, don't go there,' she said with a look of concern.

I was a taken aback. 'Why?'

'It's in the "Golden Triangle". You'll be swamped with beggars and tribal people trying to sell you drugs. I heard a few weeks ago some guys were made to pay a bribe so they wouldn't be taken to the police.'

'What do you mean?'

'Well, four of them were sitting in a café when a woman came up to them to sell some grass. When they refused to buy it, she threatened to tell the police they were using drugs and suggested they'd be thrown in jail unless they gave her one hundred dollars each.'

'No.'

'Yeah! They bargained her down to fifty dollars each but they still had to pay her. I wouldn't go to Muang Sing if I were you.'

'Thanks for the warning,' I said, but Muang Sing has one of the best markets in Laos. The tribes still wear their traditional costumes and congregate there to sell their home-grown produce.

You would have to throw me in jail to stop me going there.

Jaew Kapi – Chilli sauce with shrimp paste

This *jaew* includes fermented shrimp paste, which is sold in jars in Asian stores and many supermarkets. Once opened, keep the jar in the fridge and it will last for months. If you can sear ingredients over a charcoal or wood flame (i.e. your barbecue) it will add immeasurably to the flavour. I make *jaews* in bulk as they last in the fridge.

20 bird's-eye chillies, seared, stalks removed
1 whole head garlic, seared black and then peeled and sliced
1 shallot, seared black and then peeled and sliced
a little oil
1 level tablespoon shrimp paste
1 tablespoon fish sauce
the juice of one lime
a pinch of sugar
a few coriander leaves (optional)
a little boiled water

Spear the chillies, garlic and shallot on a skewer. Sear them over an open flame (a gas ring or even a candle if desperate) until well blackened. Rub off the worst of the soot.

Fry the seared, sliced garlic and shallot for 2 minutes on a high heat in a wok, then transfer them to a pestle and mortar and pound into a rough paste.

Add the seared chillies and pound until they are pulverised into the paste too.

Add the shrimp paste and pound again, then add the fish sauce and stir.

Now add the lime juice and taste. You may want to add a pinch of sugar and some coriander.

If the sauce is too dry, add some warm water a little at a time.

Jaew Hed – Chilli sauce with mushrooms

4 large flat field mushrooms
20 bird's-eye chillies, seared, stalks removed
1 head garlic, seared black and then peeled and sliced
1 shallot, seared black and then peeled and sliced
a little oil
a dash of fish sauce

Wash the mushrooms and grill them until juicy, then chop them roughly, retaining the juices.

Sear the other ingredients as above.

Fry the seared sliced garlic and shallot for 2 minutes on a high heat in a wok, then transfer them to a pestle and mortar and pound until they are a rough paste. Add the seared chillies and pound until they are pulverised into the paste too.

Add the mushrooms to the mixture and pound a few times, adding a little fish sauce to taste. Serve.

Kao Soi Noodles, Luang Namtha-Style

This is quick and simple dish with a savoury flavour. The rice noodles give it a lighter texture than the egg noodle-based dish, and the lime introduces a delightful sour note.

450 g (1 lb) boneless pork steak, finely chopped (or
    minced pork, not too fine)
4 shallots, peeled
1–2 heads garlic, peeled
1 teaspoon oil
a pinch of salt

4 tablespoons fermented soya bean paste (*tua noi*)

1 heaped teaspoon chilli powder (or a pinch if you can't take heat)

125 ml fresh meat stock (a pork/chicken/vegetable cube can be used in emergencies)

1 handful fresh rice noodles, available in Asian stores and some supermarkets (or dried vermicelli noodles)

a kettle full of boiling water

1 tablespoon chopped spring onions, green part only

1 lime, cut into quarters

Pawn's mother took two thick fillets of pork and sliced them diagonally against the grain with a knife. She then took the cleaver and chopped the slices into mince within seconds. Whatever you do, don't mince pork in a blender – it becomes too gooey. Set aside in a bowl.

Take a pestle and mortar and pound the peeled shallots and garlic to a paste. Then fry the mixture with a little oil and a pinch of salt in a shallow wok until the onions soften (about 3 minutes). Add the bean paste and chilli and stir for 5 minutes, adding a touch of water if it gets too dry.

Add the minced pork, stir for a minute or two and then add the stock. Let the mixture simmer until most of the liquid has evaporated; it won't take long.

As the mixture simmers, take the fresh noodles and ladle boiling water over them (to refresh them without making them go soggy), and drain. Place the noodles in a bowl.

Spoon the sauce on top of the noodles and sprinkle with spring onion. Serve with lime wedges to be squeezed to taste.

SIX

LATE NIGHT AND LANGUID

It was raining when I reached the famous market of Muang Sing. I had to step on wobbly planks laid across a gushing stream and over a style topped with barbed wire to get in, but then I stood transfixed.

An Amazonian parrot sanctuary would look beige and bland in comparison with the exotic kaleidoscope of tribal people before me.

The town hadn't changed much since 1894 when Lefèvre, a hydrographic engineer, visited it while on a reconnaissance mission with the Machiavellian French envoy, Auguste Pavie. He described the place as 'a veritable Bosnian' mixture of tribes and was overawed by the variety of produce and extraordinary costumes of the people, likening it to a fairy-tale picture from *A Thousand and One Nights:* 'a unique spectacle, this many-coloured crowd which mills around in the most extraordinary dresses and which, once the purchases are finished, adjourns to the open-aired restaurants established under the shops.' The only difference now was that people held multicoloured nylon umbrellas.

Muang Sing town is built on the fluvial plain of the river, Nam Sing, surrounded by two-thousand-metre-high mountains in which live the tribes of the Akha, Tai Nua, Yao, Luu, Hmong, Khamu, Tai Dam and dozens of other smaller groups; and all of them go to Muang Sing market to sell their wares.

I tripped through the crowd like a zombie, absolutely mesmerised. One girl passed me wearing a cylinder the size of a tin can at an angle above her temple (stuck on with wax, I imagine), encircled with silver beads and swathed in embroidered fabric and fluorescent pom-poms. She was like a piece of sculpture.

Another group of women used their hair as a headdress, twisting it into a cone on top of their heads and finishing it with a figure of eight at the front held down with a giant silver pin. These were Tai Dam (black Tai) who emigrated to the area from Vietnam more than three hundred years ago. Their shirts were pink and candy-striped with white and turquoise, like sticks of seaside rock.

Others, perhaps from another Tai Dam subgroup or possibly because of their age, wore a black scarf wrapped around their cone of hair, stitched with red and yellow diamonds, crosses, and edged with embroidered coils like little snail shells. Their jackets were dyed cochineal, emerald or black with a row of silver buckles sewn on rainbow ribbons down the front. They wore sashes and belts of floral fabric in zingy colours.

TWO TAI DAM TRIBE WOMEN

Many people carried babies who wore beautiful hats covered in pom-poms and snuggled down in rainbow-striped baby-carriers. Hmong tribe women sat behind piles of winged beans, their hair caught in twirls of black cloth and wearing coats with rings of fancy printed fabric sewn down the arms. Even the non-tribal women were wearing particularly vibrant colours – shawls and chequered scarves, floral shirts and patterned skirts. No one wore grey. The wonderful produce could barely compete for my attention, there was so much to see, but I had not had breakfast yet and those open-air restaurants Lefèvre had mentioned were still there. I made straight for them.

There are noodle soup stalls everywhere in Laos and it is traditionally eaten for breakfast, though any time of day will do. The favourite noodle dish of Laos is *khao poon*, rice noodles served cool, ladled over with fragrant, spicy sauce and topped with chopped vegetables. This is usually served on special occasions for many guests. The noodles are presented on a platter surrounded by raw (and sometimes steamed) vegetables and the soup sauce in a separate bowl. Occasionally this dish can be seen in markets, but it is really something people make at home, and in the south they add coconut to the gravy.

Many of the market stalls serve a noodle soup called *pho*, found in thousands of guises all over South-east Asia. *Pho* is originally a Vietnamese dish that has evolved to include anything from chicken, pork, duck or seafood, and has even been turned into a vegetarian version for tourists. In Laos, they commonly serve this as a kind of do-it-yourself noodle soup. Stallholders provide you with a bowl, fill it with a pile of ready-made soft noodles and then add hot stock from a vat kept simmering over a fire. Some just make a quick broth, provide a huge bowl of salad vegetables and let you pick what you want; others may add meat, liver, pork skin or a variety of vegetables such as shredded lettuce, bean sprouts, cabbage, spring onion or chopped peanuts. Either way you are left to add your own seasonings.

The trestle tables by these stalls groan with condiment bottles and jars. On one table alone it is usual to supply a bottle of chilli ketchup sauce, fish sauce and soy sauce; dried chillies in oil; shredded fried garlic; pepper, white and black; fermented prawn paste; fresh green chillies; peanuts, plus toothpicks and the usual roll of loo paper to use as napkins. The better establishments make their own mixtures such as home-made *jaew*s and *paa-dek*: cheaper ones serve MSG and white sugar to enhance their lesser quality stocks. Each person adds their own mix to create a personal dish to suit their taste or mood.

The noodles used in the broth are usually factory-made, but here in Muang Sing market I found a woman in a Day-Glo pink sweater making the noodles freshly for each bowl of soup. I sat down at her rickety wooden stall to watch, mouth watering.

She took a thick dollop of white paste from a bucket on her left with a ladle and placed it in a cloth bag she held in her other hand. It was similar to a pastry bag but this had a three-inch metal disk, punched with tiny holes, sewn to the bottom. Meanwhile, her daughter swirled boiling water in a large cauldron with a spoon, as one does when making poached eggs, and then backed away as her mother squeezed the bag over the water in great circular movements. Fine strands of noodles coiled into the pot, sank and then rose again to the surface a few minutes later like water snakes. She swiped them out with a strainer, and handed me some in a bowl with a little of the water and some chopped coriander and spring onion. It was balletic to watch.

The noodle paste is made by pounding soaked glutinous rice in a large stone mortar. In Laos many people have wooden contraptions that pound the rice with the use of a foot pedal, though it is also done by hand (usually by two people) in a pestle and mortar large enough to hold a child. It is a laborious process either way. The pounded rice is then mixed with water and left to ferment for a couple of days. The water is changed several times and then kneaded into a soft, flexible, doughy paste. After all that

work, this woman had probably walked several miles that morning with her bucket of dough, yet the soup cost pennies.

I was supposed to flavour my noodles myself with a ladle of home-made sauce from a broad enamel bowl on the bench. I spooned some on top and then added bean sprouts and the yellow flowers of a variety of kale from a plate by my side. It was heavenly, another version of *kow soi*, but made with turkey meat, a speciality of the area. I would not have dared to taint it with bottled condiments.

I was wolfing it down when an Akha woman came and sat opposite me, so close we knocked knees. The Akha tribe are particularly distinctive as the women wear magnificent skull-cap headdresses and each Akha clan has its own distinct head-wear. The headdresses are never removed, even to sleep. To say that they are an Akha woman's crowning glory would be an understatement; and this one was one of the most exquisite pieces of costume I had ever seen.

The hat came low over her forehead and was intricately embroidered with lines and patterns of coloured cross-stitching almost totally obscured by rows of glossy silver buttons, from which hung little inch-long strings of silver beads, bright cottons, tassels and tiny pom-poms; ancient coins decorated her temples and the back plate of her hat tinkled with rope upon rope of glass beads which finished in crimson feathers and gibbon fur. The wildest millinery creations at Ascot would have been put in the shade.

To complement her headdress she wore a three-layered top of rough indigo fabric: a bra-like embroidered undergarment with one strap across the chest and shoulder, a long-sleeved shirt with strips of cloth sewn at the wrists and a sleeveless jacket of the same indigo on top. A short knee-length skirt and leggings, worn with old plastic flip-flops, finished the outfit.

AKHA TRIBE WOMEN SELLING GALANGAL

We stared at each other in total fascination and then broke into laughter at our mutual inspections. How impressive to see someone wearing her heritage, and even genealogy, on her back. The Akha are one of the most conservative hill tribes in Laos and they follow a belief system known as the 'Akha Way' – a moral and social code of ancestral and spiritual worship that governs every aspect of their lives. The villages are like extended families, and each village has its own youth group. Wherever you are in the world, teenagers need a place to hang out and the Akha set aside a park at the north of their villages to keep them close.

These tribes have maintained their identity through centuries of forced itinerancy and social change; I felt a sense of reverence and not a little envy. This woman knew her people, she was still in touch with her culture and proudly wore her costume as a symbol of it for all to see. I could not say I had anything like the same connection with mine.

After the soup I trawled the market to the sound of five hundred women catching up on gossip. Nearly every vendor was female, as were the shoppers. This was the same in almost every market, and like many traditionally patriarchal societies, the women seemed to do most of the work. Apparently, the whole country ground to a halt last year when the government introduced a new holiday, 'National Women's Day', in true Communist recognition of their contribution to society. Shops shut and fields lay untended when all the women stopped labouring and pranced off on picnics.

Interestingly, the foundation of the town, Muang Sing is associated with two women. According to Dr Volker Grabowsky, Professor of South-east Asian History at West-fälische Wilhelms-Universität in his essay on the development of Muang-Sing, local folklore explains that the valley of the Sing River was first settled around 1792 by the widow of the ruler of Chiang Khaeng, the neighbouring province. She moved to get away from her squabbling sons and created a new capital called Ban Chiang Khaeng (now known as Xiang Kheng) a few miles away. Then, in 1880, the city was shifted again by another woman because of Burmese raids. It was moved five kilometres to present-day Muang Sing by Buakham, a mysterious woman who left an inscription in the monastery of Ban Nam Dai to make us ruminate upon who she might have been.

There was a small number of men in the crowd but they were in a minority and very few wore traditional costume, so they tended to blend into the background. It was still drizzling and everyone had colds. A row of Tai Dam women selling piles of the flowering kale looked at me miserably and hugged themselves against the damp. Their leaves were laid with symmetrical precision on turquoise sacks between muddy puddles and rubbish. Again, I found the idea of refuse collection to be non-existent. In Laos, everyone just throws down used cans, plastic bags, old potato sacks, beer bottles, fruit peel and rotten vegetables to get covered in mud and trodden into the ground. As a result, when it rains the market is really difficult to walk through as everyone is picking their way through the mire and poking you with their umbrellas. I was regularly struck by the contrast of the pristine rural landscape with the human detritus discarded so carelessly in towns and villages.

The produce glistened in the white light, however: there was an abundance of lettuces, watercress, greens, turnips, chillies, gourds, long beans, ginger, packets of bamboo sprouts and apples. The fruit and vegetables were mixed up with dry goods: cabbages next to batteries, MSG sold with matches, biscuits piled next to bowls of bean curd; and there were more Chinese goods like 'PRO' washing powder (the one that smells of nothing), cigarettes, tiger balm and seed packets.

I noted that tomatoes were the most popular (and rare) item that day and when someone arrived with a basketful they could hardly lay them out before they were sold. I spotted a baked-potato seller, who baked the tubers in the embers of a fire wrapped in banana leaves. I bought one – it was small and hot and infused with the aroma of the leaves in which it was cooked. They were popular too, and, like tomatoes, not indigenous to the area but an import originally brought here from the Americas.

As I was leaving the market, some people came up to me and offered me bags of grass but I just said no with a smile and they went away. No one tried to drag me off to the police station in handcuffs. Being in the 'Golden Triangle', it was not that surprising that the local drug crop was on offer to willing buyers.

I spent the rest of the day in town watching backpackers arrive looking for drugs. They were indeed mobbed by tribal women, but they were only trying to sell textiles and cheap bracelets sewn with seeds and aluminium buttons. The drug sellers were smart enough to sell their wares on the quiet.

After a noisy day, I chose a place to stay a couple of miles out of town. I fell asleep contemplating a poster on the wall. It depicted the 'perfect home' – white shag-pile carpet and lemon walls, curly baroque chairs, a smoked-glass coffee table standing on a pastel Chinese cut rug, soft-hued table lamps decorating the brass occasional tables with additional bowls of ceramic fruit and an ornamental palm tree. It was sort of Shanghai meets Florida, the total antithesis of my bamboo shack bedroom.

That night I had a recurring dream that I hadn't dreamt for years: I dreamt of the people of the horned hair.

When I was about ten I had discovered these people in a photographic article about Chinese minorities and become fascinated by them. The photos depicted women working in the paddy fields wearing two-foot-long wooden horns on either side of their heads. The horns were wrapped in the long black hair of their ancestors and formed enormous structures that seemed to defy gravity. The hair wings were supposed to represent the strength of an ox and, frankly, they needed it just to hold their heads up. I dreamt of sailing to the other side of the world to meet them and the dreams were the beginning of my love affair with the East.

Fifteen years later, I was passing by the Chinese tourist centre in Shaftesbury Avenue when a book in the window caught my eye – it reminded me of the dream. I bought the book, *In Search of China's Minorities* by Zhang Weiwan, and took it home. It was an obscure paperback of idiosyncratic articles written in the field and badly translated from Chinese. It mentioned my 'hair people', but the best thing about it was that it described the strange foods eaten by the various groups.

It was in this book that I read about the rare delicacy 'bottled bird', a kind of canned fowl unique to the Yao people of southern China (now also living in Laos). It was simple to make – small wild birds were plucked, cleaned and then packed into earthenware jars with roasted rice powder and salt in a similar way to *paa-dek*. The jars were then sealed airtight and left to age. The result was a food said to be good for curing dysentery (though it seems more likely to cause it) that was just the kind of thing I like to try.

Now that I was in Laos I was a bike ride away from China, and it occurred to me at that moment in the middle of the night that I was realising my childhood dream. I had met the people with horned hair (well, cones of hair on the tops of their heads, but let's not get finicky) and I was about to visit a village of the Yao hill tribe people. Maybe, if I was lucky, I might find some bottled bird for supper.

In the morning it was still raining and cold as I walked up a gentle incline through little rice fields to the sound of rushing water. The sky was white, the valley was as green as malachite and I was very muddy. The trees along the margins of the fields dripped great splats on my head as I passed and I pulled my shawl over my hair for protection. I was going in the vague direction of a Yao village, but I had wandered into the paddies and had to keep leaping over gushing streams. Predictably, no one was around to ask the way in the rain, but I could hear gunshots in the distance. I scrabbled up a muddy bank and through some bushes to find myself in the Yao village. Pou Don Than is in reality four villages strung together, all peopled by the lu-Mien subgroup of the Yao minority who originally migrated from southern China.

The lu-Mien still practise a medieval form of Taoism supplemented with animism and ancestor worship, and their origin myth is associated with an ancient Chinese dog deity. The society is run on patriarchal clan lines. Their houses are built on the ground rather than on Lao-style stilts. Each house has a men's door and a women's door at either end, and a third entrance is called the big door and leads to the ancestral altar. The area behind the house is kept clear to enable the water dragon spirits, which convey blessings to the household, to enter with ease.

I may have been walking into a male-dominated society, but, as I was soon to find out, lu-Mien women were no shrinking violets.

I crossed the village just as it stopped raining and people came out of their houses and greeted me. The lu-Mien women in Laos dress in colossal black turbans and wear indigo coats with startling scarlet boas, as thick as an anaconda, made from tufts of wool. The effect is most arresting. The outfit is finished off with intricately embroidered trousers and waist sashes sewn with symbols that are sometimes used by a prospective husband to evaluate the character of his future wife. A code, read only by those initiated in the Yao way, can show a girl's age, subgroup, her proclivities, and even the strength of her eyesight (all that embroidering has made the Yao notorious for their need of spectacles). Men wear a simpler costume of tunic and trousers but often opt for modern dress.

Many of these sumptuously dressed women carried babies who wore colourful skullcaps, silver-buttoned and decorated with big red pom-poms. The hats are supposed to make the babies resemble flowers, which are closely associated with children for the Yao. They looked enchanting. I continued my walk, stopping to say 'Sabaii dii' and admire their lovely little ones. The drizzle had started again when I was stopped by a woman in modern dress and half dragged into a large windowless shed about twenty foot square and with a loose dirt floor. I assumed it was to get out of the rain, but as I stepped into the darkness she surprised me by handing me a printed card, which read:

MIEN WOMEN ASSOCIATION
Pou Don Than
Muang Sing
Hand-made products by Yao women and their families
(after eight km's out of Muang Sing towards
the Chinese border turn right)

The Mien are known in Laos for their shrewd business sense, but I really was not expecting to walk into an organised women's cooperative in the remote mountains. Hurray for the women of the world. In fact, women play a big role in Yao family finances and manage business at the market with great confidence. They also monitor household budgets and are responsible for the family silver and heirlooms.

As my eyes became accustomed to the semi-darkness, I saw a dozen beturbaned ladies looking at me expectantly and several little flower children staring open-mouthed. A prospective customer had come to town.

The only furniture in the shed was an ancient eight-foot-high wardrobe in the Chinese style. The lady who found me spoke Lao and a smidgen of English.

She led me to the cupboard with great theatricality. 'Women association shop!' she said, and gave a flourish of her hand.

She took a key from her pocket and unlocked the doors. After all the ceremony I suppose I expected to find the Crown jewels in there, but it was filled with clothes and textiles. In fact I was relieved; so many ancient heirlooms seem to find their way on to the open market, sold when times are tough.

'You buy Mien clothes,' she said, helping me into one of many gorgeous red-ruffed coats. The ladies crowded around to fit it on to me.

The coat split at the waist into three different pieces, two hanging in the front and one at the back. The two front pieces were crossed over each other and wrapped around my waist to be used as a belt that was tied at the back by my willing assistants. Underneath the ruff, the coat was delicately embroidered in blue and green cross-stitches and I realised that the tinkling sound that I had heard amongst the crowd came from a round silver bell used as a clasp at the neck. Silver coils were sewn around the sleeve cuffs and two silver beaded red tassles hung from splits at my waist.

'*Gnaam, gnamm,*' said the head of the woman's cooperative, urging me to buy. She used the Lao word for beautiful. (Although the lu-Mien have their own language, many people in Laos are bi- or trilingual.) This coat had been made to be sold – it was exquisite.

Next they urged me into a pair of trousers which were so embroidered they could have been brocade. The women were having a great time dressing me as I pathetically tried to explain my search for 'bottled bird' without the ability to speak their language. One leg went into the trousers as I flapped my hands like wings and made the sign for something very small. In went the other leg as I stuffed the imaginary bird into an imaginary jar. My antics were causing much mirth, particularly amongst the children, who were hysterical with laughter.

The head of the cooperative seemed to understand what I was saying, but then she went to the cupboard and brought back a box. Inside was a piece of old silver jewellery. It consisted of a V-link chain with several little tools, bells and charms attached to one end. Some of these jewellery tools have real uses, such as pins to scratch one's head under a turban, and they are as useful to the wearer as a Swiss army knife. This one was mainly decorative and had an enamelled centrepiece of a silver fish, and, I noticed, a small engraved bird. As she picked it out for me to look at more closely, I realised she had misunderstood my miming. It was beautiful, but there was no way I was going to buy it.

There is hardly any antique hill tribe jewellery left in South-east Asia, and, bizarrely, this is partially due to the greed of two Texan brothers who come from one of the richest families in America. In the early seventies the Hunt brothers decided to buy silver in huge quantities as a hedge against inflation. They began to corner the market in 1973 when the price was low, but before long others joined the chase and the silver-buying frenzy spread far beyond the United States. Soon Chinese merchants and soldiers on the make were scouring the mountains for tribal silver, melting it down and selling it to wholesalers who then sold it to the eager, avaricious brothers. This coincided with a time of extreme poverty for the hill tribe peoples due to the Vietnam conflict, and many resorted to selling their heirlooms. By 1979 the brothers had accumulated half the world's silver. The silver market crashed, causing colossal losses around the world. The Hunt brothers declared bankruptcy and were accused of manipulating the market. However, due to the intricacies of the American legal system, they are still rich today, whereas the historical heirlooms of the hill tribes of Laos are gone for ever.

The loss makes me sick to the heart. I could never buy the pendant. I could, however, buy a coat that was brand new and obviously made to sell to tourists.

The canny women of the Mien Women Association threw themselves into bargaining over the price while I continued to struggle to question them about 'bottled bird' or indeed any Mien specialties. We had a whale of a time. None of us really had any idea what we were saying, but it felt like a party. I was bamboozled into paying way over the odds for the coat, but I was glad the money was going directly to the source and hoped it would help them. The head of the cooperative mimed that she would come to my guest house that night and 'make with bird' (hands like wings flapping). So I guessed she was going to bring me a jar.

I bounced away to my guest house to await dinner, but a minute after I left a woman whose baby I had admired came running after me. She handed me a child's flower hat as a gift. It was grubby and the silver buttons had been removed, but it was exquisitely appliquéd and topped with pom-poms. I thanked her profusely and reflected on the generosity of spirit I found in the people of Laos. When I had first arrived I had cynically assumed that the dozens of acts of kindness I observed taking place every day were related to gaining 'merit'. I was wrong. Throughout my tour I found Laotian people to be genuinely benevolent, rich or poor, Buddhist or Taoist. The idea of community lies at the centre of this: the old and the very young are seen as valued contributors to society, familial and neighbourly relationships are nurtured to the benefit of all, and people look beyond their individual needs to help others less fortunate than themselves. My own culture began to look self-referential and cold by comparison.

That evening I sat on the open-sided platform that served as a restaurant for the guest house, holding the warm red collar of my new coat to my throat against the chill. The owners were away, leaving the kitchen in the charge of two teenagers – a boy with a severe middle parting, dressed in a trendy Aertex shirt and Adidas shorts, and a girl of about seventeen wearing a lot of gold jewellery and a stroppy expression. They were bored and they wanted everyone to know it. The girl plonked my Beer Lao on the table without looking at me and sauntered to the bamboo railing with a sigh. The boy was equally unhurried as he slowly wiped the bamboo bar. This general torpor was interrupted every half an hour by a few minutes of vivacious flirting. She would steal his dish cloth and he would chase her to retrieve it, or he would suddenly start swinging on the beams of the thatched roof, pulling himself up to show his muscles. It passed the time quite amusingly, as my Mien lady had not appeared. A few other guests arrived – four Chinese businessmen, an English couple in love, and three Canadians, all friendly, vibrant and inquisitive.

By nine-thirty (late in Laos) I gave up on my 'bottled bird' and was invited to join the communal table by the other tourists. Everyone had ordered hours ago, but nothing had arrived. I went to investigate and found the teenagers chasing each other around the kitchen. They told me dinner was off as the food had not been delivered. They had rice and potatoes, so I insisted that they make something with those and they reluctantly agreed.

It was sticky rice and chips for all of us, followed by dozens of beers and topped with Mekong whisky, compliments of the

Chinese party. We were sitting in the middle of a beautiful (even when sodden with rain) plain surrounded by mountains. Maybe it was the beer, maybe something in the air, but we all felt wonderful and relaxed. We talked deep into the night about nothing I can remember, draped over our chairs like lizards, and wandered back to our rooms looking up into a sky so full of stars it hurt to behold them.

The next morning I came to with a repetitive knocking in my head. I opened the door to find a small boy proffering a dead bird on his palm. It had blue feathers and a yellow chest, and was still warm. Another misunderstanding due to my appalling miming. Struck with guilt, I took the bird and gave him some money. He skipped off, thrilled. I couldn't eat it so I buried it, vowing not to be so stupid again. Then I packed my bag and left.

The road back to Luang Nam Tha was steep and full of potholes. The bus was an open-sided pickup with a tin roof tacked on top and it was packed. I, as usual, had got the worst seat – at the end of the bench and above the wheel, looking at the road lurching away behind me.

I was so squashed I couldn't move and within ten minutes we were flagged down by yet another prospective passenger, an emaciated old man wearing a grey plastic jacket and a blue Chinese military-style cap with a dead flower tucked into the hatband. He looked about sixty-five (which probably meant he was at least eighty), with high cheekbones and a straight nose. He was carrying two large wicker baskets on a shoulder yoke. I couldn't believe he could possibly fit as there was so little room, but he managed to wheedle his way into a space between two rice sacks and we were back on the road.

He settled down and gave a cackle as he fumbled amongst the machetes, knives and various ripped garments that filled his baskets. Finally he found what he was looking for – an old tobacco box. He opened the tin and suddenly the bus was filled with a smell so piquant, so penetrating, that it hit the back of my nose like smelling salts. It was raw opium and I had never smelt anything like it before.

The peculiar thing is, I cannot recall what it smelt like at all, however hard I try. By the time I got off the bus I realised, with some shock, that I had already lost the memory of the scent completely. I have a good sense of smell and that has never happened to me before or since. I just remember that it was strong and disappeared the instant he closed the tin.

The opium was a sticky reddish gum and looked like Marmite. He scooped out a small bit the size of an aniseed ball, put it in his mouth and then took a swig of water from his khaki army-issue hip flask. Everyone in the bus watched with interest and they all went 'Aaaahhhh!' and then giggled as he drank the water down.

Most people prefer to smoke opium, but more morphine and codeine are absorbed when the latex is eaten directly. Opiate addiction has recently been proved to be genuinely physiological, rather than psychological, which makes it much harder to kick the habit, and there are an estimated sixty thousand opium addicts in Laos. Opium is primarily sold to exporters for cash, however, rather than in the domestic market. The money made is used to ensure food supplies during shortages endemic in subsistence farming. According to the government Khao San Pathet Lao agency, the yield for the 2001 Lao growing season was 117.5 tons, down 30 per cent on the year before (though the United States Narcotics Bureau puts the figure at 210 tons, increasing another 5 per cent due to the crackdown in Afghanistan). That's a huge amount of opium to try and replace with other equally valuable crops.

The drug hit the old man swiftly, and his eyes became dreamy. Then he took the yellow floral hand towel he used as a scarf and held it to his mouth. Mercifully he wasn't sick, but instead he stood up and barged on to the narrow bench to sit beside me, the *felang*. He closed his eyes and floated off to nirvana while I became painfully jammed into the bar that held up the roof.

He drifted in and out of consciousness and several times I saw his eyes roll back into his head. He kept wriggling, and we were such a tight fit on the bench that every time he moved someone would pop out of the row and have to squeeze back in again. Everyone in the bus indulged the man with smiles and giggles, as opium is an acceptable drug for the aged. When we got out at a military checkpoint, the guards ignored him.

We arrived in Luang Nam Tha at dusk. I watched the opium eater squat down, take everything out of his baskets and meticulously lay it all out in a neat line on the road to check he had not lost anything.

I walked back to the Boat Landing guest house for some good supper.

Khao Poon – Cool noodles

6–8 shallots, seared and then sliced

3 cloves garlic, seared and then sliced

4 bird's-eye chillies, seared

2.5 cm (1 inch) piece galangal, peeled and sliced

450 g (1 lb) pork belly in one piece

900 g (2 lb) pork bones or pork hock

1 pig lung (optional)

2 spring onions, tied in a knot

1 stalk lemon grass, tied in a knot

6 kaffir lime leaves

4 tablespoons *paa-dek* water

1/2 teaspoon salt

450 g (1 lb) firm white fish such as mullet or Tiapia

450 g (1 lb) dried rice vermicelli

VEGETABLE PLATTER

1 green papaya, shredded

1 handful bamboo shoots

1 handful bean sprouts

1 handful white cabbage, shredded

1 handful lettuce, shredded

8 green beans, chopped into small pieces

1 bunch water spinach

some Asian coriander

CONDIMENTS

30 dried chilli peppers, pounded

fish sauce

soy sauce

slices of lime

Place 3 litres (just over 5 pints) of water in a big pot and put it on to boil.

Meanwhile, spear the shallots, garlic, chillies and galangal on to a skewer and blacken on an open flame. Place the pork bones/hock, belly pork and pig lung in the water and bring to the boil. Skim and then add the shallots, garlic, chillies, galangal, spring onions, lemon grass, lime leaves, *paa-dek* water and salt. Bring back to the boil and then simmer, skimming occasionally until the meat is falling from the bones.

Remove the meat and lung and cut into bite-size pieces, throw away the bones and strain the stock through a sieve into another saucepan. Place the new saucepan on the heat and add the fish. Poach until done. Gently break up the fish with a wooden spoon and add the meat to the soup, keeping it on a low heat. Serve the soup in a large bowl in the centre of the table.

Now revive the dried noodles by pouring boiling water over them and leaving for 3 minutes, then rinse in a bowl under the cold tap in a colander. Once cool, take a good pinch of noodles, squeeze them dry and twist them into little nests. Arrange these on a large platter.

On another platter arrange piles of the vegetables, and spread the little bowls of condiments around the table so people can add them to taste.

To serve, give everyone a large bowl and place a nest or two of vermicelli in each. Let your guests choose their own favourite vegetables to sprinkle liberally on their noodles and then ladle the hot soup on top. Laotians like to add lots of chilli.

SEVEN

AN ALTERNATIVE CHRISTMAS DINNER

He pointed up into the trees, '*Kai mot som*, good to eat, it is the season.'

I looked up into the foliage expecting to see some kind of monkey or squirrel.

'Where? What?' I asked, squinting into the dappled shadow.

'There, look, up there,' Pawn said with impatience, as though I must be totally blind not to see it.

I looked intently.

'But I can't see anything.'

'Ant egg nest, look, in the leaves!'

And then I did see it – a glistening ball of oval leaves the colour of avocado flesh and as big as a honeydew melon. It was beautiful and delicate, and swarming with red ants.

We were in the ancient forest of the Nam Ha National Biodiversity Park on a guide-training eco-trek. There were four trainee guides, a trainer and one tourist – me.

The idea of this type of trek is to inspire environmental and cultural conservation whilst stimulating the local economy with some much-needed cash (my trek fee). It was financed by the New Zealand government to help promote global environmental awareness. I liked the idea of 'positive impact travelling': it was mutually beneficial. I was interested in visiting them and their forest without causing damage, and the local people were curious to see *falang*.

I was also there because I wanted to try tribal food and learn about the edible plants of the forest. This, at last, was my first ant nest sighting. I'd been dying to see one ever since I had first come across the larvae with Vandara in Luang Prabang.

The nest was at least fifteen foot up and hanging on the end of a long flimsy branch. I was just wondering how we would get them down when two Lantien tribeswomen appeared on the path in front of us. Their dress distinguished them as the Kim Mun Lantien Sha, a subgroup of the Yao people who emigrated from northern Vietnam in the late nineteenth century. They were wearing knee-length indigo home-weave jackets, silver-buttoned down the side and belted low on the hips with a twist of fluorescent pink cotton. Their hair was neatly parted in the middle and then scraped back into a high bun held in place by a silver tog. They had shaved off their eyebrows, which signified they were married.

The women carried two long poles, one of which had a bucket of water attached at its end. Ignoring us completely, they walked up to the ant nest tree (they must have spotted it earlier that morning), then one woman held the bucket under the nest while the other knocked it in. As they brought it down I could see a swarm of furious ants pouring out of the leaves. She kept the bucket well away from herself as she lopped the pole over her shoulder, and they were off, at speed.

'What are they going to do with it?' I asked wistfully. I'd have offered to buy it from them if I'd had the chance.

'The ants drown or run away,' replied Pawn, 'leaving the eggs and larvae which float to the surface. They're very good – ant egg soup, it's tasty. This nest is very new, very green. Later the leaves will go yellow and curl, easy to see. They are harvested by women, in the dry season only.' And then he was off again, crashing through the undergrowth, flicking fronds in my face.

I wondered if we would get to eat ant egg soup in the village tonight.

The trek had begun gently as we had picked our way in a line along the raised edges of the rice paddies. It was the harvest season and the butterscotch-coloured rice was waist-high and swayed in the breeze in rippling waves. Some of the rice had already been cut, which left squares of tough stubble toasted the colour of burnt sugar by the sun. The fields spread out in a golden oval like a tortoise shell, surrounded by an emerald corona of jungle-covered hills. No one was about at this time of day except strange, albino water buffalo that seemed to haunt the fields like spectres.

The paddies were squelchy with dark-chocolate mud that slurped over my boots and sucked at my feet when I lost my footing. Dwi, the sole woman guide, was only wearing sandals and slipped into the oozing pools more often; her socks were sodden.

'Oh well,' she trilled, 'they will soon be dry, it's only water.'

'Perfumed with buffalo piss,' added Mr Adrian, the guide trainer, guffawing. 'Did you know that McDonald's is the biggest seller of dog food in the world?'

He wasn't being ironic. His last job was as an IT consultant for the McDonald's corporation and he was a fund of information on burger trivia. In Laos, the title 'Mr' or 'Madame' is often put in front of someone's first name as a mark of respect, particularly if that person is in a position of authority.

Mr Adrian came from the United States and had perfect American teeth, but most of all his dark stubbled face was dominated by his nose. He'd found himself the job of guide trainer after chatting to someone in Nepal and was still a bit shell-shocked at the reality of the task. This was only the second time that the four trainee guides had gone out with him into the field.

Our trainee guides were Pawn, the owner of the Boat Landing guest house, Pet Sack and Set from the forestry department, and Dwi. Pawn saw the tour guide training as an entrepreneurial opportunity and was by far the most confident of the group. The other three had been attending Mr Adrian's classes and were still learning English. They had been told to practise their new language on the trek.

We were hiking towards Ban Nalan, a Khamu village that had recently shifted down the mountain a bit so they could supplement their forest foraging by cultivating wetland rice. They'd rebuilt their homes, with the help of the project, on a better plot of land in the hope of improving their standard of living.

We would sleep in the village overnight so we'd been told to travel light. I had brought only my 'jungle girl, multi-purpose day bag'.

Until recently the Khamu were also known as Kha (slaves), as they traditionally supplied menial labour to the more sophisticated later immigrants. The Khamu ancestry has been said to date back to the aboriginal Kha, predating the Tai migrations into the area by several thousand years, when the whole Southeast Asian area was inhabited by a mix of Negroid peoples. However, the Khamu now speak a language that belongs to the Austro-Asiatic family, which links them to the Cham, the Mon from the Menam region, and the Khmer of Cambodia. These people probably arrived in Laos as rice farmers, originating ultimately in southern China. When the Tai peoples began to arrive from the north during the twelfth and thirteenth centuries, the Khamu were driven into the upland regions, where many still reside today. Most Laotians, however, believe the Khamu to be the original inhabitants of Laos and, as a strange form of respect, the king traditionally recruited them as his personal guard.

Physically, aboriginal Kha were said to be of small build, to have slightly frizzy hair, darker skin and rounder eyes. I was interested to see if this physiology was evident in the Khamu and if their food differed in any way from the traditional Laotian cuisine I'd eaten so far.

'In fact, there are twenty-eight thousand McDonald's restaurants worldwide,' continued Mr Adrian from behind me. 'In one province in China, they have to write the McDonald's menu in seventeen different dialects; it takes up a whole wall!'

I hope they all burn down, I thought, as I shook my head to banish the horrible image of takeaway burgers from my mind's eye. We were now in pristine forest and I really didn't want my senses invaded by the revolting smell-memory of a Big Mac and chips.

The trail was steep and slender and you had to concentrate on your feet so as not to trip on a rock or tree root. But it was wonderful. Everything was luscious and spurting with life. The beaten red earth of the path gashed down the mountain like a stream of wine. As I climbed, I noticed fat buds pushing stickily through the soil and delicate new ferns uncoiling from beneath rocks, pushing them aside; saplings sprung out and whipped my calves; vines fingered down from the trees looking for purchase. I breathed in the zesty smell of new growth.

Pet Sack grasped a fistful of shiny, dark green leaves.

'Wild cardamom,' he said. They were shaped like spearheads; I'd noticed clumps of them growing by the path. He crushed them in his hands to release the fragrance and wafted them under my nose.

'They smell like camphor,' I said. It was black medicinal cardamom. I'd made a pact with Pawn and Pet Sack that I would help them improve their pronunciation if they pointed out good things to eat.

'We sell to Chinese, for medicine,' he said. 'Use for stomach remedy.'

'In Lao it's the third largest export,' added Pawn. 'It's grown commercially in the south, but here it's a forest product – a good source of money.'

Pet Sack dropped the cardamom and walked on. He had a soft face, his hair styled in a side parting that went in one direction above a lop-sided smile that went in the other, to charming effect. He was sweating terribly in his thick khaki forestry uniform.

I snapped off some leaves to perfume my journey and trudged on behind the others. The trek was hard but it was dark and cool under the canopy. Speckled light found its way through the trees in tiny jets that glanced off the leaves and streaked through the gloom in sparkling flashes. Whenever we stopped for breath, tiny yellow butterflies the size of buttercup petals landed on our clothes and sucked at the salt on our arms. The air was full of the clamour of frogs, crickets and birds. Occasionally a huge bumbling insect would burble past my ear.

The trail was flattening out a little and I was getting used to breathing in rhythm. A stream crossed our path on the diagonal and I disturbed another mass of butterflies that had come to drink. They were pale, iridescent green and looked like new broad beans. They fluttered away like confetti. We walked on through the dappled undergrowth and I noticed that Set had disappeared again.

Set was still learning English and really couldn't speak it very well, but while we'd been talking he'd been listening and, in the typical Lao way, wanted to help out. Every so often he'd bob off to pick something edible and carefully write the name in Lao in my notebook. Now he returned and gave me a handful of berries (*Rubus bleharoneurus*). They were yellowy-orange and hairy.

'Wild raspberries,' said Pet Sack, picking one out of my hand.

They were a little sour.

Dwi also took one. She gave me a wicked look and whispered to me with her hand in front of her mouth, 'The Lahu tribe say they looking like . . .' she pointed discreetly down . . . 'You know, down there.'

They did rather.

At last we reached the middle highlands and found ourselves looking over wide open views to the north and south on either side of a narrow ridge; in the distance row upon row of jungle-covered hills, like heads of broccoli, faded to smoky blue. We had arrived at the rice fields and sat down to eat some well-earned papaya. In between the crops I could see the evidence of slash-and-burn cultivation – occasional bare mounds like bald pates stubbled with black stumps and tufted with the odd wisp of hairy bamboo.

'God, this papaya tastes good,' I said as I sank my teeth into the juicy flesh. After the sweaty climb I felt like swooning in the honeyed aroma.

'Yeah, it's from the highlands,' said Mr Adrian. 'Tastes good, doesn't it? The lowland Lao pay much more for swidden rice, fruit and vegetables because they prefer the taste. The burnt earth adds a particular tang. It's really noticeable. You see when we try the swidden rice.'

The pink juice was dripping down my chin. I wiped it away and we were off again, sweeping through the upland rice fields at a speedy rate, dipping in and out of the grassland, into the dark, moist jungle. In shady places the undergrowth was still drenched from last night's rain.

I thought we were never going to stop for lunch so I was relieved when we reached a rest hut an hour later. Pawn produced plastic bags of grilled fish stuffed with basil and lemon grass, sour greens and chilli *jaew*. Having already noticed my look of hunger, Dwi smiled at me and took a heavy bag of sticky rice out of her rucksack. She had a delicate face, a naughty smile and a habit of looking sideways at me conspiratorially whenever men were mentioned. She unrolled some banana leaves to use as plates and laid out the food.

I was ravenous and particularly took to the pickled greens, which were tangy and moreish. As I gulped down my meal I looked around. These huts are used for several purposes: as temporary rice stores, rest houses and even homes. During the rice harvest, a whole family will come and live in one for a few days rather than traipse back to the village every night. It was a basic, somewhat flimsy structure of lateral bamboo strips lashed to a wooden frame with a roof of banana leaves. Inside, half the floor was covered with a six-inch-high platform of woven bamboo, on to which we quickly collapsed. A tin cup of tea, still warm, lay discarded next to the smoking embers of a fire. I felt like a trespasser but was assured that the farmer wouldn't mind us using his hut. Above the door, some large pheasanty-looking feathers were sticking out of the roofing in a pattern. Some kind of animist charm. The Khamu believe that elements of the material world possess spirits and that their dead exist as ghosts. These spirits may be found in many things – animals, trees, streams or even amulets – and they must be cherished and respected to ensure their protection and good-will. I'd heard that forest spirits safeguarded their fields and I asked Pawn about them.

'The Khamu only borrow their farmland from the wild spirits of the forest,' he said, sucking on a fish head. 'The land is chosen in a ceremony, and then the villagers build an altar in the middle of a field for their ancestors and village spirits to live in. They put flowers along the paths to the new land to welcome the spirits into the altar and then leave offerings of rice and chicken for them to eat. In return, the spirits offer protection from bad elements, and, hopefully, ensure a good harvest. Then, after they've finished farming the land, it's given back to the forest spirits and trees can grow back again.'

I still felt as if I was intruding. The feathers had made me feel that I was in a sacred place, like a chapel, even though it was only an old rice hut. Animist ceremonies had happened right here, which meant that there were named spirits specifically protecting this spot, and I had no idea if I was doing something offensive. Furthermore, whoever owned the hut had only just left: a plastic bag of cooked sticky rice hung from the ceiling and, beside that, a very dusty faded green cotton jacket and a raggedy shirt had been jammed into a hole in the wall. Someone had slipped them off in the midday heat and stored them away. I could still feel their presence.

'So the Khamu still practise slash-and-burn farming?' I asked, picking apart a bony fish.

'Yeah,' said Mr Adrian. 'They practise a mixture of farming methods. Wet rice near the river, and dry rice in the swidden fields.'

The Laotians were listening intently whilst rolling up small balls of sticky rice and using them to mop up pinches of fish or greens.

'This Khamu village is part of the conservation project in the park, the eco-treks are another element of it too. I don't just train guides, you know.'

'So what else are you doing?'

'We work with the tribe, helping them to develop rules for the conservation of forest resources and we've set up a village fund in case of crop failure. And it's all backed by the Lao government which is very keen to relocate the tribes and get the slash-and-burn under their control.'

Pawn was chewing violently and leaning forward.

'The people only burn a little land, they like to live in the highlands,' said Pawn.

Adrian was suddenly furious. 'Their farming is full of variety and villagers cooperate to bring in the harvest without having to depend on expensive machines and fuel. The diversity of crops planted each season means that if one crop fails another is good over the hill. Actually, there are many good things about slash-and-burn. And not everyone wants to live in the lowlands.'

Everyone had stopped eating to listen.

'The government relocation policy is really controversial. Once people leave the deep forest, their traditions are often lost for ever. Lots of people are against it but it's hard to protest openly here. Even the mildest opposition to government policy is dealt with using draconian methods – imprisonment for unspecified terms. We can't control the movements but we are trying to help. We ensure that if a village is relocated in the park, it has to be moved to an area of good land. They get a title guarantee so that they can be sure to keep it, to re-establish their community properly.'

'Good idea,' I said, picking out a fish bone painfully lodged in my tongue. I wondered, though, how strong those titles would be if a road was being built in the area, as in the south of Laos. There, people were being swept aside and forcibly relocated to make way for it.

'That's why this project is so important in Nam Tha. We are trying to work with the villagers, not against them.'

The fish, though delicious, was full of tiny bones and at that moment I got another one caught in my throat. I had to be saved from my purple-faced spluttering by Set forcing me to eat a ball of rice to dislodge it. This drama rather killed the conversation, so we set off again.

After lunch, the trek was much harder. We were scaling a seemingly vertical mountain, using a splashing stream as a path. I had thought myself reasonably fit. I'd been walking several miles a day during the past weeks, often carrying heavy luggage, but I was a novice in comparison to the Lao guides, who'd been on several fitness-training treks in the last few months. I was puffing and letting off steam like a pressure cooker, but it felt like a privilege to be there as we were now in the National Bio-diversity Conservation Area. Old forest.

We were passing through Nam Ha Park, where some of the world's most threatened mammals live amongst five-hundred-year-old trees. Asian tigers, clouded leopards and wild elephants were hidden in the jungle around us; somewhere, a sun bear, the smallest bear in the world, was sitting in a tree snacking on some fruit; and pangolins, weird scaled anteaters with fur between their scales, were snuffling into termite mounds. The place was filled with endangered species – hog badgers, guar, slow lorris, Hodgson's porcupine, mouse deer and short-nosed fruit bats to name a few; plus a whole assortment of rare rodenty things.

Not that I could see any of them.

Our stream-path was completely covered over by the forest canopy, like a tunnel. The sunlight only penetrated in sprinkles.

As I struggled up the rocky stream bed, the elusive light flitted from one object to another, highlighting things for a second with fearsome clarity: the glossy scales of a lizard as it whipped away into the bushes; the jaspered glitter of a pebble in the water; the delicate tutu frills of a lichen. The tree trunks dwarfed us, their roots curling into the leaf mould like fat snakes. The leaves closed in on us and we had to thrust them away. And when we paused to rest, the forest came alive with the roaring clamour of a million creatures that were hidden from our view.

We stopped at a natural ledge in the stream. The villagers had tied a piece of bamboo pipe to one side of a shelf, which acted as a drinking spout.

'How far have we climbed, Adrian?' I gasped at a rest stop.

'Nearly one hundred metres since we started the steep bit,' he said, looking at his special hiking watch. 'We are now one thousand, four hundred and seventy metres above sea level.'

I was dying. Like a secretary in a cheap blouse, you could see every detail of my bra. My pale green cotton shirt had become transparent with sweat. My cotton trousers clung grittily to my hot thighs and I was literally panting with my tongue out.

'Do I look red?' I huffed.

'More fuchsia,' said Mr Adrian.

Three hours had passed, and the guides had become silent. The only person still able to speak was Adrian; he wasn't even out of breath.

'You realise that one in three of all restaurant meals eaten in the world today is a McDonald's.' Nobody answered.

Twenty minutes later: 'Did you know that every minute a million zillion trillion burgers are sold worldwide?'

Leaping up a ledge: 'Actually, the burgers are just a sideline. The *real* business is real estate.'

Eventually even he shut up, but by the time I got to Ban Nalan I unfortunately knew as much about McDonald's as the plants of the forest.

To be honest, I wasn't capable of conversation – I was in agony. My body had begun to complain loudly. The thirty metres before we reached the top of the hill were the hardest; my legs just didn't want to move upwards any more. I had to concentrate all my will to get one above the other. My bag felt as if it were filled with boulders and my water clanged against my aching bottom like a wrecking ball. Compared with me, the others were leaping up the stream like goats, though Pet Sack was struggling a bit. I, however, had become all slow motion. I was moving like a sloth.

I was clearly at the 'aubergine stage' when at last I reached the summit, way behind the others. I collapsed. Thank God, that had been the final climb before the village, and the last ten minutes of the journey would be downhill. We were still in deep jungle and, though we were much higher now, I couldn't see anything through the thick undergrowth. I lay on the ground for a moment like a wet rag, unable to move. Sweat was dripping off my nose and splashing down my shirt. I could hear the blood rushing through my ears. Not wanting to make a scene, I heaved myself off the jungle floor and, still a bit delirious, almost walked through a gateway on the path to the village.

'Walk around it,' hollered Mr Adrian. 'It's taboo to walk through it, you'll disrespect the spirits.'

The gateway melded so well into the surrounding forest that it was easy to miss. It was box-shaped and made from thin, sun-bleached branches. Looped bamboo chains were strewn across the top and a star-shaped talisman, also bamboo, was fixed to the pole on the side. It looked forgotten.

I did as I was told. I didn't want to offend through ignorance. The Khamu believe spirits are active in all aspects of daily life. Bad ones are responsible for disease, natural disasters and failed harvests. The spirits of the ancestors live alongside the tribe, in their houses, village and village gate. The spirits that are most feared live outside these boundaries: spirits of elements such as the mountain, water, forest, thunder and sky. The village gate keeps them out and the talismans frighten them away.

Having avoided bringing catastrophe on the people I was about to visit, I stepped out of the forest and looked down on a scatter of about thirty-five houses built in a clearing on a curve of the Nam Ha river. The huts had woven bamboo walls, shaggy, thatched roofs, and were the same dun colour as the earth.

As we trooped into the village, there was a stampede. Hundreds of turkeys, chickens, pigs, piglets, puppies, dogs and ducks rushed out from under the stilted huts to greet us. Ban Nalan was filled with animals. At first I didn't see anyone, as Khamu houses are windowless. Then a little boy with boss-eyes and a stripy vest poked his head out of a doorway and his face split into a huge grin.

'*Falang! Falang!*' he screamed at the top of his voice.

He can only have been about two, but he zipped down the ladder of his house and waddled towards us with such speed that he was just a blur.

People sprang from nowhere.

Their clothing was a mixture of Western cast-offs worn with traditional skirts and jewellery. Little girls were wearing stripy tops and no knickers; little boys were wearing stripy knickers and no tops; women were wearing old men's shirts; stripy towels were wrapped like turbans around heads. This village must have been really mad about stripes as practically everyone was wearing them.

It was four o'clock and the adults were coming back from foraging in the forest and tending the swidden fields. We caused quite a crowd. An old lady with a twist of checked fabric in her hair and no teeth came to show me her grandchild. A tiny girl in a twelve-inch *sin* and a necklace laden with old coins stood transfixed in front of me. The Khamu were a good-looking bunch – petite-bodied, with chiselled jawlines and clear nutmeg skin. I didn't spot any frizzy hair or exceptionally different trib-al physique. The children are particularly stunning as they have lovely brown long-lashed eyes and are always smiling and hav-ing fun.

Most noticeable of all when we arrived, however, was the big, bright blue sign standing proudly in the centre displaying the 'REGULATIONS FOR USE OF THE FOREST', which listed what you could and couldn't shoot, etc. Ban Nalan is a model village working closely with the Wildlife Conservation Unit.

We were still standing in a huddle when we heard the sound of booming gunshots in the jungle behind us. Then the headman appeared carrying a blunderbuss almost bigger than himself. Mr Adrian let out a huge sigh and raised his eyes.

'God, what ha-a-a-a-s he been sho-o-o-o-ting? They're sup-posed to have handed in their weapons.'

The headman didn't bat an eyelid as he gave the gun to his five-year-old daughter. A tiny man in a grubby narrow-striped shirt and grey shorts, he sported a moustache and wispy beard. He held himself straight, smiled rarely and looked you straight in the eye. He had an almost military presence and I was reminded that the Lao monarchy used the Khamu as bodyguards and mahouts for their sacred white elephants. As proto-inhabitants of Laos, they were considered 'guardians of the land' who endorsed the legitimacy of the king but at the same time were used as menial workers and called Kha, slave: a strange dichotomy.

We greeted him formally and asked for permission to stay in his village. He agreed, and, looking at our dishevelled state (par-ticularly mine), suggested we go for a swim in the river to cool off. We were led to a newly-built wooden schoolhouse that was to be our room for the night.

As soon as we started to change our clothes, we noticed them. Leeches. It was the very end of the leech season so the few remaining leeches were desperate for blood.

Trekking through a stream does have its hazards. They were all over our boots, trying to worm their way into our feet by any devious means possible. At one centimetre long, they were small and tricky to pick up. Dwi, in her wet socks, had already suffered two attacks along the way and Set was helping her by deftly flicking them into oblivion using the lightning-quick moves of a martial arts master. I counted seven of the bastards on one boot alone.

'Roll them off me! Roll them off me! It's the only way,' roared Pawn, leaping high in the air.

'OK, OK, calm yourself,' said Dwi, as she squashed them with her sandal.

I'd expected the guides to be used to leeches, but they weren't. Pawn looked as if he was sucking a lemon as he removed his leeches between his forefinger and thumb, and when Set lifted his foot out of his shoe it was streaming with blood. I removed eighteen before they got a purchase. Then I stripped off my socks to find one hoovering about my ankle. It wasn't going to have a meal on me, so I rolled it off and attempted to fling it away, only to find it, a minute later, trying to sneak a drink underneath my ring. I squashed it.

Mr Adrian didn't have any, anywhere, as he'd wisely sprayed insect repellent on his boots and socks before setting out.

Leech-free at last, we headed for the river and a cool swim. I'd taken my boots and socks off at the schoolhouse, and as I stepped into the water I noticed that a stream of blood as long and thick as a drinking straw had coagulated on my leg – a bastard leech had managed to get a suck. To my amazement, my blood floated off down the river like a stick.

It was a beautiful spot; the water was clear and flowed fast. You had to keep a firm footing or you'd be whooshed downstream by the current for thirty feet until you could grab an overhanging tree. This happened to me several times, and my sarong kept ballooning off like a pig's bladder. It was certainly very refreshing. I became the centre of a flying-down-the-river-hanging-on-to-a-*falang* game for the village children, while several adults, scrubbing themselves down with packets of washing powder, looked on in hysterical amusement. It was such fun I didn't want to get out, but suppertime was nearing and I wasn't going to miss that.

I wandered back to the village. As Khamu houses are windowless they all have an external platform with a thatched awning for working in the shaded light. It was the time for relaxation, and most people were stretched out on their verandas dozing or chopping vegetables. Outside the headman's hut there was an iron pot stand placed over the open fire and several little stools scattered around it. I sat down on one to watch dinner being cooked. Alas, ant eggs weren't on the menu as no one had gathered any that day. Instead, we had purchased two live turkeys and now their time had come.

They lay in the dust impassively until the headman grabbed one by the neck and ripped out all its neck feathers while it screamed. He felt for the jugular. He held down its head while another much older man took out a huge iron knife and cut the vein.

'It is taboo for the headman to kill it since his wife is pregnant,' whispered Pawn.

The turkey blinked at me in panic as they twisted the sinews to release the flow of blood. It poured into a chipped enamel bowl. This took three long minutes.

The turkey was still alive when an old man took it to the wood pile and knocked it on the head with a stick to finish it off, only he wasn't looking when he brought the stick down, so he missed. He didn't notice and walked away without looking back. With a terrible, depressed realisation of its own doom, the turkey buried its head up to the shoulders in the wood pile. Everyone was ignoring it while they went about their business, going to get potatoes, chopping vegetables and stoking the flames.

Five minutes later it was still horribly alive.

Someone picked it up by the feet and threw it on a stool by the fire. It lay there with its head lolling back to reveal the vertebrae, jerking in spasms until it finally died. It was stuffed into a pot of boiling water to soften the feathers, then plucked. Cream-coloured dogs licked at the bloody splatters in the dirt.

The other turkey had watched all this; now it was her turn.

Staked to the ground with her legs tied together, she suddenly became aware of her fate and squawked and fluttered violently. Then the whole process was repeated again.

So it was turkey blood for supper. (If you ever want to make this at home follow the above instructions then add seven spoons of fish sauce, seven spoons of water, three chopped stalks of lemon grass, four chopped spring onions and five cloves of sliced garlic. Mix around and serve.)

To supplement this dish, the turkeys were chopped up (bones included) and boiled in a big pot with lemon grass, seared chill-ies and greens. The meat was taken out and put in a steamer on top of a bed of red onions and garlic. A layer of sliced potato was placed on top and covered with banana leaves. The broth was used to cook white cabbage and a lemon mint *jaew* was pounded for a side dish. It was December and it occurred to me that I was about to eat a kind of Christmas dinner.

During this spectacle, hoards of children had gathered to stare at us. Behind them, in the central village clearing, more children were playing a game with a wicker-bamboo football. Another group near me were having fun with a sweet packet full of sand. They were completely uninterested in the turkey and oblivious to any sense of it being in pain. Butchering animals was just a part of village life.

A puppy exhausted from its foraging in the turkey blood lay asleep by the fire, a tiny feather blowing in and out of its nose. An old woman with a towel turban on her head, smoking a home-made silver pipe, sat down on a stool beside me. Towels are used as a fabulous fashion textile in Laos: a nifty sarong, a dapper turban, a distinguished neck scarf; the brighter and more synthetic the better. She had a very kind, benign expression. The rest of our gang came back from visiting the *lao-lao* rice liquor still.

As twilight dropped to night almost instantaneously, the other villagers came and joined the party. While the food was cooking, a scratched plastic doll's teacup was passed around full of *lao-lao*. You had to down it in one, refill it and pass it on. By the sixth cup things were getting quite merry. Though none of us could speak a word of each other's languages we managed to have elaborate discussions using mime and comical facial expressions. We discovered who was married to whom, how many children belonged to which couples and who was the oldest resident (ninety-two) of the village. I was shown various edible leaves and nuts. A little boy wearing a rusty tin can as a hat gave me a dainty bunch of marigolds; grinning widely, he had a good look at my face, then shot away. The small glow of the fire hardly lit people's faces, but I could see the shiny glint of their eyes in the inky blackness. The sound of children's laughter filled the night.

The *lao-lao* did its magic and the stars looked particularly glittering as we all wobbled up the headman's ladder and into his hut for dinner.

There was an open fire on the floor to the right and the walls were decorated with various wildlife conservation posters. The food was laid out in bowls on banana leaves and blue plastic rice sacks on the floor, and included a big plate of herb leaves. Everything tasted excellent; I can recommend turkey blood as a dish of kings. Actually, the flavour was mainly of the lemon grass that had been chopped into it, and it was very salty. Everything else tasted of strong gamey bird or the turkey broth that it was cooked in – potatoes and cabbage – and the minty *jaew* added just the right piquant touch to lift the roof of your mouth off. But the real treat for me was the sticky rice grown in the swidden soil. It smelt divine and it tasted even better. The smell was strong, fragrant, like clean wet earth; there was a hint of fresh sap and a whiff of jasmine flowers. It tasted nutty and there was a mere touch of a smoky tang to it. It was delicious.

Although this village looked well fed, malnutrition, particularly a lack of vitamin A, is common in the mountains. Adrian told me that nearly all the fruit and vegetables I saw growing in their gardens were destined to be sold at the market for cash. During the meal I tried to glean if there were any dishes that were specially related to the Khamu, but the headman shook his head as though I'd asked a crazy question. People here ate what they could find. An average meal in the village consisted of rice, greens gathered from the forest, a bit of chilli for flavour, and maybe a little fish if any were caught in the river that day. Meat was only eaten to celebrate an event, festival or when it was sacrificed to appease the spirits. We were dining on 'special occasion' food and I don't think Adrian, I or even the

Laotian guides thought about this as we were used to eating meat every day. We had casually bought, not one, but two turkeys and had therefore become a significant 'event'.

So everyone was eating with gusto, and we'd all stopped talking to concentrate on the feast: spoons were dipping into everything. I picked up a choice bit of turkey in the near dark of the two small candles and bit.

I had picked up a head and, as the eyeball popped surprisingly in my mouth, I felt a terrible sense of guilt. That eye had looked at me in panic only an hour or so before. I swallowed quickly. Across the floor I noticed a bowl of turkey broth. A splash of blood had fallen in it from a passing spoon and was dispersing redly in the liquid. It reminded me of the shower scene in *Psycho* when the blood swills down the plughole. I sent a turkey prayer up into the night.

By eight o'clock it was all over and the whole village was asleep. Our group were all sharing one room and each bed consisted of a mosquito net draped over a plastic mat, a sheet and a blanket. There was one net for every two people, so I shared one with Dwi.

I slept for three hours and then woke, dying to pee. I had wisely gone to bed with all my clothes on, but when I stumbled out into the pitch-black jungle, the temperature had dropped dramatically and I nearly froze my bottom off. My little torch wobbled in my shaking hands. In fear of rats or God knows what else, I yanked up my trousers as fast as I could and leapt back up the stairs.

I returned to the hard floor with my thin blanket. A cricket had dropped by and it sounded as if someone was tapping on an old manual typewriter in the next room. Puffs of freezing air wafted through the floorboards carrying with them the smell of mushrooms. I was chilled to the core. I was so desperate for warmth that I even considered curling around Dwi, but then thought better of it. I lay still, trying to imagine I was lying on a boiling hot beach. I'd read somewhere that it was through this method that a woman had survived hypothermia when she fell down a snow-filled ravine, but it didn't work for me. I lay frozen listening to the sounds of the jungle; the night was filled with an underscore of a million frogs which would suddenly swell into a deafening crescendo then, just as suddenly, subside again. At three o'clock a dog, far away, barked three times, 'Woof, woof, woof.' Nearby one yelped back, 'Aaaaaiiiiii', 'Woof, woof, woof'. 'Aaaaaiiiiii', 'Woof, woof, woof'. On and on they barked until I wished I had the headman's blunderbuss. At four the cockerels started.

I got up with the first glimmer of light.

At dawn, the village looked ethereally beautiful. The vast sur-rounding trees, dripping with vines, slowly emerged from the early morning haze. Small birds flew from the branches. Dogs yawned and stretched, pigs snuffled together trying to sit in the embers of the fires. The river gushed and burbled in the distance and I washed my hands in a sparkling stream. It was paradise.

I decided to have a walk around before everyone got up and drifted across the village dreamily, noticing several little turds of indeterminate origin lying around after the night's activities. Every house had its own garden, and I was curious to see what they were growing for market. Several circular compounds con-tained orange and pomello trees, bananas and trellises of winged-bean plants; all were surrounded by bamboo fencing to keep out the pigs. Others were cultivating chayote, chillies, cab-bages, pumpkins, potatoes, onions, shallots, lettuces and other edible leaves that I couldn't identify. Little boxes of herb plants, raised on stilts to foil chickens, were placed conveniently by doorways.

The Laotians are big on salads, and one of the first impres-sions I had in the country was of the huge variety and abundance of salad vegetables. Absolutely every Lao household has a salad and vegetable patch around their house or on a nearby river bank. These beautiful, verdant gardens are tended lovingly, and neighbours vie with each other to produce the most attractive displays of delicious produce. Lettuces, watercress, tomatoes, cucumbers, amazing varieties of beans, mints, basils, morning glory and hundreds of unidentifiable jungle leaves jostle for space in a riot of colour. I was never served a meal without a side dish piled high with crunchy lettuce, raw vegetables and exotic herbs.

I floated on towards the outer boundaries of the village. The houses gave way to store huts and small wet rice plantations leading to the river.

And everywhere there were little black pigs: extremely curious black pigs.

Wherever I looked, a little piggy face would be staring back at me with an interested expression. I passed huddles of them vying for position in the warm embers of last night's fires. Covered in ash, they examined me through sooty lashes. They poked their heads from behind houses, baskets, trees and bushes. When they caught me looking at them, they would disappear for a moment then sneak back again. We were playing hide-and-seek. They followed me into the forest and kept vigil while I explored. Noses snuffled out of the leaves; there were grunts in the undergrowth. When I looked back, two or three would be trotting behind me. They were really delightful.

Back in Ban Nalan, people were beginning their early morning spitting ablutions. The village was waking up and I was peckish. I turned back. An old man sharpening a knife on a stone with a cup of water greeted me from under a house.

'*Sabaii dii!*' I called back.

The sun was up, throwing shafts of smoky light on to the thatched roofs. Dogs were barking, children were yawning and old people were stretching their bones. The women were starting their cooking fires.

And it was turkey for breakfast.

Grilled Fish Stuffed with Basil and Lemon Grass

450 g (1 lb) whole fish, sea bass or fresh trout, gutted
3 stalks lemon grass, finely chopped
1 handful basil
1 lime, squeezed
1 teaspoon oil
a pinch of salt
a pinch of dried chilli (optional)

This is an extremely simple, fragrant recipe.

Take one-third of the lemon grass, all of the oil, salt, chilli (if used) and lime and mix together in a wide shallow bowl.

Meanwhile, gut and wash the fish, and make three diagonal slits in the flesh on each side with a sharp knife. Dry it with a paper towel.

Take two leaves of the basil, scrunch them with your fingers, then rub them all over the outside of the fish, throwing what's left into the bowl. Put the fish in after it and make sure it gets a good covering of the oily mixture. Leave for an hour or more.

When ready to eat, stuff the gut cavity with the basil and remaining lemon grass. Place on foil with the sides turned up to catch the juices and grill for 10 minutes on each side, or until the flesh is cooked through and the skin is brown and crispy.

Pickled Greens

1 kg (2 lb) spring greens, chopped into 5 cm (2 inch) pieces
2 cups rice vinegar
2 tablespoons salt
a pinch of sugar

Wilt the greens for 10 minutes in a steamer. Meanwhile mix the other ingredients and bring to the boil so that everything dissolves. Let the mixture cool.

Stuff the wilted greens into sterile glass jars and pour the cool boiled liquid on top. Stand for two days at room temperature, then eat them.

To serve hot, stir-fry to heat through (1 minute) and add a splash of fish sauce. They should taste sour and tangy, not bitter.

EIGHT
STARVING IN UDOMXAI

I decided to fly back to Luang Prabang to avoid staying in Muang Xai in Udomxai province. If I took the bus, it meant a four-hour journey over rough roads, staying the night in Muong Xai, and then a six-hour journey the next day.

I had my last breakfast, another bowl of Pawn's mother's excellent *koa soi* noodles, at the Boat Landing. The family were at their customary corner table eating barbecued meat, *jaew* chilli sauce and sticky rice. Little Bear was handed around for his usual morning cuddles from friends and family. Noi held him to his chest and nuzzled his head with his chin.

I idly read my airline ticket.

NOTICE
1. The passengers must be at the airport at the two hour time indicated [i.e. 10 a.m. for my flight at midday].
2. The late passenger are not allowed for the confirmed flight and the seat will be given to the stand by passenger, the company is not responsible for this case.
3. Each adult passenger is allowed to have 20 kg of luggages, and a youngster is allowed 10 kgs. The handbag should not be over 05 kgs for each.

I was all right for once – no handbag, and I only had my little rucksack.

The *tuk-tuk* arrived at nine-thirty, nice and early as everyone was very anxious that I didn't miss the plane. Ten minutes later

I was at the airport, a dusty field with a concrete box building at one end and a grubby restaurant shack at the other.

It was derelict.

This did not bode well.

I crossed the field in the bright sunlight and went into the airport building. The place was empty: no people, no bags, just a huge old weighing machine, like the type you used to see in antiquated chemists or boarding school sanatoriums. With a heavy feeling I called out and someone replied from behind one of the doors. I followed the sound and went into an office. A man in a khaki uniform smiled at me, showing a lot of gum. He had a wispy beard and milky eyes.

'I'm here to catch the plane to Luang Prabang. I've already paid for the ticket,' I said.

'No plane,' he replied, still smiling.

'But I booked last week at the Lao Aviation office.'

'I know, but you only passenger, plane cancelled.'

Oh God. If you miss a twenty-minute flight in Laos it takes days to get to the same destination by road.

'But I need to go to Luang Prabang today.'

'Not possible. You only passenger, sorry, very unusual, you very unlucky.'

I still couldn't believe I was the only passenger.

'I know, when's the next plane, please?'

'Next plane Saturday.' It was Wednesday. 'You take bus.'

'But it's ten o'clock. I've missed it by three hours.'

'There's another one, local, eleven o'clock, you go to Muang Xai then you take another tomorrow to Luang Prabang. You stay here, I get *tuk-tuk*, go to Lao Aviation office to refund ticket then bus station, everything OK. No worry,' and he was gone.

A whole night in Muang Xai. That meant awful food. Without exception, everyone I met who had been there had complained about it. It was ugly, modern and there were no decent restaurants. In fact, I'd heard that you could only get Chinese food there and that it was poor quality Chinese food at that. Since I was following a trail of delicious Lao cuisine, I'd firmly scrubbed it off my list of places to go. Now I was going to be forced to stay there.

The *tuk-tuk* arrived from nowhere and whisked me off to the bus station with a quick pit stop to get my refund, as promised. The bus hadn't yet arrived. It was twenty past ten.

In Luang Nam Tha, the bus station is situated near the market. It is a wide dirt space littered with the usual detritus of old plastic bags and tin cans. On one side stands the ticket office, on another a covered bus shelter with benches, and next to that there is a male and female toilet shack painted a pretty powder-blue but firmly locked with padlocks.

A few snack shops line the far side, cobbled together out of wood and packing cases. The owners live behind the shops and a washing line of stripy knickers was strung up beside them. To pass the time I wandered over to buy some water.

Each shop sold exactly the same things as the next, almost as if it would be insensitive to compete by selling something original. I viewed the rows of Vitamilk, pork scratchings, tinned Nescafé, packets of dried noodles, Ivy orange juice, Coca-Cola in glass bottles, biscuits with a hole in the middle, '50%' coconut milk in tins, cigarettes, shampoo, Nestlé condensed milk (its tins printed with drawings of slices of white bread covered in whirls of the goo), toothpaste and three old baguettes in a glass case. I bought some water and sat back down at the shelter to wait.

Looking to the right I noticed a big placard posted in the dirt. It was hand-painted in Lao and English.

FRIENDSHIP PLANTING GARDEN.
CO-OPERATION BETWEEN LAO PDR AND
JAPANESE ENVIRONMENTAL AID PROJECT.
DATE OF PLANTING 1/6/2000

The sign stood in front of a mound of earth grown over with seedy grass. A broken-up packing case lay beside it, and, seeing an opportunity to dump, someone else had abandoned a load of rotten wood nearby. Broken bottles and cans completed the picture. I wondered how much money had been given for that considerate foreign-aid project, and where the money had gone.

The bus arrived promptly at eleven o'clock. It was painted 'Lao blue', a bright mid-blue (the colour of Savlon tubes) that seemed to be the favourite colour for everything: plastic sacks, roofs, trucks, house paint, *tuk-tuks*, clothes dye, flower pots. The bus was actually an open pickup truck covered by an iron frame welded on to the raised edges of the back. There were two extremely narrow benches on either side with a little padding, and a roll of plastic curtain was studded to the frame behind them in case of rain. My heart sank a little. I'd been hoping for a minibus, as the roads in the north are notoriously bad.

An old hand now, I raced to the cab at the front to try and get the roomy seat by the driver. Too late. Someone had already placed her large black handbag on the seat, thereby reserving it even before the bus had pulled into the station. Damn. The driver grabbed my rucksack and slung it on the roof, and then drove off showering me with dust.

I went back to the shelter and sat down in the hope it would return.

An hour later it did, loaded with Chinese floral mattresses – rose-covered beauties which were weighed down on the roof with rolls of corrugated iron whose shaped ends looked like giant cookie cutters. Plastic sheeting was placed on top and the whole ensemble was tied down. Then the rice sacks had to be loaded, then a cauldron and some chickens and, finally, us. I noticed the owner of the black ladies' handbag was a septuagenarian monk.

The inside of the bus was plastered with First Choice condom stickers showing a happy condom with arms, legs, a smiley face and spectacles. He was giving the thumbs-up sign. We all packed in, and at the last minute we were joined by Marge and Terry, two Australians in their late forties who I'd met briefly in Muang Sing. They travel the world for ten months of the year buying jewellery and ethnic bits to sell when they return home for the remaining two months. They finance themselves by renting out their beach house while they're away. Some other tourists had told me they were terrible skinflints. I liked them. They looked as if they'd just spent three weeks at a seventies rock festival. Marge was covered from head to toe in Afghan silver jewellery from their last buying spree; she was thin and good-looking with wild, wiry hair. Terry was a long-haired baldy. He wore a grubby khaki flak waistcoat and carried a wonderful battered leather camera bag he'd had for twenty years. It had become his talisman.

Finally, at one-thirty, we left.

And went straight to the petrol station.

Then the journey started for real. The road from Luang Nam Tha to Muang Xai is at least tarmacked, but from there it's all downhill, literally. It winds its way through the mountains in twists and turns, cutting across deep gullies with sheer drops. There are lots of potholes and it was just after the rains, so some parts of the road were washed away into lumpy stretches of mud and rock.

The views, of course, were marvellous. We drove through sumptuous forest, where every plant and tree seemed different from the next. Two-hundred-foot-high clumps of bamboo swung in the wind as we passed, and I suddenly caught the narcotic fragrance of hidden flowers. The clean air jump-started my senses: going by bus was fun.

Unless you had the driver from hell. We did, and the landscape was a bouncy blur.

He drove like a maniac. Ten minutes into the journey we passed a horrible car crash between an army jeep and a minibus. They'd collided from opposite directions on a corner and the

minibus driver had gone through the windscreen. He was standing in the road, looking dazed, with a blood-soaked shirt held
over his nose and mouth.

However, our driver was not deterred. We leapt over potholes
that made my whole body lift twelve inches in the air. I'm not
often scared, but now I was terrified. I kept imagining terrible
rollovers down the mountain, reaching the bottom alive but broken, trapped in a mass of tangled metal. You really had to cling
on for your life. At times I just gave up sitting down and hung on
to the ceiling bars like a monkey.

Four and a half hours later we arrived in Muang Xai. It was
dark and I'd pulled my right shoulder.

Confusingly, Muang Xai is more commonly known as
Udomxai (oo-dom-sigh), and has become a boom town. During
the Vietnam War it was a little speck of a place. Chinese troops
were stationed there and the Americans avoided bombing them
to avert an inconvenient diplomatic incident between the two
superpowers. After the war the Chinese and Vietnamese migrants
stayed on to take advantage of the road-building projects being
funded by the Chinese government and the money started to
pour in. It's in a prime position for trade, situated at the cross-
roads between the routes to China, Vietnam, Luang Prabang and
Pak Beng (from there to Thailand). Better roads means better
transportation of Chinese goods to new markets and, more
alarmingly, the easier removal of irreplaceable woods, herbs and
animals that have been wiped out in neighbouring countries and
which sell for a huge amount on the global market. Udomxai
trembles with the reverberations of the heavily laden trucks that
trundle through it night and day. Though it was late by the time
we arrived, they were still passing through with their cargoes of
colossal tree trunks, poorly disguised under tarpaulin.

Even in the dark I could see it was modern and ugly.

I felt like my arm had been wrenched out of its socket and
then jammed back in again. We jumped out of the bus as though

we were stepping out of a Moulinex blender. I staggered around a bit, remembering the feeling of solid ground. My rucksack landed with a thud beside me (swiftly followed by six mattresses), and as I swung it on I felt a burning pain in my shoulder. I was going to have to do something about this, and quickly. Luckily, one of the delights of Laos is the availability of herbal steam sauna/massage parlours; most big towns have one. I decided to seek relief as soon as possible.

'That was a journey from hell,' said Terry as he yanked his rucksack from under a mattress.

'Yeah, I'm bushed,' replied Marge, turning to me. 'Why don't we all stay in the same guest house? Maybe we'll find some action later on.'

I wasn't sure I wanted any action.

None of the guest houses looked very appetising, so we decided to try one recommended in a guidebook. It was off the main road, so hopefully would be quieter. We walked for half a mile with our rucksacks and entered the white tiled lobby of the hotel. I went up to the reception desk.

'Hot water?' I asked. I really needed it.

'Yes, yes,' said a plump Chinese man with bad skin. Beside the desk, there were a couple of very heavily carved and lacquered chairs made from orangey coloured wood with a matching glass-topped coffee table. The TV beside them was blaring.

'But only two rooms left. One has a double bed, the other three beds, you all share.'

We looked at each other. After that journey I didn't want to share with anyone. I just wanted a massage, food and then sleep. I could see by the look on their faces that Marge and Terry felt the same, and I knew they couldn't afford the three-bed room (the price a of a sandwich in Soho), so I thought I'd simplify things and take it.

'I'll take the three-bed room, but I don't want anyone else coming in to share later, OK?'

'OK,' he said and led me up the tiled stairs.

'I'm going to try and find a massage,' I called back to Marge.

'Fancy meeting up for dinner at about eight?' she asked.

'Umm, all right, knock on my door.'

I was shown my extravagant room for three. As we entered, the grit on the floor made a crunching sound, the light switch was hot and everything seemed to be covered in a grubby film of dust. But it was better than some I'd been in. He pointed to a door in the corridor and said 'bathroom', then left me to it.

I was dying for a wash, so I dumped my rucksack on a bed, grabbed my sponge bag and went for a shower.

The bathroom was filthy and smelt of sewage. It was about three and a half foot by eight and was lit by a fluorescent tube. The walls were half tiled and were once white but were now stained pee-yellow and brown. Above the tiles, three of the walls were made of concrete and the other of asbestos panels; all were blackened with soot as if there had been a fire in the past. The electrical wiring was completely exposed everywhere and sagged across the ceiling.

At the far end, opposite the door, a pattern of holes in the wall let in the mosquitoes. Below stood a pale blue ceramic squat toilet on a raised tile plinth. Beside it there was a concrete dunking tank with a floating plastic scoop for flushing the loo by hand, and an empty loo brush holder with murky drips running down its sides. Unsurprisingly, there was no loo paper.

A pale green plastic bathroom mirror unit hung on the left wall. It included a little projection full of holes to fit six toothbrushes, and a broken shelf at the bottom which sagged at an angle so that nothing could stand on it. Very useful. I looked at the electric shower next to the sink opposite. It was made by Joven and had a picture of a pink cartoon whale splashing about. 'Whale of a Time' it said in jolly writing.

The water could only be cold, and it was. We were still high in the mountains and now the temperature outside had dropped to freezing. 'At least I'll wash my face,' I thought, 'and then I'll shower at the massage place before my sauna.' I turned on the sink tap and my feet were instantly drenched in icy water. The drainage pipe led nowhere; it was just hacked off six inches underneath, so the water splattered out at knee level to the floor.

I gave up. I can sleep on the floor, wash in the river and shit in the jungle, but I really can't stand modern filth. As I left I noticed the stained loo brush standing wetly by the door frame.

The man at the reception desk told me there was a massage place but no sauna. If I wanted one then I could go to the Chinese massage parlour on the main street. I followed his directions to a row of grubby shops. All the store owners were sitting outside on the street playing mah-jong and watching the evening action. They had pulled out plastic chairs and coffee tables and there was quite a party atmosphere until I came along, when everyone stopped talking to stare at me. The massage parlour was an open shopfront at the end of the row. Three Chinese girls were sitting on a suite of olive-green plastic furniture that had been placed outside. They were tarting up for the night, sharing make-up compacts and doing each other's hair. One was pretty, one moon-faced and the other plain as a pudding, but all were plastered in make-up. They acted sultry and annoyed when I asked them for a massage. They looked me up and down in disgust.

Admittedly, I can't have looked that appealing. I'd been on the road for ten hours; I hadn't washed my hair for four days; my mascara, applied in an attempt to look less like an alien (my eyelashes are white), was halfway down my face; I was wearing my entire capsule wardrobe, six items of clothing that hadn't seen washing powder for some time; and looking down I realised that I was covered from head to toe in a thin coating of red dust from the road. My Jungle Girl bag wasn't looking too good either: bleached from the sun and streaked with salt marks from my sweat, it hung limply across my chest, and I'm pretty sure it smelt.

The girl with the big moon face and matt black hair down to her bottom got up with a huge sigh and roll of her eyes. She pointed to a curtain at the back of the shop and we walked through. The parlour was painted shell-pink and contained three red plastic massage beds in a row. The only light source came from a single red bulb in a double brass fitting on the wall. The colour drained all the blues and greens out of my perspective and gave the room that surreal, dreamlike quality that is used so artfully in brothels. For decoration they'd stuck a huge poster on the wall depicting a bunch of yellow roses lying across a table with a tea-light candle and a piece of ribbon casually strewn about it. All these items were in really soft focus so as not to spoil the main focal point of the picture – a spent champagne cork.

Who takes these photographs? Laos is covered in them. Someone, somewhere, right now, is lining up a cheap vase of roses and gypsophila next to a couple of champagne glasses, trying to decide whether to add the fluffy kitten mewing in the box by their feet or throw in a couple of party poppers. The result will then be turned into a billion posters and greetings cards that will allow the photographer to retire to a beach house in Malibu and drink pina coladas for the rest of his life (he'll probably photograph those too).

I put my bag down and mimed washing my feet. She pointed to a door covered in white peeling plastic which led out into a black Dickensian corridor and up a flight of stairs to another corridor with a stinking concrete bathroom at one end. Unbelievably, this bathroom was far worse than the one in my hotel. I picked over the uneven, filthy floor past the squat toilet to the dunking tank and turned on the tap. The smell of urine was making my eyes water. I washed my feet pretty quickly.

I returned to the parlour to find that the cute girl in lots of make-up had come to watch the show. Both of them looked at me with distaste, but after seeing the state of their bathroom I felt less ashamed of my disarray. I began to take my clothes off but was stopped by their squeaks. It seems I was to have the massage fully clothed.

I lay on one of the beds and the pretty girl sat on the one next to me, swinging her legs. She was about fifteen and had perfect doll features under her mask of white make-up – big eyes, a tiny nose and a pouty parrot mouth with full lips. She was wearing a tartan miniskirt and matching tartan jumper, with white stockings and high heels, all ready for the disco. She stared without shame and made rude remarks about me in Chinese until her father's voice called and she shot out of the back door to avoid him.

The music was turned on. As opposed to the tinkly Asian music we hear to 'relax' in Western beauty parlours, here it was schmaltzy Western pop and pop-classical played on a saxophone to the background of fifty violins. We started with 'The Way We Were' with a karaoke accompaniment from the men outside, followed by 'Auld Lang Syne', which cheered me up a bit as nobody recognised it.

By now I was feeling humiliated. I was sure other people didn't get massages with all their clothes on, and she was prodding me viciously through my jeans. I can honestly say it was the worst massage I've ever had. My shoulder did feel a little better for being whirled like a windmill, but she'd pressed my temples so hard I was afraid my eyes were going to pop out. I found little bruises all over my body for days afterwards.

I plodded back to the hotel, starving.

I'd only had a bowl of noodles all day – eleven hours before. Even though I was hungry, I'd given up hope on the culinary treats of Muang Xai. Food had not been the motivation for my visit to this town, and just for once I didn't have the energy or inclination to search out a decent meal on my own that night.

I found Marge and Terry waiting at the hotel door.

'Oh, great, we were just coming back for you,' said Marge. 'We've been all over town and the food's so expensive.'

'More expensive than Muang Sing!' Terry chipped in with a horrified expression.

'A bowl of fried rice costs 15,000 kip, it's disgusting, the whole place is a rip-off!' she ranted, jewellery jangling.

'No worries, though, we bumped into Katie and Dan, they found a café by the bus station that does noodle soup for 4,000,' said Tony in a state of euphoria.

'It's Dan's birthday – he's twenty-four. They invited us along to dinner and we asked if you could come.'

'Thanks, I'd love to,' I said half-heartedly. I'd have eaten dirt by this point but would have preferred to dine on my own.

'Yeah, they're real nice, and on the way back to get you we met some Lao having a birthday party; they're drinking heaps of *lao-lao*, the one with the brown lumps in it, and they gave us loads free,' said Tony.

'It's going to be a good night tonight and cheap, too,' said Marge as we set off down the road in the dark.

On the way we passed them, six men at a table with a huge, five-litre bottle of Ya Dong *lao-lao* on the table between them. Ya Dong is a type of bark that's supposed to be medicinal; it turns the liquor light brown and makes it taste earthy. Many bars and homes keep a bottle fermenting on the side and top it up with pure *lao-lao* as it empties. Tonight they were drinking so fast that they were already topping it up, and they called us over to try some. In anticipation of the food to come, I slugged down a glassful to deaden my taste buds. Marge grabbed a small tumbler, filled it to the brim and swigged it back to the delight of the crowd.

'That's my fifth already,' she said greedily. 'Ah well, we had a month off the booze in Afghanistan, didn't we, Terry?'

He followed suit. 'Yeah, love; we're making up for it now, though.' He turned to the party. 'We go eat,' he said, making eating motions, 'then come back, drink more. I feel like gettin' shit-faced tonight.'

We all slapped each other on the back as the *lao-lao* spread warmly across our chests, and went off into the night.

'Nice people,' said Marge.

We reached the bus station and found Katie and Dan at a café shack. It was very dark, lit only by two small candles and the wood fire under the stove. They were sitting at either side of a plastic-covered table. Dan was 'travel thin' with an open, optimistic smile and a bit of stubble. Katie had long, blonde dreadlocks and the face of an angel. She was a beauty, with perfect skin and even features, but at this moment her eyes were rolling back into her head, which rather spoilt the vision.

We joined them. They had already ordered their noodle soup for 4,000 kip and Dan had started his, head lowered, with very droopy eyes. Katie wasn't touching hers.

'You can have one for 4,000 or 5,000 – don't know what the difference is.'

Ever wanton, I ordered a 5,000 one and immediately regretted it; it probably just meant more meat.

Dan's eyes were like slits.

'God, Katie's had three *lao-laos* and she never usually drinks alcohol.' Her head was lolling over her soup. 'Only takes drugs, alcohol doesn't agree with her.' There was absolutely no way Katie was suffering from the effects of *lao-lao* – they'd both taken a birthday hit of opium.

'Happy Birthday!' shouted Marge. 'I got you a present.' She produced a seed pod bracelet she'd bought in Muang Sing.

'Wow, thanks, Marge,' said Dan. He needed quite a lot of help to tie it on. 'Thanks a lot.'

Our noodle soup arrived. The owners of the café, a family man with a round belly, his portly wife and their thin, nervous son aged about ten, had been sitting in the corner, agog. We comprised a scene of total fascination for them: five dishevelled *falangs* behaving strangely, one with wild hair like a hat. As the wife put our bowls down on the table, her eyes nearly popped out of her head with the strain of taking everything in, then she returned to the corner and settled down to watch us as if we were a television show.

I was right about the soup. In the dim light I was unable to see much, but it tasted of livery hot water and I couldn't identify the meat (please, no beetles), except that I knew it would be impossible to swallow it. I swamped it with fish sauce, soy, lime juice and chilli, but it made little difference. We chatted about Muang Sing and birthdays and a joint was passed around. Marge was practically shouting and Katie looked as if she might be sick; she'd gone very pale. I seemed to be the only person who noticed.

I looked down miserably at my noodles. 'Shall I order some beer? I'll get it,' I volunteered hopefully.

Marge raised her eyes to the heavens. 'What the hell? It's much too expensive. We can eat here and get smashed on their drink later.'

I looked down guiltily. Not wanting to seem reckless with my money, I acquiesced.

Katie leant over to me, her elbow missing the table. 'Marge said you live in Brixton, great place, I used to live in Brixton.'

'Yes,' I replied. 'Are you all right? Maybe you need a glass of water.'

'I'm fine, but cold water would be good,' she said, her upper body rotating gently in little wobbly circles. 'I used to live in a squat on Railton Road, do you know it?'

'No. I'm going to ask for some water. *Sabaii dii, nam duem,*' I called to the family.

I looked at her with concern. Her eyes were rolling off in different directions and she kept giving off deep sighs and throwing her head back. 'Then I lived in another one off Coldharbour Lane,' she continued. 'You must know it, lots of artists lived there, it was great.'

'Afraid I don't.' I was more concerned with picking out the lumps from my soup and putting them in a pile on the table with my chopsticks.

'Then we shared one in Stockwell, on Mordaunt Street, great parties, know that one?'

I was getting bored.

'My friend Michalev used to live in a squat somewhere near me, but I can't remember where. The loo had been blocked with cement and it had a kind of courtyard,' I said, completing my pyramid of cartilage. I really couldn't eat the soup.

'Yes, that's it! No! It didn't have a courtyard. What about Bridgewater Lane?'

Mercifully the water arrived and saved me from a detailed history of the squats of Brixton. Katie took some tentative sips. 'Drink it all,' I said.

'Who are you, her fucking mother?' spat Terry from across the table. 'Are you the mumsie type?'

I jumped at his sudden vitriol. 'Not really, but I think she's going to be sick.'

Right on cue, Katie got up from the table and stumbled into the blackness. For several minutes we could hear the sound of her vomiting in spasmodic episodes that punctuated our conversation. No one seemed to care, and it reminded me how self-centred and hedonistic travellers can become. A few days before I'd heard an appalling story that had ended in tragedy.

Edgar, a twenty-something Dutch boy, had gone on a four-day trek in northern Thailand. He had been travelling alone for six months and was relieved to hook up with a gang of travellers in Chiang Mai. He'd picked up a diarrhoea bug about two months before, but as it was sporadic and he'd only lost a stone in weight he wasn't worried. He told his new friends about it. They all got on so well that they decided to stay together for a few weeks and go trekking. They bought a huge bag of grass and procured a couple of guides who were willing to help in the opium department, and set off. It began well, and Edgar was amazed at how the jungle looked so surreal and vivid when he was walking stoned out of his head. That evening he tried opium for the first time and after the initial three vomits he was amazed at that, too. The tribal people were so fascinating.

The next day was a wonderful repeat of the first, though a bit more strenuous. He found it hard to keep up with the others. The following day was harder still and he really began to lag behind. He called to his friends but they were too far in front to hear him. Every so often he had to sit down to get his breath back. The opium had made him constipated, his stomach hurt and occasionally his vision seemed to slip sideways. It seemed like hours since he'd seen his friends and he began to call more desperately. Miles away, as they broke for lunch, one of the group suddenly noticed that they hadn't seen Edgar for a while. In fact, come to think of it, probably not for about three hours. They retraced their steps. An hour later they found him, face down in a stream, dead. There was no clue as to the cause of death.

The story had been told to me by Peter, the person who discovered him. When the guides realised Edgar was dead, they ran away in panic and fear of the authorities. One guide is always supposed to walk at the end of a trekking group for safety reasons, so in this case they would have been implicated in the death of a tourist. The travellers had to find their own way back with the dead body, pay for him to be embalmed and buy a coffin. They had to contact his parents in Holland and help to arrange for the body to be flown home. Peter's eyes were still hollow with the shock of it.

'Well, that was great,' said Marge, ignoring Katie as she returned. 'Why don't we go back and join those blokes for *lao-lao*? Dan, it's one of their birthdays so we can tell them it's yours too.'

To the huge disappointment of our audience, we paid for dinner and left. I was relieved to go as I felt embarrassed by what the Lao family must think of us, shouting and vomiting all over the place. I held Katie by the arm as we meandered down the road and back to the birthday party at the restaurant.

ANT EGG SOUP

The six were still there drinking copiously, and, to my dismay, a scatter of empty plates in front of them was all that remained of what had once been a seemingly delicious feast. Even old fish bones looked good to me now. My stomach rumbled, but alas the kitchen was closed. It was nine o'clock and they were the only customers in the restaurant. The television, in its enormous display cabinet at the back of the room, was blaring out Thai satellite shows. My favourite advert was showing. A man wearing only Y-fronts was gyrating in time to disco music. On every beat he thrust his pelvis forward and his knickers changed colour as animated stars burst all around him.

The birthday crowd was very pleased to see us; they were drunk, and three of us were women. Huge drinks were immediately poured. We ordered some *lao-lao* to top up the communal bottle, cold water for Katie and a much needed beer for me. Marge downed four tumblers in ten minutes and became stupendously drunk. Katie went off to be sick again.

Everyone wanted to know where we came from, to tell us where they came from, and to make us drink as much as possible. The self-appointed leader of the group was sitting next to me. He was called Goud and owned the restaurant. He had a fat face and very podgy hands. His dyed black hair flopped forward and he kept having to push it out of the way. He winked one eye when he smiled.

Leaning too close, he said, 'Are you a madame or a mademoiselle?'

'A madame,' I lied, and trotted out the old lines. 'I've been married one year, I love my husband very much, he's doing business in Vientiane.'

'Oh, my English no good, you speak Russian?'

'No.'

'I speak fluent Russian. You mademoiselle?'

It turned out that Goud, like many Lao, had learnt Russian in Moscow on an educational Communist exchange programme.

He'd then spent six years in Czechoslovakia, though we couldn't work out what he'd done there.

'Ahh, Prague, *craseevi, craseevi* (Russian for beautiful).' He winked at me again. 'Let's go disco.'

'Here's to the birthday boys,' yelled Marge, standing up. 'Do ya know there's two birthday boys here tonight?' She dragged Dan to his feet; he had gone white and could hardly stand. 'He's twenty-four, how old's your one?'

Goud yanked his birthday boy to his feet too. 'Phumi, yes, he forty. Let's go disco, good.'

Phumi was thin as a chopstick and looked, like most Lao, ten years younger than his age.

We all drank another toast. Dan slumped back down in his chair, his eyes barely open. Goud kept winking at me and trying to get me to drink more *lao-lao*, while I secretly managed not to drink too much of it by slopping it on the floor and sticking to beer. Dan had taken Katie back to the guest house to collapse, then returned, without her, to drink more. Terry and Dan had been throwing back the liquor. Dan kept rambling on that now he was twenty-four he should get a proper job, like his parents wanted him to. Terry told him not to be stupid, he was still young. Marge was on a roll, telling funny stories to the applause of an appreciative audience who probably couldn't understand a word she was saying. Meanwhile, Goud was invading my body space with pleas to go nightclubbing and repetitive questions about why I was alone.

Quite suddenly, Dan got up from the table and was spectacularly sick by the side of a pickup truck outside. At the same moment Goud clasped my knee with his hand, 'You, me, disco,' he said with another big wink.

'I think it's time to beat a retreat,' I yelped to Terry and Marge, 'I'm knackered after that journey.' I was dying to get away from Goud.

'Yeah, yeah, let's go too, love,' suggested Terry.

Marge stood up a bit reluctantly. 'Yeah, all right, I'm pissed enough, but I think we should walk Dan back to his guest house, he doesn't look in a fit state.'

'Oooo, now you're the mumsie one,' sneered Terry in a high voice.

'Well, look at him.'

Dan was doubled up over an impressive splatter of yellow vomit. He was lurching from one foot to the other and groaning. The birthday party were laughing their heads off. We all got up to leave and they tried to make us stay. Goud was fraught with disappointment because I wouldn't go to the disco with him, but I calmed him with the excuse that we had to look after Dan. A moment later, I turned back and they had all forgotten us in their enthusiasm for a new drinking competition.

Circumventing the sick, we took Dan by the shoulders and walked him towards his guest house. He couldn't quite remember where it was and he was sick again twice along the way, so it took some time. Marge had become loud-mouthed with the drink, and Terry obstreperous in return. They bickered all the way, with Dan trying to appease them. 'Hey, guys, don't argue, be cool.' Finally and clamorously we got there, and Marge took him up to his room. She seemed to stay up there for ages. In the interim, Terry's conversation was taking a lewd turn and I wanted to go home to bed. It was freezing and I was wearing all my clothes: jeans, two tops, fleece, shawl and the pièce de résistance, big socks jammed into my trekking sandals. I was not a beautiful sight.

Terry was moving closer. 'So,' he leered, 'slept with any Lao men yet on your travels? They like you, don't they?'

I wanted to say, 'Actually, I'm a lesbian'. Instead I told the truth. 'No. I have a boyfriend, we've been together for six years, I'm missing him.'

'When the cat's away,' he said, edging closer. 'It gets boring sleeping with the same person night after night, you need a little variety, don't you think?'

Marge popped her head out of the upstairs window and bellowed, 'Want to come up for another drink?'

I cringed at the thought of her waking the whole district.

'No thanks,' I stage-whispered back, 'I think I'll go to the guest house.'

'All right, I'll come down. I'm so shit-faced, I'm crapping,' she shouted.

She returned, gave us a suspicious look and took Terry's arm. As we reeled back, we recounted the events of the night and became hysterical, doubled up with laughter until we couldn't breathe. They were laughing because they thought the evening was funny; I was laughing in horror. Why had I allowed myself to spend time with these people? They were either whining about how they were being ripped off by the locals (haggling over a matter of pence) or gloating about how much they had managed to pay for something. I was sick to death of meeting this kind of traveller. As I toured the country they always asked me the same questions. Not where had I been? What had I learnt from the experience? Who had I met? What were they like? But how much did my room/food/bus fare/beer cost? And was it the cheapest I could find? They seemed to travel with such avarice, it disgusted me. They wanted everything for nothing and gave so little in return. What had that Laotian family thought of us, sitting in their café, drunk, drugged and vomiting? I was ashamed to think of it. I had sat by while they had behaved appallingly over dinner and then taken blatant advantage of Lao hospitality, slugging back someone else's *lao-lao* with obvious glee because it was free. It was all so thoughtless.

The last thing I heard as I closed my door was Terry recounting a story to the startled night porter about the wheels of sperm stains he'd seen sprayed on the walls of his last guest house. God I was glad to be leaving in the morning.

At last I was in my triple room with the gritty floor and the sandy beds. I pulled out my cotton sleeping sock, lay it on top of a bed and got in with all my clothes on. I was out in a nanosecond.

I awoke with a jolt. It was pitch-black and it took me a moment to remember where I was. Then I heard it. A crunchy, rattly sound. I went rigid, like I used to when I was scared as a child. I lay straining to hear the slightest sound. There it was again, a crunchy noise. And again. I worked out that if I slowly rolled down my sleeping sock first, I could make the light switch in one bound. My heart racing, I leapt for the switch with a battle cry and looked wildly around in the glare of fluorescent light. There on the floor was the thin plastic bag containing my flip-flops which I'd thrown on the floor earlier that evening.

In the bag was a big rat.

It poked its head out, actually snarled at me (I recoiled) and shot off into the corner and down a hole I now noticed under the bamboo vanity table. Regathering my strength, I hurled the table aside, picked up the wardrobe and jammed it against the hole. Then I checked for more holes, and, satisfied there weren't any, went back to bed with the light on and a heavy walking boot at the ready.

I'm not actually frightened of rats, it's the fact they're prepared to walk over you that I find so hateful. Rats seem to go out of their way to traverse the byways of the human body, and what's worse, they like to do it at night. I can't count the number of times they've scuttled over my feet in cafés, jumped on my knees in trains or tried to nose their way into my sleeping bag. Most animals run like hell when they see people, but not rats (or cockroaches for that matter). If that rat had dared to come back into my room, I would have flattened it.

It was four-thirty in the morning. I lay awake until five-thirty when the light began to dawn. Someone went to the bathroom next door and started clearing their phlegm very loudly, so I packed and got up. I was supposed to wake Marge and Terry, who were leaving for Thailand, but I couldn't. I never wanted to see them again. I paid the bill and sneaked past their door.

I was so hungry I could have eaten a water buffalo. The bus left at six so I had no time to find breakfast. I managed to buy a pack of stale biscuits-with-a-hole-in-them (which I wolfed down in one go) and some chewing gum before jumping on a bus to leave town.

No recipes from Muang Xai, for obvious reasons.

It was my fault. This was what happened when I got deflected from my culinary trail – I got the Lao equivalent of a rancid British motorway service-station breakfast: a bowl of rank noodles and some unidentified flotsam. I suppose that if I'd searched thoroughly I could have found some good food, but it would have been tough. The cafés had sold out. They were all serving the same limited menu of poor quality dishes to people passing through, too lazy to care. Sadly, I see it happening all the time, all over the world.

I find it difficult to understand why we put up with it. Why do we accept insipid, pappy pears that never ripen (Britain accepts continental fruit that other countries, such as France, would never even take delivery of), and preprepared food pumped with chemicals? I think, in England, we have little choice. Price, lack of availability and massively biased, misleading advertising has crushed the natural food producers of Britain, who struggle to survive. It now takes more time, effort and money to eat locally grown real food than purchase processed pap from abroad. In the name of 'choice' we end up eating cattle fodder, dressed up to look enticing, exotic and international, while our own traditional produce and recipes quietly die out. In Laos, there is still real choice to eat well naturally, and I loved that. Practically everything is grown locally, seasonally and without chemicals, and prepared in a traditional and tasty manner. Ironically, the main reason for this is the lack of interest of the multinationals due to the difficulty in finding a profitable market in such a poor country. Laotians are proud of their culinary traditions and, even more so, of the purity of their produce, so it was tragic to come across a rash of crappy cafés.

As I looked out of the back of the truck I felt that the events of the evening before had reflected my feelings about Udomxai, and it didn't look any better in the morning light. It's a used ashtray of a town, made rich from Chinese road construction workers and the Yunnan prostitutes that help make their stay away from home a bit more pleasurable. Ugly white stubs of concrete buildings line the main street like crinkled cigarette butts, their skirtings stained nicotine-brown by the ever-blowing grit and dust. It is dominated by a huge brothel masquerading as a hotel, and every evening the population flocks to the spittoon of the hotel's nightclub, whose tinny music vibrates for miles around, hoping to find relief among the painted disco-princesses of the night. The town has a redolent air of bad sex and corruption. The people are haughty and sour-faced. It doesn't feel Lao.

I turned away with a sense of relief; it was only another six hours to Luang Prabang.

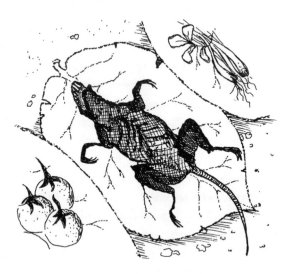

SNARLY BARBECUED RAT

NINE

A FEAST AT THE WATERFALL

I scrambled down the steep river bank and over people's salad gardens planted in the fertile mud, mainly sliding on my bottom.

After the disastrous trip back from Luang Nam Tha, Vandara suggested we go to her country 'retreat' near the Kung Si falls, a famous Lao picnic spot where a spectacular, many-layered waterfall cascades into a series of cool, turquoise pools just begging you to take a swim. The village below is surrounded and watered by these pools, and it was there that Vandara decided to build her second guest house, right in the centre of the village action. The falls are thirty kilometres south of Luang Prabang, so to avoid another vile road journey we decided to go by river.

Vandara and her husband Mr Humpheng managed the descent much more elegantly but we all had to wade up to our thighs in the swirling brown water to reach the canoe. I clambered in heavily, nearly knocking over the boatman standing at the prow in a torn T-shirt. The boat was about twenty foot long and three foot wide, with open sides and a tin roof. I sat on a tiny chair six inches high with a back that hardly reached above my coccyx, and gave Vandara Phia Sing's recipe book, which was already beginning to fall apart from so much handling, and was grubby with fingermarks and splatted with sauce. Vandara smiled as she took it from me. She was fascinated by it – the only royal Lao cookbook in existence – and had been trying to find the time to look at it since I had arrived.

The boatman pushed off using a long pole, like a gondolier, before starting an outboard motor that belched oily black smoke into the pristine air. Vandara handed me my favourite snack, coconut-banana rice balls. Laotians usually eat them for breakfast; they're made with sweetened sticky rice rolled in shredded coconut, and contain a morsel of soft, yellow banana. I leant back and sketched the passing scenes, popping rice balls into my mouth to keep me going.

It was the season for the river bank gardens, and they were luxuriant: brilliant green squares on the freshly silted banks separated the river from the jungle and were scissored with little streams that flowed into the Mekong from the mountains beyond. People were staking out their plots and harvesting their bean crops. Gangs of naked children played in the sandy mud and raced along beside us shouting, 'Where you go?' and ' *Sabaii dii, falang! Falang!*', their mothers keeping an eye on them as they tended the vegetables or washed clothes in the river. We passed an old man standing in the shallows with a circular cast net weighted at the edge with a chain. He slung it over one arm and casually threw it out across the flow with the other, then quickly gathered it up under water and pulled it out like a bag. Tiny silver fish shone for a second in the sun.

We were still near the town so were puttering past 'cultivated' forest, banana groves and, behind them, in the hills, the shabby messes of teak plantations. I'd been amazed when I'd first seen young teak trees: I'd thought I was looking at a field of tobacco. Their large elliptical leaves were the size of serving dishes, all dried up, brown and mottled (it was the winter season). They were fifteen foot high, and so spindly you could practically get your thumb and forefinger around the grey trunks – nothing like the majestic hardwood I'd been expecting. The cultivated trees grow to house stilt size in ten to twenty years depending on the soil, but people often cut them down before that in desperation for instant cash. Numerous charities donate seedlings as an investment crop, and foreign con men, seeing an easy opportunity, are targeting Laos and buying up the plantations. It's good money – a twenty-five-foot log costs £140 in Laos, the export price is £455 and it sells in England for £8580 (2001 price). The profit is enormous, even more so as they're investing in futures. They pay instant money to own the wood, the trees are tended for them by the villagers, then fifteen years later they collect the timber having paid a tiny yesteryear price for it. A businessman in Luang Prabang told me this had happened just the other day to a donation of a thousand saplings he had given locally. I wondered if I was looking at them.

Vandara made little yelping noises from behind me when she recognised recipes in Phia Sing's book, or added comments.

'Oh, yes, I make like that . . . He uses so much pork fat! Very old-fashioned to me! . . . No, bad for the heart, I don't use . . . I use mince, Natacha, just a little.' And so on. I wished I'd bought twenty copies of the book to hand around, it generated such enthusiasm.

Vandara was a true instinctive cook, never quite satisfied with a printed recipe. She was generous, too. She happily shared her recipes with me and gave me endless cooking tips.

We slipped along, the gardens disappeared and animals replaced people on the river banks. Black water buffalo lay about almost totally submerged, just their wide horns sticking out of the water like the handlebars of the Harley Davidsons in *Easy Rider*; I wanted to grasp them and ride away in an arc of spray. A troop of monkeys shrieked at us yobbishly as we passed them; one stood on a boulder, watching, until we disappeared around a bend. I even saw a curd-yellow smudge of bird fly by – usually you only see birds when they're lying dead in the market, as children start to catapult anything with wings out of the trees as soon as they can walk.

Unfortunately, every mile or so, I'd see a 'plastic bag tree' hanging its scraggy branches in the water. A new species that's evolved in the last few years, it grows close to the waterline and fruits plastic bottles and flowers tatty brown shreds when the river level drops at the end of the rainy season. Despite the sight of bags skimming along the river, it was idyllic. There was a hazy blue tinge to the atmosphere which lent a dreamy quality to the landscape. The banks on either side of me were thick with trees and palms, backed by the familiar vista of rolling hills.

After forty-five minutes we stopped at the bank to find a truck waiting for us, and drove for twenty minutes, arriving at Ban Tha Baen just after lunch. It was all but deserted, so we made our way to the guest house without much fuss. The village is built in the shadow of the falls, and at its heart there are two pools. The top pool is shallow, larger and easily accessible, so most of the daily washing action goes on there. We crossed a bridge between them to reach Vandara's guest house. I was struck by the loveliness of the place. It was breathtaking: the natural colours of the stilted, thatched houses against the palms; the wood smoke rising in wisps and melting away into the mountains; the watery-white light of the winter sun; the balmy smell of incense tinged with lily flowers; and the sound of rushing water, everywhere water, babbling, burbling, rippling and trickling.

Vandara's place overlooked the main pond and followed the design of a classical Lao house – a single-storey wooden build-ing supported on stilts with a steep two-sided roof thatched in cogan grass (*Imperata cylindrical* – a pesky, invasive grass that has to be either used or burnt to death to stop it strangling every-thing). In the past, the upper living quarters were divided into a closed-off sleeping section (now several guest rooms) and a wide-open veranda for lazing about on. The lower area was used for storage, cooking and working in the shade. Historically, the Chinese and Vietnamese built their houses on the ground while Tai peoples' houses were always raised above the earth. The original reason they were raised on stilts was to keep the owners dry during the rains and protect them from wild animals, but as man-eating tigers are a rarity these days, Vandara has walled in the underside to create a ground floor for more bedrooms.

She loves gardening and flowers were everywhere. The entire doorway was enveloped with emerald green leaves and clusters of huge, white, bell-shaped 'angel's trumpet' flowers that trembled at every step, frondy shrubs and bushes with Tyrian purple leaves, and my favourite, the magical double-petalled 'blushing hibiscus' or 'clock flower' which blooms white in the morning, tinges shell-pink by midday and gradually turns deep red by nightfall. At that moment they were as pink as prawns.

Vandara's niece greeted us at the door. I introduced myself but I didn't quite catch her complicated name. I dumped my bag in a room and tucked in my mosquito net while it was still light. I'd been promised a cookery lesson later in the day, but first we decided to take a walk to Vandara's allotment. To reach it, we had to cross a series of little bridges and walk around several pools scattered among the houses. Poinsettia was in season, huge ten-foot bushes of it, the blousy red flowers reflected in the sky-blue ponds. Everything was so succulent and lush.

As we walked, kids bounced around us shouting the usual 'Falang! Falang!' As many people were still at work, most of the remaining village activity was taking place in the areas underneath the houses where children played, chickens scratched and puppies sniffed around for scraps. Old people were lying on the verandas of the houses keeping an eye on the gangs of children, and they waved as we passed and called out greetings. Vandara was in her element and had a beatific smile on her face. She'd often told me how much she loved this village. Several years ago she and her husband had been visiting it when he suggested that she build a guest house. Since then she had become involved in helping the villagers establish crafts to sell to tourists at the main waterfall, so they didn't have to leave to find work. She's popular.

' *Sabaii dii*,' called out an old lady wearing a purple man's shirt.

'She's a hundred,' said Vandara with a toss of her head.

'Really?' I asked, craning my neck back to look at her.

She lay on a low bed, energetically sifting peanuts from their shells by shaking them in a wide, flat basket. She looked lithe and fit; I'd never have guessed her age. It occurred to me once again that, as a people, the Laotians generally look much younger than they actually are. I had noticed they all dye the grey out of their hair (both men and women), but they scarcely line in older age. The graceful countenances of their older people made our faces look like used teabags in comparison. I commonly met people in their sixties who turned out to be eighty-nine.

'There are many people of a hundred in the village and all over Laos. It's the healthy lifestyle and good food, no chemicals, as I said before,' she added.

The official life expectancy is fifty-one for men and fifty-five for women. The hard lifestyle of subsistence farming and a high infant mortality rate lowers the average (and, from the amount of lao-lao I've seen people put away, also liver failure I suspect). That aside, I met loads of centenarians.

We left the village and took a path that cut through the jungle, walking to the sound of rushing water. I glimpsed turquoise froth through the trees. Although it looked wild to my untrained eye, most of the vegetation I was passing was cultivated: papaya, banana, mango, durian, pomello; rattan and basket ferns; betel nut palms; and hundreds of bamboo stems – all meshed together in the twists and curls of vines whose tendrils palpably caressed me as I passed them.

After a few minutes the path opened out into shallow steps leading to water. Twenty mini-waterfalls splashed around trees and fallen logs and spurted through bushes. Out of the watery mud rose a huge clump of bamboo with at least a hundred milky-green stems as thick as grown men's thighs. It stretched seventy feet into the sky, where its delicate feathery leaves reached for the sun and scattered shards of light back down to us below.

I love bamboo – there is something mystical about it. And it truly is weird.

Bamboo is one of the oldest forms of plant life. There are over one thousand species and they flower with shocking infrequency; some flower only every seventy-five years, others (like *Dendrocalamus strictus*) every twenty to forty years, and one (*Bambusa vulgaris*) every one hundred and fifty years. But what's really peculiar about them is that their flowering is synchronised. All the individuals of a given species reproduce at the same time wherever they are located in the world, whether in the forests of Laos or in someone's oriental theme garden in Milton Keynes. I mean, how do they know?

We crossed a plank set over a rushing stream in the dappled shade and reached Vandara's hill. She showed me her herb and vegetable patch, which was laid out in the usual Lao way so that colours, textures and tiers were balanced to be a pleasure to the eye. It was scrupulously tended. As we walked among the herbs she told me what grew at this time of year and identified some of the plants that were alien to me. I recognised some of them: mints and basils, chives, dill, garlic, cabbage and mustard greens.

'This, I think you call holy basil, this is a mild one I grow specially,' said Vandara, plucking a pointed green leaf from a neat row of basil plants that alternated green and purple. 'You try.' It tasted like the basil we are used to at home, but it had a stronger perfume and an undertone of clove. I often bought it in London to sprinkle over soups or add to rice.

'Yes, you can buy it in Asian supermarkets in England,' I said, 'and this purple one, but there seem to be so many types here – the one that's lemony and the one that seems a cross between mint and basil.'

'I know,' she said, picking a purpleish leaf. 'Look, this is sweet basil, taste stronger, more like star anise.'

We moved on to a plot of pointy greens.

'*Hom pay*!' cried Vandara. 'You know?'

I didn't know, but I soon would as it was in season and it turned up in many dishes throughout my trip in Laos. It was a dark green salad leaf with a serrated edge, which looked and tasted a bit like rocket, only sharper. I liked it steamed.

'Oh, Vandara, there are so many wonderful plants and leaves that you can't get in England. How am I going to make your recipes in England?'

'Improvise,' she replied with a big smile. 'You have many things like us. Look.' She swept her arm across her plot. 'Potatoes, tomatoes, aubergine, spring onion, ginger, lemon grass, *kha* (galangal), coriander. Maybe not same quality?' she added with a wink, 'but you can get. Anyway, if you don't have lemon grass, use lime juice, maybe it won't taste just the same but you can experiment. We do when we can't get exact thing.'

She was right, of course. Actually, when I returned home I found that with a little perseverance I could get many of the unusual ingredients I wanted. *Hom pay* (also called saw-tooth herb), for instance, is sold in the Vietnamese supermarkets in Hackney around Christmas time.

We continued our walk over several more hills until we came to her papaya and banana trees. It was the season for papaya and they hung from the trees like huge green party balloons, at least four times the size of their poor relations found in Western supermarkets. Hidden amongst the trees were little paddocks of pot-bellied pigs or roosting chickens. The bananas were flowering and the palms were sprouting huge purple-red buds that bobbed down like triffids. The paths were narrow and often crossed with streams, or they doubled back on themselves as they wound around trees. It was difficult to tell where the plots ended and the jungle began. It had begun to rain, so I snapped off a giant 'elephant ear' leaf to use as an umbrella and we skidded back to the house. It was four-thirty, and time to cook.

The guest house had a traditional kitchen situated, as always, at the back of the building and open to the sky, with a small thatched roof area for emergency cover against a sudden downpour. There was a wood/charcoal-burning stove and a big pot topped with a woven basket (for steaming sticky rice) standing on an open fire. The floor was scattered with slices of tree trunk for chopping on and little low stools to sit on when preparing food. One wall of the kitchen supported thick plank shelves for surface space, and water was supplied through a hose from the water tank. The other wall was simply a bamboo fence which held back the jungle. Other people's chickens casually wandered in and out (until six o'clock when they went home, regular as clockwork, to get their dinner). The sounds of people returning from work, cocks crowing, dogs barking, children laughing, yet another centenarian's birthday party and the background burble of water echoed all around us as we cooked. In this village everyone knew everyone else's business.

The niece was already squatting on the floor, grating coconut milk. She was using a 'rabbit' (*ka-tai*), a small wooden plank with a projecting sharp edge to shred the coconut flesh into a bowl ready to extract the milk.

'We cook a Lao feast tonight,' said Vandara. 'Greens with sesame, Lao tomato sauce, aubergine farcis in omelette, sticky rice and lime soup. And something special – my Paradise Chicken.'

This was an honour; it was Vandara's signature dish, passed down to her from her grandmother. She had mentioned it many times and only made it on special occasions.

The soup broth was already simmering and her niece had laid out bowls of washed vegetables on the plank sideboard. I was set to work chopping lemon grass and garlic while the niece poured water over the grated coconut bowl and squeezed out the milk with her fists. Vandara grabbed a scrawny chicken, already plucked, from a tray and attacked it with a machete. Chickens in

Laos taste fantastic; in fact I'd almost forgotten what real country chicken tastes like – much stronger than the ones I buy at home. This one had particularly enormous feet that verged on the ridiculous, as they're Vandara's favourite bits. She put the chicken pieces in a bowl and added the lemon grass, sliced galangal, garlic, fish sauce, and a liberal sprinkling of rock salt.

'It is supposed to marinate for a few hours but we have no time today, half an hour will have to do,' she said, giving it a good stir.

I'm not one of those cooks that likes to shoo everyone out of the kitchen and arrive at the table with a banquet: I love cooking with other people. When I was growing up, the kitchen was the hub of the house. We were given tasks to do by my mother, and we'd catch up on each other's daily news. Now, when I invite people for dinner, I sit them down at the table so we can talk while I cook. I'll rope them in to chop the onions and use them as tasters. It's a bonding experience, particularly, I think, between women. I've had some of my most intimate conversations over potato peelings, and made lasting friendships while sharing culinary secrets in foreign kitchens.

The next two hours were a whirr of activity – chopping, pounding, searing, steaming and smelling – while I desperately tried to take recipe notes in between tasks. Every vegetable and herb we were preparing had been grown around the village and picked in the last few hours; the rice was 'new season' and gave off wafts of grassy-nutty aroma across the kitchen. Downy feathers clung to the still warm eggs as I cracked them into the wok while the local chickens looked blandly on. I was in my element. As we worked Vandara kept feeding me with pieces of sweet papaya.

'You see, taste my papaya, it is the best.' It was. 'No dirty-nappy taste like chemically grown papaya. This comes from my own trees, everything we grow in the village is good, you can smell it, it's organic. We are lucky, like I say before, everything we eat is natural.' She was very proud of the quality of Lao food and always had lots of ideas on how to promote it. Her latest was to produce a sort of cookery book of her own.

'I want to make a box of card recipes from natural Lao paper, using Lao crafts, to sell like a set,' she said, dumping a load of cooked sticky rice on a tray. 'Not like a book like Phia Sing, more like a present.'

She rolled the huge mound of steaming rice with asbestos hands. 'This releases the wet steam, stops it going –' she screwed up her face – 'soft and . . . how you say?'

'Soggy,' I added, as she broke off balls of rice and dumped them in little bamboo rice baskets.

'Yes, I will make a set, with three, four or five recipes, like one meal, like we do today.'

'That sounds like a great idea. People could give them as gifts, something special from Laos. But you'll need to tell them how to cook sticky rice, we don't really eat it in the West.'

'I know, but how to prepare depends on the quality and how many you cook for, too long and it's really bad. I have ideas how to tell.'

I really admired Vandara. She was ever practical and was constantly sponsoring Lao crafts. She was involved in all sorts of self-help schemes with the village, and wanted to set up a native-run craft centre in Luang Prabang.

The time shot by as we chopped and chatted. We had to bring out oil lamps to finish the cooking as the electricity supply (the first in the village and only installed a month ago) had inexplicably been cut off. It was dark by the time I ascended the steep stairs with a tray of food.

Vandara's husband was already sitting on cushions on the floor of the veranda, and while we were cooking another guest had arrived. Tim was a young English lawyer. Pure public school: from his pressed pale-blue shirt (casually open-necked, 'I am on holiday, after all') to his leather-belted jeans and sockless, loafered feet. He had worked in Hong Kong for the last five years which had persuaded him towards the use of strong aftershave. He beamed at me when he shook my hand affably with both of his.

We served the meal on a traditional tray that fits on to a low circular bamboo table. This was laid with a home-weave cloth and matching napkins, a brass fork placed on the left and a spoon on the right of each plate (no chopsticks – the Lao only use them with noodle soup), and each diner was given their own individually woven and coloured basket of sticky rice. Vandara laid out all the dishes at the same time, and, as is often the case in Laos, most of the food was served lukewarm due to the warm climate. She also poured everyone a cup of green tea. As well as the dishes above, we ate tiny river crabs scooped from the falls. They were steamed for a few minutes in their own juices and their delicate flesh tasted sweet and minerally like the water. The meal was all the more delicious as I had learnt how to make it.

'So what are you doing here?' Tim asked me.

'I came for the food. Lao food is wonderful, and especially Vandara's cooking. You're lucky you caught her here.'

'I know. That is why I came to Vandara's too.' He turned to her. 'This chicken stew is so light! I love the way you do the steamed greens!' Vandara's face broke into a grin.

I agreed. 'I know, it's nutty, spicy and fragrant all at the same time and it's so simple.'

'I'd love to learn,' he continued enthusiastically. 'I do a bit of oriental cooking myself, as half my family is Asian.' Vandara and I exchanged a glance. This came as a revelation as he was six foot, blonde and blue-eyed. 'My brother is married to a Chinese girl and her whole family are always around the place.'

'So you cook a lot of Chinese food?' I asked, interested.

'Well, to be honest, not that much really, but I have a few signature dishes. But I eat a lot of it. I'd love to add some Lao food to my repertoire. Do you think you might show me how to cook too, Madam Vandara?'

She replied cheerfully, 'Of course, it would be my pleasure!'

Everything was so spectacularly good it was difficult to pick a favourite dish. This food would surely be immensely popular if you could ever find it in a London restaurant. I would serve the tasty little omelettes filled with garlicky, smoky aubergine purée as an appetiser or first course or main dish with equal satisfaction. You could eat the chicken stew every day for a week and not get bored, and the Lao tomato sauce made Mexican salsa seem insipid by comparison.

We ate by candlelight, chatting about the village and her visitors. Vandara voiced concern that tourists were hearing about her guest house on the grapevine and had begun to drop in unannounced instead of booking through her in Luang Prabang. Her niece looked after the place when Vandara wasn't there, but she didn't speak any foreign languages so it had caused problems. An older couple had become incensed by the sporadic electricity and lack of hot water. They'd complained bitterly, offending everyone in the process. Lying back on a bolster, the scent of angel's trumpet flowers in the air, relaxed by the sound of rushing water, I couldn't imagine how anyone could complain about this place.

Suddenly there was a kerfuffle below and I looked down through the carved balustrade to see what the commotion was about. Outside in the garden next door a crowd had gathered around a cage, a rough box of chicken wire about six foot square that had been built around a small tree. Something was rushing around inside it.

Vandara stuck her head over the balcony. 'Next door owns a monkey, his name is See.'

'Why is he in a cage? As a pet?' I asked.

'Yes, his mother was shot in the forest and my neighbour, he save him.'

The monkey's fur looked almost green. Later I discovered that See was a long-tailed macaque. They're quite common in Laos and I'd seen wild ones earlier that day coming to drink from the river. They usually form large sociable groups of up to seventy, and they're gregarious to the point of being pests when they raid people's gardens and houses looking for food.

I went downstairs to investigate. He looked young and was the size of a large cat. His fur was mottled with grey, and he had a soft white belly and a quiff of dark hair on top of his head. His small pink face was fringed on either side by sideburns which made him look like a Teddy boy. He was racing around, but he stopped for a second and took me in (the newcomer) with very intelligent yellow eyes.

Obviously bored out of his mind, he had stolen a live chick.

He'd grabbed the pretty little thing as it passed by his cage, and now fifteen adolescents were trying to get it back off him. They were all girls and they were in hysteria. Their faces were contorted, laughing and screaming at him. The three oldest were ringleaders who took turns to poke into the cage with a stick. Two of them, smart in their school uniforms of navy *sims* and white shirts, were laughing so much that it marred their attempts to catch the monkey. The other, a plump girl in a conical rice hat, took the job more seriously. She grabbed the stick and waved it threateningly around in his face.

He flung himself around the cage like a spring, clasping on to his prize with increasing pressure. The rice-hat-girl dragged the stick along the wire net noisily, then jabbed it into the cage like a fencing foil. See was getting more and more agitated; the bird in his fist was making smaller and smaller peeps and its head was beginning to loll. He leapt away from the stick with athletic bounds, clinging to the roof of the cage for one moment, then spinning around his tree and bouncing off the walls the next. Rice-hat-girl finally managed to trap him in a corner by holding him across the chest with the stick. Her piggy eyes looked vicious. The mob cheered and moved in. Several little hands reached in to try and unpick his fingers from around the bird.

See looked frantic, squashed in the corner; he was panting and scared. He didn't want to give up the fluffy yellow chick and tightened his fist, unaware that he was squeezing the life out of it. Rice-hat-girl tightened the stick across his stomach, hurting him. See bared his teeth and clutched tighter. Rice-hat-girl started to prize each of his fingers off the chick. See's fingers pinged back like elastic. She screamed at him. He screamed back. Then suddenly she yanked the chick out of his hand. It was already dead but she didn't care. She was triumphant. She was victorious. And the children danced behind her as she left without a backward glance.

See was in a total state – he leapt around his cage in a froth. One girl, straggling behind, looked at him sadly. She offered him a Bic lighter. He clung on to the wire and his hand shot out to grab it, then she followed the others.

Now it was quiet I offered him some bananas. He grabbed them but threw them on the floor with the lighter. He was much more interested in my rings, which he tried to pull from my fingers. Just then, Vandara's neighbour returned, calling to him, and he immediately calmed down and made little grunty noises. He walked up and down his cage and then lay sprawled on the ground, legs akimbo, until the neighbour came and gently offered him some dried corn kernels. Softly, See took one at a time from his hand and ate them while they cooed together. The neighbour left and I retreated to the house and watched him from the balcony.

Vandara told me they had tried to repatriate him to the forest three times, but he kept coming back to the village.

'Last time, he stayed in the forest for one month, then he followed some tourists back to the village so they built him the cage. Now he stays.'

'So he's here by his own choice,' I said sadly. 'How awful that he's lost the will to live in his natural forest.' I hate seeing intelligent animals in cages.

I looked down at him. Calm now, See was sitting on the floor playing with the orange cigarette lighter, which had lost its workings.

In Laos they have a different attitude to animals than in England. It's a rural country and they take the farmyard view that animals are workers or food producers. In towns most people have pets, but I'd seen a few disconcerting things like chickens tied up in a bunch by their feet and then hung from the back of a moving motorbike with their heads an inch from the ground; and live frogs sewn together on strings, each with a leg broken in case they escaped. People drink raw blood here. It's not everyone's idea of paradise. Of course it's nothing compared with what I saw in Vietnam. In Saigon I'd seen squirrels half garrotted on wire nooses to make them dance; snakes ripped apart while still alive; and someone stamping on a chicken for fun. Really.

It was eight-thirty, the show was over and the people in the houses around us had gradually fallen into silent reverie. People don't stay up late in Laos. Vandara's husband and niece had crept off ages ago. I said goodnight and climbed down the steep steps to my room with a torch. After the excitement of the day, I fell into a heavy sleep.

In the morning I heard the deep thump of the monks' call to prayer and opened my eyes to see a spider the size of a dinner plate in the corner of the ceiling. I quickly closed them. When I opened them again the spider was gone, which was worse. They're harmless and supposed to be lucky, but I was a bit perturbed that it might decide to join me in bed, so I got up. I had three mosquito bites on the soft underpart of my foot, and one where my sandal strap stretched across on my big toe.

It was six, and I followed the niece out of the house. She was carrying food offerings for the priests – we'd made extra last night for that purpose. In the dawn light the pools were the colour of bluebells.

The village was much more lively at this time in the morning. Children were getting ready to go to school and playing throw-the-flip-flop; ladies were weighing sacks of new rice; people were brushing their teeth in the main pond; turkeys were pecking at baskets of chillies left to dry in the sun; and little girls were catapulting birds out of the trees. We passed a pool of water lilies of such shocking pink as to be almost rude. A woman was collecting buds and putting them in two plastic buckets linked by a yoke across her shoulders. We reached the *wat* compound, and I parted company with the niece to set off early for the famous Kung Sii falls before all the tourists arrived.

A TURKEY ON SENTRY DUTY BY DRIED CHILLIES

After walking for fifteen minutes I passed through the empty picnic area, greeting villagers setting up their food stalls. I reached the falls, and the sight of it stopped me in my tracks for a few minutes. It may not be the tallest waterfall in Laos, but it was certainly arresting. It was many-tiered, and curved walls of white water spumed over the bell-shaped limestone sediment like billowing curtains. The sound of the water was deafening and the air was filled with spray which coated the surrounding leaves and trees with pale silt, giving them a ghostly appearance. Admittedly the trail was a bit treacherous, as I had to pick over detritus and fallen logs whilst clinging to the rock face, and everything was covered in a fine mineral silt, but the silt was not slimy, more crunchy, so it helped to give me purchase.

Little spurts of waterfall crashed over me, soaking me, and I had to clasp my bag under my armpit to keep it dry. Sometimes I was protected by the ghostly trees, at other times I looked down a sheer drop. Suddenly the path opened into a little plateau in the middle of the fall and a depression large enough to splash about in. I sat on a log with my feet in the cool water and looked down at the rushing steps cascading into opaline pools fringed with elephant ear leaves. I had the whole place to myself, and basked in the joy of it for an hour or so. The light filtered through trees which dripped water in glittering droplets. Dragonflies whirled about in the rock pools and it felt good to be alive.

Then the tourists arrived.

It was Saturday, so there were a lot of them, nearly all Laotian. I had been really looking forward to taking a swim, but it seemed crowded now so I returned to the village to swim in a private place I'd spotted that morning – a deep, butterfly-shaped pool with two waterfalls and a little island in the middle. I crossed on to it via a wobbly plank, stripped to my swimsuit and jumped in. God, it felt good. I couldn't touch the bottom, and swam hard in the same spot against the current, pushed back inch by inch until I was exhausted. Then I got out and lay on a rock shelf in the frothing gush of the water. I massaged my back, then my bottom, and then turned about to let the water pummel my itchy feet. Vandara appeared from around a clump of bamboo. She was wearing a sarong and carrying a plastic net bag of soap and shampoo. We washed our hair in the waterfall – a first for me.

'This make your hair and skin very soft,' she said, scrubbing vigorously behind her ears.

It was true. When I'd dried myself, I prodded my arm and it felt like I was sticking my finger in flour. My whole body was as relaxed as a noodle.

Vandara had to go back to her other guest house, but I decided to stay on for a few days and unwind. Village life in Ban Tha Baen was very appealing; I could see myself living here for ever. The rest of the world seemed very far away. There were no telephones, no computers and I hadn't heard the news for ages. I still didn't know who had won the American elections and I didn't care. Where was America anyway?

Laos had got to me as I had been told it would. Slowly and sensuously the spirit of this place took me by the soul. All my cares vanished; time lost its meaning. And that hadn't happened to me for a long, long time. I fell into a kind of lyrical, dreamy state. And I liked it.

A Waterfall Feast

Vandara's Paradise Chicken
Lao Tomato Sauce
Soop Pak – Seasonal Mixed Greens
Aubergine Farcis Rolled in an Omelette
Sticky Rice
Preserved Lime Soup

Vandara's Paradise Chicken

Laotian chickens can be tough and need a much longer time to cook and tenderise than ours. Our chickens are so soft and juicy that I have compensated by shortening the cooking times below (15-minute rather than $\frac{1}{2}$ -hour intervals).

1 whole gutted chicken (head and feet optional), cut into
   6 pieces with bone
2 stems lemon grass, roughly chopped
10 cm (4 inch) piece galangal, cut in slices
3 garlic cloves, thinly sliced
1 teaspoon salt
2 tablespoons fish sauce
$\frac{1}{3}$ tin coconut milk diluted with $\frac{2}{3}$ tin of water
$\frac{1}{3}$ tin coconut milk diluted with $\frac{1}{3}$ tin of water
$\frac{1}{3}$ tin coconut milk
1 tablespoon coriander root, roughly shredded
4 lime leaves, roughly torn
2 tablespoons chopped spring onions
300 g (12 oz) pak choi or water morning glory

Put the chicken pieces, lemon grass, galangal, garlic, salt and fish sauce in a heavy saucepan and let them marinate for at least two hours, preferably more. Then put the pan on the stove with the lid firmly on and let it steam in its own juices for 5 minutes.

Add the coconut water diluted with 2/3 tin of water nearly covering the chicken, and replace the lid. After 15 minutes add the coconut milk diluted with 1/3 tin of water. After another 15 minutes add the coriander root and lime leaves. Wait for a few minutes then add the last coconut milk to thicken the stew.

Finally, remove from the stove, add the spring onions and pak choi, stir for half a minute and serve. Vandara particularly likes the feet.

Lao Tomato Sauce

This is the most wonderful sauce, thick and pungent. It is better to pound the mixture in a mortar – I have tried using a blender, but it changes the texture and, I think, lessens the dish. The sauce is served on the side and added to taste. I have to make it in huge batches because family and friends easily eat a jar at one sitting. In England I eat it on bread.

1 cup *paa-dek* or 5 salted auchovies, rinsed and chopped (optional)
1 cup boiling water
a ball of ground pork mince, the size of a hen's egg
20 cloves garlic, peeled
8 red chillies, 4 cm (1 $\frac{1}{4}$ inch) long, split and seeded
10 small tomatoes, peeled and chopped into thin slices
1 tablespoon fish sauce
6 tablespoons oil

1 handful *hom pay* herb, chopped, available in Oriental
    stores Nov – Feb (optional)

In a shallow wok, fry 1 cup of *paa-dek* (or the anchovies) for
about 3 minutes on a high heat until almost dry, then add 1
cup of boiling water. Sieve to make 1 cup of liquid, removing
fish bits, bones etc., and put back in the wok.

Add the pork, spooning the sauce over it as it cooks. Continue for about 6 minutes or until the liquid has reduced to
about 4 tablespoons. Take off the heat and save.

In a new wok, cook the 20 cloves of garlic in oil until golden,
add the chillies and toss for a bit. Remove them and pound the
chilli/garlic in the mortar. Throw the tomatoes into the same hot
wok used to cook the garlic and reduce for about 10 minutes.

Meanwhile, add the pork and fish sauce cooked earlier to
the mortar. Finally, add the tomatoes and pound to a rough
consistency. Add fish sauce and herbs to taste.

Soop Pak – Seasonal Mixed Greens

This is a dish that can be adapted to any type of green leafy
vegetables, like spinach, spring greens or broccoli tops. Vandara's greens had quite a sharp taste, reminiscent of kale or
even sorrel. Powdered sesame adds a delicious nutty flavour
and makes the leaves taste really fantastic, especially if
eaten with Lao Tomato Sauce.

2 tablespoons sesame seeds
6 seared chillies, split and seeded
1 kg (2 lb) greens – spinach, kale, whatever is in season
a little *paa-dek* (optional)
4 tablespoons finely sliced galangal

Dry-fry the sesame seeds until golden, then pound in the mortar until they become powder. (If you do a lot at one time, you can keep the powder in a jar and use it to add an interesting flavour to other dishes.)

Sear the chillies in a flame, add to the mortar and pound.

Meanwhile, steam the greens until tender then chop vigorously. Mix in the sesame powder, chilli, a little *paa-dek*, if using and the galangal. Toss and serve.

Aubergine Farcis Rolled in an Omelette

This aubergine purée makes a delicious accompaniment to lots of dishes. On this day, Vandara made a thin omelette in the wok using 4 eggs, shallots, soy and *hom pay*. She filled it with the farcis and rolled it up. She told me that they usually make several small omelettes and place one roll by each person's plate.

    6 small purple aubergines
    3 cloves garlic
    2 tablespoons chopped shallots
    a ball of ground pork mince, the size of a hen's egg
    1 tablespoon fish sauce
    2 tablespoons soy sauce
    2 heaped tablespoons chopped garlic leaves or two
        cloves chopped garlic
    2 heaped tablespoons chopped mint
    1 bunch *hom pay* herb [optional]

Place the aubergines on an open flame and burn the skin a little. Then steam them until soft (about 5 minutes), cut them up and pound them in a mortar for a bit.

In the wok, fry the garlic, shallots, pork, fish sauce and soy sauce. Add all the cooked ingredients to the mortar and pound to a pulpy sauce. Add the herbs and pound again.

Spread the purée on the centre of a thin omelette, roll and serve.

Sticky Rice

See *How to Cook Sticky Rice* in General Recipes, p. 330.

Preserved Lime Soup

This soup is Vandara's favourite. The main ingredient is preserved limes which come in jars in any oriental store.

> the pork bone from your butcher
> beef bits from a butcher plus a bit of beef blood if possible
> 1 whole ginger root
> 1 whole galangal root
> 3 lemon grass stems
> a little *paa-dek*
> 2 preserved limes

Make a stock from the pork bones and beef bits. Meanwhile put the ginger, galangal and lemon grass directly into the embers of the fire (or in a flame if you're at home) for 5 minutes until fairly charred. Add to the stock with the *paa-dek*.

Simmer for 40 minutes, then add the preserved limes. Simmer for another 20 minutes.

Serve with a big plate of mint, watercress, lettuce, basil etc. on the side.

In Laos soup is served in one large communal bowl and everyone reaches across and takes a spoonful as they wish.

TEN

THE PLAIN OF JARS

I had been sitting in the hot aircraft hangar for two hours when the party of Communist officials arrived.

I had been full of hope as the bus whisked us away from the new Luang Prabang airport building so efficiently on time, but sitting on a hard poly-prop chair staring at a hazy runway for what felt like days had dampened my spirits somewhat. At last salvation had arrived, and I knew what to do. Have a party.

I stood up, introduced myself and offered to go and buy some beers. Forty minutes and many Beer Lao's later, we were completely drunk and all really great friends. This was a blessing because when the plane arrived it was brought in to land by a man with two ping-pong bats. It sounded like a mosquito and looked appalling – an ancient Chinese army surplus, patched up with duct tape. It was a Chinese Y-12 twin-turboprop utility aircraft with accommodation for seventeen passengers – unpressurised for extra discomfort. The crew consisted of one pilot.

We staggered on. I took my seat and then abruptly lay down, as the back would not stay upright. None of the seat belts worked, the windows were made of flimsy plastic and wires dangled ominously from the ceiling where the oxygen masks were supposed to be. There was no radar.

We took off, and soon I was looking down at the jungle below me. The sun was beaming into the pilot's eyes, so, to my astonishment, he picked up a gigantic padded envelope from the mess of papers on the seat beside him and wedged it into the windscreen, almost entirely obscuring his view. This did not seem to bother him, even though he was navigating by sight alone, and he just took a peek around the side of it every so often. This got me a little ruffled. I spent the journey obsessing that I had forgotten to bring my water bottle, and that if I did manage to survive a two-mile drop from the sky into the jungle I would probably die of thirst before I was found by a rescue team.

Half an hour later we arrived safely, and everybody clapped and cheered as though their lives depended on it. Apparently this is the traditional response on landing in Laos. But flying, precarious as it was, offered an unusually quick travel option, and I had to admit that after spending endless days bumping along rocky roads to go just a few miles, I also felt like clapping, not so much from relief but because I had avoided the terrible bus journey.

I was alive and in Phonsovan, the new capital of Xieng Khoung Province (the old one was obliterated by American bombs). It is not the most beautiful town in Laos, but it has character. Nothing is higher than two storey. The roads were being rebuilt, so a fine dust hung in the air watering the sunrise and bruising the sunsets the colour of dried apricots. Many people were walking around wearing masks.

The reason tourists come here is to visit the Plain of Jars, a prehistoric site of ancient stone vessels a metre or more in height, carved by a lost civilisation some two millennia ago. I was there to see them too, even though I'd been told that the food up here was a bit ropey as the area also happens to be the most bombed province in Laos. It was central to the conflict during the Vietnam War for a number of reasons: the province strategically flanked Communist Vietnam, parts of the Ho Chi Minh guerrilla trail snaked between the borders, the Hmong tribe (anti-Communists backed by the US) had their headquarters in the hills, and the Americans had a secret airbase on the plain. Laos was a neutral country, but the Americans, afraid that all the countries in

Indo-China would fall like dominoes to the Communists, defied the Geneva Accord and secretly began to move their military there from 1964 and stayed until they were kicked out in 1975.

Vandara had told me to stay at the Maly Hotel owned by her friend Sousath. He greeted me warmly with a heavy handshake weighed down by the mass of his many gold rings inset with jewels – ruby, sapphire, moonstone and (he claimed) diamond. He was wearing fly-like, iridescent, wraparound sunglasses, a flashy belt, a bulging flak jacket and an enormous gold chain that hung to his waist.

His father had been a Pathet Lao Communist official posted to Vientiane during the war, but the rebellious teenage Sousath missed his home village and ran back to the war zone. Like the Artful Dodger, he darted between enemy encampments – Pathet Lao, Vietnamese, American, Hmong – charming cigarettes and supplies from the royal army and giving them to the Communist troops, learning all the languages and not forgetting to make a little money on the side. He was unrelentingly on the make, but his ready wit and genuine enthusiasm for the archaeology of Laos charmed me through his crafty attempts to extract my money.

'Welcome, Natacha,' he said, stepping over the ten-foot bomb that flanked his hotel door. 'Welcome to our Plain of Jars! Come, come inside.'

We passed the reception desk, which was covered in a selection of defused bomblets, and went into the dining room for some tea. The room was decorated with shiny pine panelling and a poster of a swimming pool bar in Bali. Pride of place, however, was given to a wall of framed newspaper and magazine articles with Sousath's name marked out in neon highlighter pen, just in case his guests might accidentally overlook the obvious fact that he was one of the greatest self-publicists in Laos.

'I've been in many, many books,' he said, winking. 'You read the articles. You see, people come to me as I know everything.'

We sat down to tea, which was brought to us by Sousath's beautiful and somewhat resigned wife, Sivon, who was wearing a red Chanel-style jacket with her *sin* skirt. I noticed that a small bomb in the centre of the table was being used as an ashtray.

'That's a bombie,' said Sousath. 'There are so many we recycle them. They still go off all the time. Last week three teenagers were killed near the Jars Site One.' He frowned. 'It is always children.'

America was never 'officially' at war with Laos, but as the Ho Chi Minh trail crossed the border of the two countries, they bombed it anyway to root out the Communists. The pilots' respect for Laos was so low that they used to dump excess bombs on Lao land when returning from Vietnamese raids, just to empty their load. As a result there were more bombs dropped in Laos than on the whole of Europe in the entire Second World War – three hundred thousand tons fell in Xieng Khoung Province alone. The results were catastrophic for the civilian population.

The CBU26 cluster bomb was most widely used (though twelve other kinds of clusters have been found) – a huge bomb-shell containing six hundred and seventy tennis-ball-sized bomblets, each of which contains three hundred metal fragments that strike people at such pressure and speed that they cause horrific damage. The main bombshell opens in midair, scattering the balls over a kilometre or more; ten to thirty per cent did not detonate on impact.

Those undetonated bomblets are still lying around in their millions like super-landmines, buried under top soil, hidden under leaves and grass. They get less stable as time passes. A slight touch and they go off. At least a hundred people a year are killed or injured in this way. Typically, the casualties are poverty-stricken farmers forced to clear new land, but forty per cent are children and one-quarter of the deaths are toddlers who pick up the balls thinking they are toys. I found it hardly bearable to imagine.

I looked at the ashtray – an amusing object that once was capable of killing a child.

Sousath brought me back out of my rumination. 'Do you want to buy home-made real Asian pearl?' he asked, eyes shining. 'The best valuable souvenir.'

'No thanks, but I do want a guide.'

'Oh, I guide you! I have good car,' he said, practically rubbing his hands together with glee as he handed me his card, which, in florid writing, proclaimed:

SOUSATH-TRAVEL AND mALY HOTEL

THE mALY

'your home away from home'
- Organizer of adventure tours in Laos
- Special professional guide and translator
- Historical and Indochina war background Guide

Always with an eye for an opportunity, he had my number. I was not going to buy pearls, but I was interested in his knowledge of the area, and maybe, he deduced, I was prepared to pay for it. Things had not changed much since he was selling cigarettes to the troops at a premium, and he read my interests with the skill of a market trader.

'Now we have some whisky.' He filled my glass to the brim triumphantly. 'Tomorrow, I take you to the jars. I made the government open the jars site for tourists. My idea. I told them to open. They didn't want because of the bombs but I persuade them.'

I had a feeling that every good idea in Phonsovan came from the wellspring of Sousath's brilliant business mind and that I was going to hear a lot more of them, but he was a likeable enthusiast and the main thing was I had my guide.

'It was hard, it cost 20,000 dollars to clear only Site One of three tons of bombs. But I say, you need tourists, they come, they bring moneeee . . .'

We drank and ate Sivon's delicious bamboo shoot soup as I listened to Sousath's grand plans for organised tours of the area. When I went to bed I was surprised to find a television in my room. I still did not know the American election result so I turned it on. Unfortunately there was only one satellite channel showing a cheap Australian soap opera. No doubt in the hope of pulling double the audience, it combined the two most popular soap genres by placing a police station on the premises of a hospital. It was so mind-blowingly boring that I fell asleep after two minutes.

I am ashamed to admit that I was expecting to be disappointed when I walked up the hill towards the Plain of Jars, as several tourists I had met had been unenthusiastic about them. But when I stepped over the ridge and saw three hundred of them at once, my mouth dropped open in awe. They varied in size from hip height to ten feet, some scattered, others snuggled together in groups across the barren landscape.

Sousath watched my reaction with genuine delight. 'You see, Natacha, it is a special place.' He bounded off down the hill. 'I think you see it too.'

I felt drawn to touch them as though they were sentient things; and when I did, they were warm – the morning sun had heated the stone. I found myself leaning on them, stroking and hugging them, resting my head on them and gripping on to their round rims. They felt comforting, familiar, ancient.

And when the wind is strong enough, they sing.

'They make a sound. We call the sound *hong hai ha fa*. It is hard to translate. It means "to cry towards the sky with longing", or something like that.'

They looked very similar to the earthenware water storage jars still used all over South-east Asia today. Each jar, however, was individual. Some were fat with oval openings, some narrow, some with rectangular holes. Once they all had lids, but now they were open to the wind and rain, though there were a few lids left, half buried at the edge of the site. The large jars are known as the 'urns of the aristocrats' and were supposed to have been the burial jars of the kings and queens of a great, lost civilisation. A local legend claims they belonged to a race of giants who came from southern China.

'Four metres tall, the average height of this race,' said Sousath. 'Enormous. Khun Jeuam was the leader, one of seven sons of the Chinese king. He was looking for a new place to rule. He came here and one thousand soldiers join him and make war on their neighbours. When they had won, it became a big kingdom and they celebrate by making a thousand stone jars to make rice wine. Then they all have a party and hold dog races.' He smiled widely at the thought of such a huge celebration. 'The place was called by the local people *kang ma len* – "the field of the running dog", not the Plain of Jars, as they used to race dogs here. After the King died they kept the tradition of dog races for many century.'

'Have the jars ever been studied by archaeologists?' I asked, my back nestled against the warm stone.

Sousath's face lit up and he was bursting to show off his knowledge. 'Oh yes! A French lady came in the 1930s and wrote a book. She said the jars were very old, from around 500 BC to first century, two thousand years old!' he exclaimed. 'She die in World War Two. Her name was Colani.'

Madeleine Colani was a pioneering archaeologist and formidable character. She dashed around Indo-China with her sister, Eleonore, accompanying her as her dogsbody. Allegedly, she used to lower Eleonore into dark potholes by rope and refuse to retrieve her unless she had found something interesting. Colani broke new ground when she discovered, among other things, the Hoabinhian, a hunting-foraging people who were based in Vietnam eighteen thousand years ago. She also spent a good deal of time in Laos.

She wrote two volumes on the Plain of Jars entitled *Mega-lithes du Haut Laos I et II*, in which she wrote that she excavat-ed eleven jars. She found them to be filled with small amounts of black charcoal sludge. Rainwater had emptied the jars of their contents, some of which had been washed outside and buried by time. She found orange comelian, blue and yellow beads (*perles de verre*), human calcified teeth, bones, burnt teeth, and a jaw-bone. She also discovered bronze and iron tools that she believed were used to carve the stone.

She concluded that the jars were used to store cremated remains. The results of the dig were supposed to have gone to the museum in Vientiane, but when I went to investigate I found no trace of them and there certainly wasn't anything left inside the jars on the plain now. The precious artefacts had just disap-peared into the ether of Laos's bureaucracy.

Sousath knew all about her. 'Colani was the one who named this place the Plain of Jars. She say they lay on a route stretching from the Vietnamese coast, near Da Nang, to the North Cachar Hills of India, six hundred miles to the north-west!' He stretched his arms wide in excitement. 'She say that some stone jars dis-covered in north-eastern India had roughly the same design as our urns in Laos and in Sa Huynh. In Vietnam she found urns of baked earth containing some human remains. Similar. And there are stone circles, too, a big one like your Stonehenge. Lots, maybe three or four.' I was amazed he had heard of Stonehenge, but I was learning fast that, like a London cabbie, Sousath picked up titbits of knowledge from his clients and used them to brilliant effect; he had a reputation to keep up.

'Where's your henge?'

'About one hundred eighty kilometres away towards Sam Neur. I took some tourist camping to see it.' He burst out laughing. 'We camp outside and all night long the rats ran over our sleeping bags. The tourists were not very happy.' He wig-gled his hand across his chest from left to right several times to illustrate the rats. 'The henge is very old, Lao history goes back far in time.'

Indeed, complex societies in the neighbouring kingdoms of Angkor (in Cambodia), Champa (in Vietnam), and Pagan (in Myanmar) were already well established at the turn of the first century AD.

'Colani suggest that prehistoric salt traders followed a caravan route from India through to Luang Prabang, our Plain of Jars and into Vietnam, and the people who lived along it shared a similar culture, burying their dead in jars. Now someone say there are stone jars in the island of Sulawesi, near Bali. Maybe they go down there too.' A group of affluent Thai tourists had arrived and were posing uncomfortably in miniskirts on the stone rims.

'Now you see the Jar Cave,' exclaimed Sousath, dragging me down the hill.

The moment I entered the cave I felt like I was inside a jar. It was the right shape and there were two small holes at the top that let in the light.

'There used to be one hole,' said Sousath, 'but the rain made another one.'

When Colani discovered the cave she noticed that one wall was blackened and there were signs that the interior had been chiselled and shaped. She found cinerary vessels and believed that the cave was used as a crematorium. The burnt remains were then placed outside in the jars with their personal effects.

There was a hallowed atmosphere in the cave and I turned about in wonder.

Suddenly, and to my surprise, Sousath said, 'In 1994, there was another excavation, a Japanese man came here.' He liked to spin out his revelatory nuggets of information.

'Really? I haven't read anything about that.'

'Oh, I show them where to dig, I know where,' he continued pompously. 'We find a man carved on the side of a jar, he face

the north-east towards the big stone circle. I help find everything: beads, broken pottery, skull and bones. They all buried
underneath the jars, not inside. Lots of beads – aquamarine and
sapphire.' His eyes bulged at the thought of their value.

'Where are they now?'

'All sent to Vientiane.' Nothing from this dig in the Vientiane
museum, either. (However, the founding Communist president
Kaysone's chest expander is given pride of place.)

When we returned outside I almost felt like I had stepped
back in time to the 1970s war. The horizon was completely
obscured by great clouds of smoke and the barren landscape
around the jars was smouldering in patches as though it had just
been bombed.

'God, what's happened?'

Sousath's face twisted in disgust. 'Oh, they are burning the
"American" grass. They have to do it once a year.'

'What's American grass?'

'After the Americans bombed, they spray Agent Orange on
the ground to defoliate. The earth has become poisoned. Nothing grow except this grass. It is invasive, and grows two metres
tall.' He put his hands to his throat. 'It strangles everything.
They have to burn it, sometimes bombies go off as they burn,
even when the land has been demined. There are so many.' He
practically spat, 'I hate this grass.'

I turned away. For maybe two thousand years these wonderful objects that had taken such imagination and civilisation to
create had rested peacefully in their sacred landscape of lush
vegetation. Yet it had taken only a few years of modern warfare
(in a neutral country) to sterilise the land of its natural flora. It
was a despicable disgrace.

The next morning it was so cold my breath hung in the air.
Sousath had to go to a village sixty kilometres away to see a
headman in a Khamu settlement.

'I help the village get some pump and plastic water pipes from the river to the fields. They are going to be thanking me with a *baci* ceremony. I bring my wife and one son, the other son is sick in bed. You want to come for the ride?'

Indeed I did. The heart of all Lao celebrations is the *baci* (pronounced bassee), a special blessing, the origins of which lie in Lao animist prehistory. As the Khamu tribes are animist and considered to be the first inhabitants of Laos, I thought I might be seeing it in its primal form. Of course, I had to pay for the privilege, but it wasn't much.

Sousath introduced me to his nineteen-year-old son, who had recently named himself James after his hero, James Bond. The day before I had heard him playing the guitar like a pro and singing, 'We had joy, we had fun, we had seasons in the sun . . .' in perfect English. He had inherited his father's affable manner but with a more languid style. He donned a pair of iridescent wraparound sunglasses like his dad's before getting into Sousath's quality four-wheel-drive car. Plenty of people had big cars in Phonsovan.

'There are lots of entrepreneurs in this town, lots of military, road construction business, and lots of corruption,' said James casually.

Suspiciously, everyone buckled up their seat belts tightly and Sivon wrapped a headscarf securely around her head.

'We go down Route 7 towards Vietnam. We can do some sightseeing on the way. We have plenty of time. The village is near the hot spring. You can go to the spring resort now. First prime minister Kaysone's wife built it. But if you go to resort you have to pay, whereas in my village you can bathe in the spring water for freeee!' He clapped his hands together at the thought of scamming the official site.

We set off, and within two kilometres of the town the road disintegrated into a series of ruts and potholes of gargantuan proportions. I had heard that it sometimes took three days for the public bus to reach our destination, and now I understood why. Even in Sousath's luxury car it was hell. The landscape looked awful too.

'The legacy of Agent Orange!' shouted Sousath over the noise of the engine.

The herbicide, Agent Orange, was used by the Americans to defoliate trees and shrubs to expose the enemy. It contains dioxins, some of the most toxic chemicals known to man, and was used widely in Vietnam and Laos. US servicemen, who at most served only a few months' tour of duty, have suffered from cancers, skin disorders and liver problems as a result of contact with it. In May 1984, in an out of court settlement, the manufacturers agreed to pay $180 million in damages to servicemen for exposure to Agent Orange. The hateful Monsanto company was the key defendant and had to contribute 45.5 per cent of the total payment disbursement. It has been linked to Parkinson's disease, spina bifida, miscarriages and deformities. There are no records of how it has affected the people of Laos, though I personally noticed dozens of children with hare lips and other minor deformities in this area.

'Round here, eighty per cent of the land was sprayed. The soil is bad, we have to bring topsoil from far away so we can grow things. This bit is very bad, later it get better.'

Even after 1975 the poisoning continued with other chemicals as the government issued vicious military campaigns against the defiant Hmong minority. In an attempt to root out the guerrillas, the Communists enlisted the help of the Soviet army, who tested trichothecene (known as 'yellow rain') against the Hmong. According to the the US Army Biological and Chemical Weapon Information Service, a minimum of 6300 people died in Laos as a consequence. Ten per cent of the Hmong population were wiped out and thousands had to escape for their lives. The after-effects of this particular chemical in Laos are unrecorded.

We'd began to pass substantial villages and the recycled war scrap became more prolific as we sped by fence upon fence made up of bomb casings jammed into the earth in macabre rows and dozens of battered torpedoes recycled to encircle market gardens. Everywhere I looked there were bombs reinvented as pig troughs, window sills, house stilts, and even flower pots.

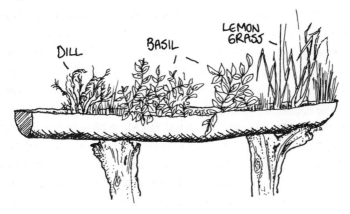

HERB GARDEN IN A CLUSTER BOMB SHELL

After three hours of hip-dislocating bumps, we stopped to visit the Tham Piu cave. It was famous as a shelter used during the war by the villagers of Ban Na Meun. One day in the late sixties, an American pilot on a secret mission fired a single missile into the cave thinking it was being used as a Vietnamese field hospital (nice target!), and almost the entire village was wiped out. They had been hiding there to avoid the bombs during the day, and tending their rice fields under cover of darkness.

There were trees here, and butterflies. We made our way through a trail in the woods towards the foot of a sheer cliff and a new concrete platform. A sign read in English:

Deploring to the spirit of villagers who got hit by rocket on
24/11/1968 from an American Imperialist

Beside it lay a black donation box with 'Thanks for your sacrifice' written on the side. I gave a donation and we climbed the steep path to the gaping mouth of the cave. As I entered I noticed a little wooden house on stilts. It was covered in dried flowers, incense sticks and candles. One sees these spirit houses all over Laos, usually standing on a post by the gate of the house. They look like perfect little doll's houses and are often exquisitely made. Offerings of incense, food and flowers are left before them for evil spirits, who, thus placated, leave the real house and family alone.

One of the candles must have set this one alight some time ago as it was partially burnt; the three little statues that lined the back were almost stubs of charcoal. I went to have a closer look at the offerings and realised, with some shock, that they included two charred human rib bones.

'Ah, those found by tourist two month ago,' said Sousath casually. He was prancing around the entrance to the cave, reluctant to enter. Sivon and James had stayed in the car.

I had to pick my way over the debris left by the explosion and could still see the remains of the wooden platform, the base of a two-storey dwelling used by the villagers when they had moved their village inside. It was dark and sinister. The ceiling of the cave was a hundred feet above me, but it still felt oppressively enclosed. I kept thinking of all the men, women and children who had burnt and suffocated to death in the rubble. One man killed four hundred people with the touch of a button; it was horrible to imagine.

Sousath did not want to go in. 'There are bad *pii*.' Sousath was an animist himself and *pii* (pronounced pee) are spirits, often malevolent, that inhabit nature, objects and, sometimes, people. Nearly all Lao, even Buddhists, believe in them to some extent.

'I am animist, not Buddhist. My necklace not the Buddha but animist,' he said, pulling out a big gold locket from the many chains around his neck. 'This spirit represent iron flowing in water, very strong. You won't find many Buddhist temples here. In rural area there are witches that can put a nail in your stomach.' And on this obscure note, he stomped back towards the car. 'We go to village now.'

The Khamu village was similar to the one on the trek in Luang Nam Tha, but this one was four times the size and, judging from the tools and farm implements, obviously wealthier. Sousath led us past the village and through the trees to the hot spring for a 'water sauna', but once we were at the river location he declined to go in the water and sped off to do some business, taking his wife with him. I had put a swimsuit on under my clothes and awkwardly removed them beneath a *sin* skirt while James ogled my whiteness.

The spring consisted of four bubbling holes in the fine mud of the shallows. It did not look too prepossessing but I plunged in anyway. The springs were boiling hot – enough to burn your skin – but the water around them was deliciously warm against the chill of the air, and we larked about for half an hour, floating in the gurgles. We returned to the village glowing with mineral health.

Sousath and Sivon were sitting on the outer veranda of the headman's stilted house, deep in conversation about water irrigation. We climbed the ladder to join them.

'Good, yes? The water gives you massage and all for freeee,' he laughed.

'Yes, it was lovely, thank you for taking me there.'

The headman, a small man moving obsequiously around Sousath, had disappeared on our arrival and now returned with a large earthenware jar.

We sat down and I could see the headman's wife inside the house, pounding something in a bowl. Her eleven-year-old daughter, wearing a disintegrating T-shirt with Elton John on the front, was adding wood to the open fire inside.

'Rice wine,' said James with a grin, removing what looked like a bird's nest of straw from the top of the jar to reveal a grey mash. 'It is not as strong as *lao-lao*, more like beer. Try some?'

The headman stuck a couple of bamboo straws into the jar and I took a suck. It was mild and slightly sour and tangy – easy to drink.

'They steam sticky rice, then wash until clear, sieve it, add yeast and stir. There are two kinds, one is sweet and the other is sour. After three days compress it, add water and seal with ash and grass to ferment.'

Many people from the village had come to see us, particularly children, who played beneath the house and looked up at us shyly. A gang of teenagers were chasing two cockerels with a machete; they would be cooked and used later in the *baci* ceremony.

The headman's wife brought out a snack of sticky rice and the raw green bean salad she had been pounding. The bean salad was fabulous – a mix of beans, garlic, salt, sugar and lime that seemed to hit all the taste buds at once. Later, in the south, I tried several versions of this dish, and now it is one of my favourites. I add tomato and peanuts and people go wild about it. We were given some moulded aluminium spoons to eat it with which Sousath claimed were made from American war planes shot down in the war and recycled to make utensils, and we continued our conversation on animism.

'Animists, like me, believe in the spirits of nature,' he said grandly. 'They live in a big tree or a big cave. People here, they live with nature. They know they should not hunt more than you need. You must ask spirits before you hunt and show them you kill for survive, then it is OK. It is all very eeeeco,' he added, taking a long draft of rice wine.

A grandmother in a pink shirt stopped to stare at us as she rocked her grandchild tied in a floral scarf. Several other children joined her, many carrying smaller ones in old towels or on piggyback. They stood stock-still like a Victorian portrait, framed by the banana groves behind.

'You see, I know what is going to happen in the future.' At this, Sousath's wife sighed almost imperceptibly. 'In next month, for instance, I feel I'm going to have luckeee or get hurt. Last month the spirits say I should not travel a long distance but I did and I had a crash. You must listen to them. River, for example, it is our belief that you should not make it dirty 'cos the river spirit will be angry. You must not go to forbidden areas in the forest and the Jars you must not touch them.' He smiled. 'That's why they are still there. Some things I believe,' he flicked his hand casually, 'others just superstition.' In my experience so far, I found that everyone I met, without exception, believed in *pii* with some fervour, and they were even venerated in ceremonies within Buddhist temples.

It was dusk, and the headman brought out a small pineapple-shaped bombie to use as a candle holder and another sweeter jar of rice wine. In the fast fading light only the luminous stripe down the leg of a boy's tracksuit trouser leg gave away the huddle of children staring at us in the darkness. Inside the fire blazed, glinting through the bamboo-weave walls. I was excited, as it was nearing the time for the *baci*.

The *baci* is more usually called the *su-kwan* in informal circumstances. *Baci* is a corruption of a Cambodian phrase *bha sri* meaning 'the rice of prosperity', and is the proper term for a ceremony involving royalty or high statesmen. The name *baci* has been adopted more recently (particularly by the government for the benefit of tourists) to cover all special event ceremonies and has a stronger Buddhist structure that some believe is corrupting the original ceremony.

The *su-kwan* has its roots in animist prehistory and means the 'calling' or 'welcoming' of the *kwan*.

The Laotians believe that the body is made up of thirty-two 'parts' or 'organs' and that thirty-two *kwan* protect each one of these parts. The *kwan* constitute one's spiritual essence and are part of the body from birth. It is difficult to illustrate exactly what they are as they are intrinsic to the body and life force, yet separate. These *kwan* have a wandering nature and are only too glad to abscond from the body without warning, causing illness and distress until they return. When someone dies they fly off and join with others to be reincarnated into someone else.

The *su-kwani* is a ritual binding of the *kwan* to their owner and is a way of conveying good luck and goodwill to all the others present. It is an extremely warm-hearted ceremony and epitomises the generosity of spirit of the Lao people.

Sousath explained, 'We do this when someone comes to visit, or a member of the family goes away, or at wedding, when someone is sick, New Year, even as a "treat" for a child who is causing problem. Every time. It is very affectionate ceremony, like a warm welcome.' Or as my friend Khamtoune explained later in England, like when you open a bottle of champagne to celebrate an old friend who has come to visit. I found the subtle differentiation between the *baci* and the *su-kwan* to be extremely confusing and was never sure in which ceremony I was taking part.

'People believe the *kwan* they like to roam around so much, be free, bit naughty. It can be led astray by bad spirits, it must be reminded to come home as often as possible. We go inside now, you see.'

We entered the living room to find a low wicker tray-table positioned on a plastic rose-covered mat on the board floor.

The tray contained the two unfortunate (and now boiled) cockerels, two bowls of cooked sticky rice, and on either side of those a couple of bottles of *lao-lao* with Ya Dong bark. A small bowl of the best uncooked rice lay in the middle of the table with thirty white cotton strings placed on top of the grains. This was the *phakwan* – feast for the soul. In grander ceremonies the *phakwan* might include an elaborate sculptural flower display arranged on a cone of banana leaves on a plate containing whisky, eggs, cakes, incense, candles, fruit, biscuits and more. The cotton strings would later be tied around our wrists to bind the wishes of health or luck.

We all took our seats on the floor around the table and everyone crowded about us. There were about thirty or forty people in the hut, and much animated chat. The place of honour, opposite the master of ceremonies, was set for Sousath, as he had helped the village buy the vital water pipes to irrigate their fields. Sivan, James, the headman, the chief of a neighbouring Hmong village, his son and I completed the circle. The room was dimly lit by three guttering oil lamps. The man in charge of the ceremony stepped out of the gloom. He was in his eighties, with a sculpted face and cadaverous hollow cheeks. This was the Mor Phom, 'wish priest', an elder with knowledge of the ancient texts.

Money was produced and placed on the bowl of uncooked rice and the white cotton strings were replaced on top.

Sousath nudged me and said in a stage whisper, 'Moneeee for someone to wish good luck.'

Many people came and added more 1,000-kip notes (10p) to the pile.

In the background darkness the women were casually chopping away, and I could hear the children outside playing and laughing, but I could feel the excited anticipation of the throng in the semi-darkness.

We were asked to place our hands on the table, like at a séance, and the old man began to chant loudly. The words were not Lao but some other ancient language.

'First he invokes the divinities of heaven, earth, mountain and water to come and gather the offering set before us,' whispered Sousath. 'Then he call the soul to come.'

Someone took one of the cooked cockerels and pulled it apart into a bowl, adding some sticky rice. We were asked to eat it to 'acquire the spirits within us' and given a glass of *lao-lao*. The bowl was passed around and we ate a morsel and drank from the communal cup.

The chanting rose to a loud songlike mantra as we passed the food. Sousath said, 'He say something like "We choose this day to put on this tray, chicken and rice. Good food and delicious dishes and alcohol for you to share. Come back and eat rice with your uncle and chicken with your ancestors. Come back this day, oh soul who has gone to wander. Do not linger on the way with the *pii* or in the mountains. Come back and stand before the *phakwan* (tray) and stay home from now on!"'

The invocation continued until it was deemed that all the *kwan* had returned, and then the wishes formula was recited.

The old man took Sousath's hands and chanted over them, tied a cotton string around one wrist and then repeated the incantation as he tied the other.

'Be as strong as the antlers of a stag, as the jaws of a wild bear or as the tusks of the elephant. May your life last a thousand years, may your riches be abundant. Should you suffer from fever, may it disappear. May everything yield before you and may you be free from want. May you have long life, health, happiness and strength!'

Sousath then took some strings and tied them on to his wife's wrist, and the ritual continued around the table finally including me. Meanwhile, the other people in the hut were taking strings and tying them on each other's wrists. A couple of people came and tied me with more until I had three on each wrist.

'You must keep them on for at least three days or more, or you will have very bad luck,' Sivan told me earnestly. 'You then can untie them, or pull them off only. *Never* cut them off, it is very bad to do so.'

The old man stood and said a last incantation, and Sousath gave him a thousand-kip note. The bundle of money on the table was given to Sousath in return.

'I have to take it for ceremony,' he explained.

'What is it for?'

'Planting,' he said. 'I plant in the bank, flower is interest.' His big eyes rolled, and he gave me a broad toothy smile, laughing heartily like a fat Chinese Buddha.

The ceremony was over, so the table was cleared and the rest of the chicken chopped up for the party. Bowls of forest greens, chicken broth, *jaew* and sticky rice completed the feast, which was almost identical to the one I encountered in Luang Nam Tha.

Sivan said to me, 'First time I came to village I make big mistake, very big. I did not know that Khamu women do not eat until the men are finished. We ate so much, leaving the women with little, this is their custom, cannot change.'

Indeed, the women and children were sitting around the fire not eating. We (including Sivan and myself) were asked to join the feast, however, as we were guests.

I had a tiny morsel, as I wanted to leave food for the women, and then suddenly the guests got up and it was time to leave. The table of food was picked up and taken to the women, and everyone in the house descended upon it as though they hadn't eaten for a week.

The trip back over the terrible roads in the dark seemed endless as I swung wildly from side to side in the car. When we arrived at the hotel, we all disappeared without a word in a state of bruised exhaustion.

The next morning Sousath took me to the airport to catch the eight o'clock plane that I had booked the week before. At the time of my arrival I had been very careful to confirm my departing flight (I was learning to deal with Lao bureaucracy by now), but the man had written my confirmation on a tiny scrap of paper, which had made me suspicious. I got there early to make sure I got a seat.

Sure enough, I was not on the list so I could not fly.

'The spirits say you should not go, Natacha,' said Sousath portentously, but he helped me get another flight as more tourists were due at his hotel that afternoon. After much flutter, I was rescheduled on the two-thirty flight – thankfully, the ATR plane maintained by a French mechanic. I left my bag and I went back into Phonsovan with five hours to kill, and sat down to read at a café. Seven Vietnamese road builders were working on the storm drain outside. They wore khaki pith helmets and cotton masks against the dust.

At lunchtime I was given the special *felang* menu that had been translated into English. It read:

Placenta salad
Fried flour chicken
Tripe salad
Latna ·
Soup eggs not salted
Spicy fried chicken stomach
Beef bile sour
Maw poo

The café was full of locals, and, not surprisingly after reading that menu, no foreigners but myself. I toyed with the idea of placenta salad followed by maw poo but thought better of it and pointed to something someone was eating at the table next to me – delicious spicy beef cooked by Miss On. I then went to the kitchen to watch it being cooked again for my benefit.

When I returned to the airport, my bag had been joined by sixteen suitcases, three industrial-sized laundry bags, four stuffed rice sacks, nine cardboard boxes in various sizes, a multi-purpose electric wok and a motorbike. A man added to the pile by dropping a long canvas bag to the ground with a clunk that sounded suspiciously like a bundle of rifles. The plane had been rescheduled to leave at four-thirty; it was becoming a long day.

We took off at five-thirty as the sun was setting. From the window of the plane the pale depleted earth looked ruinous beneath us: craters pockmarked the landscape like acne scars and sickly trees stubbled the hills in struggling tufts. Then we rose through the fluffy cotton clouds and up towards a sky as shell-pink as a picture in a Sunday school prayer book, and it seemed like the hellish landscape had all been a bad hallucination.

It was real, though; and people have to live there, among the unwanted detritus of a long-forgotten war. Cluster bombs are as just as horrific as landmines, and America was still dropping them on Afghanistan in 2002 and Iraq in 2003. Human rights campaigners have called for countries using them to bear responsibility for their clear-up, and then a total ban on the weapons; but a UN conference on the subject in 2003 came to nothing.

Raw Green Bean Salad

This is an excellent dish for summer. Make it for lunch as a side dish, pack it into a picnic basket or just eat it as a light snack. It is Rachel's and my favourite recipe.

  1 large clove garlic, peeled
  1 bird's-eye chilli
  1 heaped teaspoon rough salt
  1 level dessertspoon brown sugar
  2 tablespoons unsalted peanuts
  450 g (1 lb) raw green beans or long beans, topped and
      tailed, cut into 2.5 cm (1 inch) pieces
  1 tablespoon fish sauce
  3 flavourful medium tomatoes, quartered, or 8 cherry
      tomatoes, halved
  juice of one lime (or more, to taste)

Pound the garlic, chillies, salt and sugar in a pestle and mortar until they are a rough paste. Add the peanuts and pound to break them up (not too fine). Add the bean pieces and fish sauce and pound them until they are bruised so the flavours infuse. Add the tomatoes and pound a few more times. Squeeze on the lime and serve immediately.

Miss On's Spicy Beef

  1–3 bird's-eye chillies
  3 cloves garlic, peeled
  2 shallots, peeled and chopped
  1 tablespoon vegetable oil

2 lime leaves

a handful of chopped steak

3 level tablespoons coconut powder

$\frac{1}{2}$ onion, chopped fine

$\frac{1}{2}$ teaspoon salt

$\frac{1}{2}$ teaspoon sugar

250 ml ($\frac{1}{2}$ pint) meat stock

3 green beans, cut up into 2.5cm (1 inch) pieces

Pound the chilli, garlic and shallots to make a well-mixed paste. Heat the oil in a wok until hot, then add the lime leaves and pounded paste.

Now add the steak and the coconut powder, the onion and the salt and sugar. Toss for 30 seconds to coat everything and then add the stock.

Cook at a high heat and add the green beans. Keep stirring at a high boil. Put a lid on the wok, leave for a few minutes and then remove the lid. The liquid should reduce to a thick gravy.

Remove from heat and serve with sticky rice.

ELEVEN

THE FESTIVAL OF THE GOLDEN STUPA

The next morning, in Vientiane, I wandered on to the street to find some breakfast and was stopped in my tracks by a newspaper headline. LAO AIRPORT BOMB INJURES 4. I bought the Bangkok paper and read on:

> A bomb exploded in Vientiane airport yesterday, injuring four people. The bomb went off just outside the domestic air terminal of Wattay airport around 10 a.m. It was not immediately clear if there were any foreigners among the four people injured. The explosive contained shards of metal and had been placed in a plastic bag on the back of a bicycle. Yesterday's blast was the latest in a series of mysterious bomb explosions at high profile targets in the Lao capital. No one has claimed responsibility for the attacks which have injured dozens of people.

My stomach turned and I instinctively felt for the lucky cotton strings around my wrists – I had been in the domestic air terminal yesterday and if I had caught my correct flight from Phonsovan that morning (with the usual bureaucratic delays on landing), I would probably have been leaving the building at the moment of the bombing. By the time I got to the airport in the evening, there had been absolutely no sign of an explosion, not a trace. The smiles of the staff stretched wide and all evidence of subversion had been swept away. If I had not seen the foreign newspaper, I would never have known that anything had happened; and that is just how the Lao People's Revolutionary Party would like to keep it.

I had been warned about the bombs before I visited Laos, but no one seemed to know much about them. Supposedly there had been twelve explosions in the last year, but, then again, nobody was sure. Once I arrived and started asking questions, things became even more obscure. Vientiane natives shrugged their shoulders and claimed they were firecrackers thrown by children. Some seemed to think it was the Hmong tribe trying to claim their independent homeland in the north. Bureaucrats avoided the subject altogether. I heard other wild theories: that they were thrown by Thai travel companies jealous of their tourists crossing the border; that the royalists were secretly back in Laos; that it was the Chinese, the Vietnamese or the Burmese, or, even more amazingly, the government bombing itself in a struggle between the ruling octogenarians and the younger upstarts, those pesky septuagenarians who were pushing for reform.

I could not understand why a terrorist group would detonate bombs and *not* want to claim them, but as I continued on my trip I realised why. I had almost forgotten that I was in a one-party state. On an everyday level it is easy to forget this when in Laos. The rural people (85 per cent of the population) continue as they always have. There is a private sector operating, almost independently, on dollars and baht, and the annoying bureaucracy can be eased away with backhanders, but when you break the law, the government comes down on you hard.

After the revolution, people with even the most tenuous connections to the opposition were taken away and put in re-education camps to toil and starve for, not months, but years, even decades. Many died incarcerated and the people have not forgotten. Prison in Laos can be draconian in the extreme. Even now, in the twenty-first century, I hear rumours of prisoners being kept in pits, defecating, washing and eating from a bucket sent down on a string. Vientiane Prison is supposed to have a hole in the ground like the Black Hole of Calcutta, and, allegedly, pockets of insurgents in the forests up north are being flushed out and shot on sight by the army. If a group admitted to the bombings, who knows how many would be rounded up to smash the ring – so no one dares to lay claim. They just cause enough disruption to needle the skin of the government without breaking cover.

Luckily, I had just missed their latest stab.

The reason I was back in Vientiane was for the food. The next day would be the culmination of one of the biggest, loudest festivals of the year – the Boun That Luang – which takes place on the full moon of the twelfth month in the Laotian calendar at the Pha That Luang (the Great Stupa), the most important national monument in Laos.

The festival is a time to make homage to the Buddha, the People's Democratic Republic (of course) and the guardian of the city, Nang Si – a pregnant woman who sacrificed herself as a gift to the spirits when the new capital was established by King Setthathirat in 1563. Legend has it that as they were founding the first new *wat*, Wat Si Muang, by lowering a stone pillar into an auspiciously placed hole, Nang Si leapt into the gap as it was dropped into position and was crushed to death. Her fervent act has been venerated ever since. The festival lasts several days and starts at this *wat*, where devotees come to honour her, and then it proceeds to That Luang compound for more celebrations with offerings of candles and flowers, fireworks and games that last until after the full moon.

I wanted to go because the editor of the *Vientiane Times* had told me they had planned a special marquee selling all the traditional foods of Laos, and I was not going to miss that.

I had arranged to meet my friend Soun Vannithone, a talented chef I'd met in London, outside the gates of the *wat*: luckily his visit home briefly coincided with my stay in Vientiane, so I was in for a culinary tour with an expert. However, I was an hour early so I went into the That Luang *wat*, a compound the size of four football pitches.

There were stalls everywhere, even pressed right up against the crenellated temple walls. Children were running about with balloons, and families were posing for snapshots of their big day out. The stalls sold an incongruous array of goods from toys to manufacturing hardware; thin women sat gossiping on sacks, selling those packets of dried noodles that nobody buys opposite the flashy State Enterprise for Agriculture and Industrial Development stall that included a selection of concrete roofing tiles. In front of it, inexplicably, stood a life-sized statue of a charging Spanish bull. A group of monks, all wearing large wire-rimmed, Kojak-style seventies sunglasses, stood transfixed at a stand with a blaring television. On a rostrum, teenage girls with hair as shiny as volcanic glass promoted 'Pop Fruity Shampoo – to make your hair smell delicious' (oddly, written in English and Lao) to passers-by; and Chinese tractors posed in formation next to lines of coloured forklifts. All the stalls were edged with carefully tended tins of flowers.

Again, the curious mix of the religious, secular and state jumbled together in the midst of a big party struck me as peculiarly Lao. There is a common expression repeated by foreigners and Thai – that Laotians are either preparing for a party, having a party or recovering from one. It is not meant as a compliment, but, frankly, I think it is the Laotian *joie de vivre* that makes them secretly the envy of their neighbours. Laotian people know how to enjoy and celebrate life in a way that gladdens the soul. It is infectious, and partly what makes travelling in the country such an absolute joy.

The crowd was building and I was swept along to the crisply restored, golden stupa, the mass of pure gold leaf bedazzling in the sunlight. One hundred and fifty feet high and shaped like an elongated lotus bud, the That Luang sits in an elaborate stepped cloister, the entirety of which is also glowingly gilded. It is supposed to encase a piece of the Buddha's breastbone brought to Laos from India by emissaries of the Moghul Emperor Asoka in the third century. The structure dates from the middle of the six-teenth century, but the renovation was so shiny it had stripped away the history for me. As the symbol of Laos, the That Luang is supposed to contain the sacred *kwan* of the nation.

I could hear music, wooden xylophones and a rhythmic chanting, and I soon distinguished musicians in the crowd leading a procession of thousands. Beautiful girls followed the music-makers, their hair swept into high buns and clasped with rings of gold. They wore thick silk *pha sin* skirts and sashes in gorgeous colours – bronze, apricot, lime, gentian, cherry-red and cyan – and silk the colour of squashed damsons, creamy gardenia petals and blushing mangoes, all stiff with gold thread. They seemed to glide across the ground and their tapering fingers spiralled in the air to the sound of flutes and gongs.

Traditionally, the That Luang festival was a time when the notables and civil servants of Laos used to take a pledge of loyalty to the king of Vientiane. He would take three days to reach the stupa and the royal procession must have been a marvel to behold. Even without the king, it was still magnificent.

Behind the beauties came hundreds of boys and girls in elaborate tribal dress, and following at the rear came men incongrously dressed in plain street clothes and pork-pie hats, carrying the traditional *phasat* – castles and pyramids made from banana plant stems decorated with wax flowers, notes of money and offerings to the temple. These *phasat* were six feet tall and had to be carried on stretchers held between two men. Trails of kip notes interwoven with flowers were attached to the amazing teetering towers and flew behind them like party streamers. *Phasat* are given to the temple to gain merit, good luck for the future (this life and your next) and to please the spirits of the ancestors. They can be small and simple, but these ones were superlative and worth a fortune. A whole extended family might share the cost of one of these to bring good luck for the next year.

The procession stopped at the That Luang and the people dispersed to walk around the stupa three times to bring good luck. I bought a thin candle and lotus bud and made my wishes for the coming year as I circumvented the stupa, laying my offerings before four Buddha statues of descending size, surrounded by shimmering trees of gold and silver, leaves atremble to the footsteps of the devoted. I had to tear myself away to meet Soun.

Outside, hundreds more women were queuing to get in, holding, with difficulty, their bright sun parasols (tartan was particularly popular) in one hand and delicate marigold pyramids in the other. Beyond them, commerce and jubilation carried on as usual with the odd rifle-toting teenage soldier wandering through the crowd trying to look sufficiently sombre.

Soun is punctual and was where he said he would be. He is a handsome man with a broad face, long lashes, high eyebrows and a generous mouth. Now, turning fifty, he sports a snappy crew cut, but in his youth he had long curls and looked like a Laotian Jim Morrison. He has the dextrous fingers of an artist and uses his hands to illustrate his conversation. When he laughs (which he does often) he looks down with bashful giggles.

I had met Soun a few months before when I went to his restaurant at the Page pub in Pimlico with Alan Davidson. Alan had been introduced to Soun when he was an art student in Laos in the early seventies while searching for an artist to illustrate his book, *Fishes of Laos*. Soun had had to escape from Laos after the Communist takeover in 1975, and Davidson had sponsored his refugee status in England. He still works as an illustrator, but a few years ago he developed his second creative love – cooking – into a business by opening a restaurant in a London pub. In the last year, his gastronomic empire had expanded to three restaurants.

I was dying to get to the traditional food tent, but he told me they were still setting it up so we went to have a beer to pass the time.

There were dozens of café-bars set up on the perimeters of the festival, each with identical plastic chairs and Beer Lao bunting. We stopped at one that was unremarkable except for the confidence its owner exuded as she pounded her pestle and mortar making the favourite Lao snack meal – green papaya salad.

Su Phon wore a smocked barmaid's blouse with puffed sleeves and a wry smile. Her hair flicked out on either side of her face like a bell and she wasn't going to take any nonsense from anyone. She looked nineteen, and as she stood there, so self-assured, I imagined she had dozens of lovelorn admirers languishing in her village, draped on their verandas desperately awaiting her return from the festival. And she made a mean papaya salad.

Papaya salad in Laos is always made with *paa-dek*. It is also a dish of huge popularity in Thailand, particularly in the north-east, where it has many incarnations according to the preference of the chef. It can be made with fish sauce instead of *paa-dek* or shrimp paste and sometimes has added ingredients such as dried prawns, tamarind, chopped green beans and, often, sugar. In Laos, I found it tended to be made simply, with unripe green papaya, lime, *paa-dek* and no sugar, but it is a recipe that is constantly evolving. Su Pon had added a sour fruit, *mak kaw*, 'hog plum', a small orange fruit sometimes available in Asian stores. The dish was juicy and tasted hot, sour, salty and sweet all at the same time, with a hint of the piscine. It was very refreshing with a beer.

'Sometimes in England we make it with raw turnip when I can't find green papaya,' said Soun. 'You would not know the difference, really!'

'I don't think I've ever eaten raw turnip.'

'Oh, it is very good, the texture is the same and the sauce takes all the turnip smell. Sometimes I make with cucumber too, but you have to eat fast or it goes too soggy. In England we can't always get the ingredients we want, we have to improvise.'

While we ate, Su Phon cooked omelettes at speed on a butane-powered double-wok gas stove which included a built-in holder for four bottles – fish, soy, and oyster sauces, and vegetable oil. An old mayonnaise jar of *paa-dek* (everyone prefers their own fermentation) stood proud on her trestle prep table with bowls of vegetables, bags of fresh noodles, a massive pestle and mortar and the biggest basket of sticky rice I had ever seen. An oil can, cut with air holes, served as another wood stove for the stockpot. And the entire kitchen was held up with crates of Beer Lao and a sickly soft drink called Miranda. It was as basic as could be, but the food coming out of it was first class.

Soun was sitting back watching the festivities with a big smile, obviously enjoying his hometown celebrations in between mouthfuls of papaya. I asked him whether he wanted to return.

'Oh, it is difficult.' He put his hand to his mouth and then slugged back some beer. The papaya salad contained a lot of chilli. 'Ai! Ai! This is hot! Lots of chilli like Thai! Sorry,' he continued. 'Now I can come for holiday but I am not allowed to own property unless I return for good. And my wife and children are in England. Soumali is still at University, Marina also wants to study.' Even when émigrés do return, there is a great deal of jealousy and suspicion to contend with and good jobs go to those who support the government. Those who left and come back relatively rich and successful are not necessarily welcomed back with open arms.

When the Communists took over in 1975, Soun was made deputy of the art college in Vientiane, and then set to work on dull propaganda illustrations. Soun's flourishing career as an artist hit a cul-de-sac as his creativity was quashed and contact with the foreigners who could give him commissions was banned. To make matters worse, the Communists then split up his family. At this time, the government moved people around the country according to their skills, regardless of familial ties, as the Party was now supposed to come first. The policy was as spectacularly unpopular as were the re-education camps, forced collectives and village relocations. People left in droves. An estimated five hundred thousand (15 per cent of the population) left between 1975 and 1990, when policies were relaxed due to economic necessity. Laos lost almost all of its intellectual elite and has never really recovered.

After two years working at the college, Soun heard rumours that the Party was displeased with him for consorting with Westerners for artistic commissions and realised the family must leave Laos. His wife, Kaochang, had to drug the milk of their two children with sleeping pills so they wouldn't make a noise, and they left by canoe across the Mekong in the dead of night. They were caught on arrival in Thailand and immediately imprisoned as illegal immigrants in a squalid Thai jail. After three weeks, Soun drew a dramatic drawing depicting his family's misery in the prison and was noticed by a UN aid worker.

'We were moved to a UN Thai refugee camp where we live for the next nine month. I knew nobody anywhere to help except Alan Davidson. He was very kind to us. He sponsored us to come to London and we all live in his house until accommodation was found. Then we were all move to Worthing and I worked as a house painter to make my own money for the family. I don't want to live off the state.'

We finished our snack and continued our conversation as we walked through the crowds towards the food tent.

Once the family was settled, Alan commissioned Soun to illustrate Phia Sing's *Traditional Recipes of Laos*, which led to a string of assignments. Soun then worked for Penguin, Cambridge University Press and the National Trust and illustrated Alan's *The Oxford Companion to Food* (a gargantuan project that took the next twenty years to complete).

'Ah, here we are.'

A sign painted with 'Lao Traditional Food Stand' was staked to the ground near a small open-sided marquee. A circle of trestles stood underneath it, with a makeshift kitchen-cum-storage area in the centre. Most tables held a gas wok burner, and a couple of dishes were being prepared on each one. We did a circuit of the tables.

'There is not that much here, mainly snack food,' said Soun, frowning.

I was also disappointed. There was fried fish, fried chicken, grilled fish, fish balls, boiled eggs, many banana leaf packets, noodles and a few stews. You would find more in the market at the end of a bad day. I was hoping for regional stands, but no such luck. Soun called me over.

'Well, at least here you get some typical Vientiane food, Vientiane-style *or*, different than the one you had in Luang Prabang, you try *bon paa*. *Bon*, we eat almost every day in Lao.' He flashed his film-star smile. We bought our supper from the pots with some sticky rice and a plate of raw vegetables, and sat down at one of the plastic tables.

'This *or* is made with pork in the Vientiane way with aubergine and winged bean.' He lifted a spoonful to his nose and took a great sniff. 'Ah, the smell is good! In this recipe there are five pounded ingredients – galangal, lemon grass, garlic, shallots and chilli. We do not sear them in the fire before pounding as in the Luang Pra-bang *or*. When I make this I smash for about five minutes. Cook the paste, add pork and then water, just a little to not quite cover the meat. Then add vegetable – aubergine, beans. Then a little chilli pepper, lime leaves, whole, not shredded like in this one.'

Soun was in his element now, pounding the air with his imag-inary pestle, chopping the meat. The other diners were enjoying the show.

'My mother when she made *or* would add some soaked sticky rice to the mortar and make a paste and thicken. Some people like *or* to be running, some like it sticky, my mother used more liquid as she had a big family to feed. You can use cornflour to thicken instead, but I like to just leave it liquid like this.'

With my usual gusto for good Lao food, I was vigorously mopping up the juices with sticky rice.

'My grandfather say in the past an *or* was made in a piece of giant bamboo. Nowadays they make it in a pot, never a wok.'

Giant bamboo can be made into a useful vessel as the joints of bamboo are solid, while the lengths between are hollow. Soun told me that villagers would cut a length the circumference of a man's thigh below a solid joint, leaving an open top, and then cut again below the next joint to leave a solid base. This resulted in a natural container which was filled with meat or fish, vegetables and herbs, and then sealed with a plug of grass. The bamboo was then jammed in the ground at a slight angle near an open fire and left to cook slowly. Occasionally, Laotians still use this method to cook in the forest.

Next we tried the *bon paa*. *Bon* means 'to mix', *paa*, 'fish', and this one was a rough mash, and warm, almost a cross between a salad and a stew. It is a basic household dish in Laos, a jumble of fish or beef, chilli, shallots, aubergines and garlic, loosely combined. Other ingredients are then added to the taste of the cook. *Bon* can be fish or meat, but in Vientiane the fish version rather than beef is preferred and it is usually eaten with plain rice (rather than the sticky variety) and a large plate of fresh and lightly steamed vegetables such as green beans, cucumber and carrots. It can be eaten as a dish in itself or pounded more finely to a paste and used as a dip for the steamed vegetables.

It was spicy, and each ingredient seemed to hit my taste buds separately. The shallot, garlic and chillies had been seared and gave that smoky flavour that I so like in much Lao food.

As we ate I continued to quiz Soun about his life story.

On arriving in England, Soun's fame as an artist spread and he was featured in the *Observer* magazine and had several exhibitions. However, artists are notoriously badly paid and Soun fell back on cooking.

'I thought I could run a restaurant, quite easy.'

Five years ago he started Soun's Kitchen at the Racing Page in Richmond, and his daughter Marina launched another one at the Page pub in Pimlico. Nine out of ten people want pad thai noodles and green curry when they first eat at his restaurant, and it takes time to educate the pub clientele to choose unfamiliar Lao dishes. However, if you call a few days in advance, then either he or Marina will cook Lao food for you and you'll be in for a treat.

Now the restaurants are thriving and Soun fits in his artistic commissions in the early morning. Soun was too modest to mention to me the award he won within a year of moving to Worthing. In 1980 he received the first Worthing Award for having done the most to promote the seaside town during the year. They felt that his drawings of the area and subsequent publicity had helped raise the profile of the town: a pretty remarkable achievement for a refugee.

We finished our plates and continued to chat about food. He told me how his mother used to make *soop pak* (seasonal vegetables) with seven vegetables almost every day as it was cheap and there were so many of them. They used to complain, 'Where is the meat, we want meat.' But in those days you ate what was available and in season.

'If you have beef for lunch, you make it into something else for dinner. In Lao we never waste food.'

Soun had to return to his family, so I took a *tuk-tuk* to Wat Sok Pa Luang (forest temple), famous for its herbal sauna. The *wat* is a centre of instruction for vipassana mediation and a traditional herb garden. The sauna was the initiative of an octogenarian nun known as Mother Khow Keow. She took her vows aged seven, and, finding that she had a natural affinity with plants, has been seeking knowledge concerning their usage and healing powers throughout her life. It was her idea to use plants in a traditional Lao way and create a place where people could retreat whilst educating the young. The massage boys all grow herbs in the vicinity around the temple, and she leads meditative walks with the abbot in the gardens once a week.

I ambled down a path through trees and flowers and then sat in a shed on stilts letting the perfumed steam of thirty-two medicinal herbs soak into my skin as it rose up through the floor. I drank the herbal tea and lay down for a gentle massage in the forest as the sun went down on the bald heads of a row of nuns who had come to view me. I relaxed completely.

The next day the celebrations on the day of the full moon began early. Vandara had come to Vientiane to celebrate the festival and visit her two children who were living with her sister-in-law while they attended school (a common practice in Lao families as Vientiane has the only good schools). I had arranged to be at the house, which was located on the outskirts of town, at five thirty a.m.

Vientiane, like Luang Prabang, is really a series of *ban* (villages) stuck together, and I found myself in an affluent leafy suburb. It looked like a different city, a world away from the dusty streets of the centre. Here, most of the houses were modern and stood in tropical gardens with sprinkler-fed lawns. High gates protected the inhabitants and guard dogs threw themselves against them as I passed.

I found the house with difficulty and was ushered into a spot-less home with a tiled floor, big suites of unyielding wooden furniture and many cabinets full of fancy crockery and glass-ware. Photographs of Vandara's nephew, a doctor and head of the national basketball team, were displayed proudly about the living room. It was the most affluent Lao house I had entered since arriving in the country.

Vandara gave me a big smiley welcome. '*Sabaii dii*, Natacha, it is so good to see you again,' she beamed, whereupon she pro-duced an exquisitely embroidered silk *pha baeng* (shoulder sash) woven to her own design. It was the colour of port wine and sewn with a wide border of personalised geometric designs. 'I wanted to give to you a *paa sin* (skirt) but I not sure your size. You can wear this to the temple and take home to remember Lao,' she said, looking down shyly. It would have taken a long time to make, and I felt great appreciation for the gift and a lit-tle ashamed that I had nothing to give in return.

The family – her brother and sister-in-law, her aunt, her two children and several other unspecified relatives – was bustling around filling their traditional silver bowls with apples, biscuits, sticky rice and 15,000-kip notes.

'You see, Natacha, I don't look very well today. Yesterday I went to a conference on Lao crafts and we had Western lunch afterwards. We had chicken with a cream sauce.' Her mouth turned downwards at the thought. 'I got poisoning. I've been

ANT EGG SOUP

very ill last night.' I thought of all the people who refuse to eat
the lovely fresh local food in fear of their delicate stomachs when
ironically they are more likely to be poisoned by the dairy products in French dishes.

We filled our silver bowls and carried them to the That Luang
with hordes of other families. Hundreds of monks were lined up
along the edges of the *wat*, ostensibly spartan with just their begging bowls and money plates, but on closer inspection they each
had an enormous bin bag or grain sack secreted behind them in
which to pour their goodies – some had two or three sacks.

The devotees brought woven plastic mats, and families used
them to stake their territory in a sea of coloured squares. Poorer people brought newspapers or old plastic bags to sit on and
had plastic bowls sprayed with silver paint.

I was most interested in the nuns who were sitting on the
ground. They were shaven-headed and wore gleaming white
robes. Technically they are lay people, as Theravada Buddhism
does not recognise the ordination of women, but they are
allowed to reside in Lao temples and follow the ascetic life. They
are regarded as inferior to the monks and this is probably why
they were sitting rather than standing like the men. Nuns receive
less support from the lay population, as having a nun in the family may almost be ignominious as it goes against tradition. To
become a nun is often a refuge for women from a bad marriage
or abuse, and this too is seen as shameful as they are supposed
to cope. I decided to give my offerings to them.

There were at least fifty women in the row, and most of them
were very old and grumpy. One, more hunched and ill-humoured
than the rest, kept snuffling into her bowl as though checking the
quality of the goods. Next to her, a beautiful young nun sat
serene with her hands clasped in her lap, an oasis of calm in the
proceedings. She got my alms of flowers, balls of sticky rice, a
note of money, a silver-wrapped biscuit, a boiled egg, a little
cake and an orange.

238

By the time I got back to Vandara's family, their mat was an island in the increasingly deserted courtyard. It was eight o'clock and everyone was rushing home. The monks' bowls were being loaded into plastic crates and carried away, mats were rolled under arms and silver bowls swung empty in the hands of children.

We went back to the house to say our final goodbyes, as I was due to go south the next day. I enjoyed a last taste of Vandara's home-grown papaya and coffee, and then it was time to leave. We took photographs in the well-tended garden and I felt sad to go.

'You are like my family,' she said, and gave me a long hug. We waved bye-bye.

That evening was the night of the full moon. I arrived back at the festival to the sound of disco music. The golden *that* was lit up vividly with fairy lights, the sky was indigo and a huge full moon hung just perfectly over the point of the stupa as if part of a painted backdrop. As I looked up, a stray plastic bag caught up in the breeze crossed the moon before flying upwards to the heavens.

In the past, the evenings of the festival would be filled with the music of *khene* (bamboo pipes) as musicians played in the 'courts of love' – makeshift sheds where young men would compete with each other to sing love stanzas to girls who would reply in kind. Sometimes the words were improvised and sometimes they were taken from the famous love poems passed down through generations by word of mouth. Several men would compete to win the heart of a particularly beautiful girl, and the most popular combatants were those able to twist the words of their opponent with speed, wit and cruelty to win a joust that could last as long as three days.

These love poem competitions used to be a common occurrence at festivals and were a rare chance for boys and girls from distant villages to meet and flirt in public. The tradition is rarely practised now except in rural villages, though public displays of love in Laos are still bound by strict etiquette and formal reserve. The 'love courts' are a poetic remnant of Laos's highly stylised and sophisticated cultural past, and it is sad that the tradition is dying out.

I was hoping I might get a chance to hear these romantic serenades, but instead of 'love courts' I came across a promotional Land-Rover endorsing 'First Choice Imported Condoms' the ones with the bespectacled condom logo showing the thumbs-up sign. More stalls had sprung up selling coat hangers, batteries, hairbands and Chinese toys. All the children had come with their parents to enjoy the fun of the fair, and the throng was peppered with helium balloons and luminescent necklaces sold by small boys. It was a family night out with chicken-on-a-stick and fireworks behind the stupa to set the evening aglow.

Two stages on either side of the courtyard drew a crowd so thick I could hardly move. On one stage lithe young gymnasts twirled fire on a string. On the other, a band that consisted mainly of saxophones and electric organs played music with an oddly ska beat. A clown in pink shorts and a sequinned jacket replaced the gymnasts. He tripped over, juggled batons and accidentally dropped them, to the hilarity of the crowd. I pushed my way out with difficulty. On the outskirts of the square the stalls were doing a brisk business; wads of young men looked hungrily at the speaker and stereo stall. The roadside cafés were filled with totally plastered revellers having a fantastic time. I was pushed and a little knocked about as there were so many people, but there was no aggression in the crush – everyone was laughing and joking, greeting strangers as they passed and teasing their friends. Even the drunks were benevolent.

This was Lao people at their best: happy and full of a sense of fun. It was a big party, after all.

Su Pon's Green Papaya Salad

The dish should be juicy and taste hot, sour, salty and sweet, with a hint of the piscine. It is also divine with raw turnip which tastes extremely like green papaya once mixed with the other ingredients.

- ½ green papaya, skinned and shredded into matchstick-thin strips
- 2–6 bird's-eye chillies
- 4 small cloves garlic, peeled
- a pinch of salt
- ½ lime, cut into eighths, rind on
- 3 tablespoons *paa-dek* water (1 tablespoon fish sauce can be substituted)
- 4 cherry tomatoes cut into quarters
- 1 *mak kaw* fruit (optional)

Take a green, unripe papaya and peel it with a vegetable peeler. Put a dishcloth in one hand and place the papaya on top of it in your palm. With the other hand use a cleaver or heavy chopping knife to chop at the flesh leaving many roughly parallel cuts. Cut slices from the chopped surface and you will end up with fine shreds. (Alternatively, you can use a mandoline or buy a special shredding tool at an Oriental store.)

Now take a pestle and mortar. Add the chilli, garlic and pinch of salt and pound roughly (about 20 pounds) so the chilli is still in quite large pieces, not a paste. Add the papaya and pound gently, using a spoon to turn the ingredients in on themselves. Add the lime pieces and *paa-dek* or fish sauce. Pound gently, and then add the tomato and the *mak kaw* fruit. The tomato should just be bruised. Pound again and serve. You can add more lime or fish sauce to taste.

Soun's Vientiane-Style *Or* with Pork

Or means 'to braise' and refers to a type of slow-cooked stew. In the past an *or* was made in a piece of giant bamboo. Nowadays they make it in a pot, never a wok. In Laos the cook might add a little sugar to this dish to balance the bitterness of the aubergine, but it is not necessary here. You can use less chilli if you prefer.

Lao people usually use lime leaves whole to flavour an *or*, rather than slicing them finely as is more usual in Thai cooking.

2.5 cm (1 inch) piece galangal, peeled and cut into
    matchsticks
3 stalks lemon grass, soft part, finely sliced
2 cloves garlic, peeled
2 small shallots or $\frac{1}{4}$ red onion, sliced
4 bird's-eye chillies, stalks removed and roughly chopped
$\frac{1}{2}$ teaspoon salt
$\frac{1}{2}$ pork loin, cut in 5 cm (2 inch) slices across the grain
1 tablespoon *paa-dek* water or English *paa-dek* water
    or bottled anchovy water (optional)
4 golfball-sized green/white aubergines, cut in quarters
3 lime leaves
2 long beans, 4 winged beans or 8 green beans cut
    into 5 cm (2 inch) pieces
1 dessertspoon pounded sticky rice or cornflour (optional)
sweet basil leaves
1 handful spring onion, chopped

Prepare the first five ingredients by placing them in a mortar with half a teaspoon of salt and pounding them for 5 minutes until you make a fine paste. Put the paste into a heavy-bottomed saucepan and dry-fry it on a medium heat for about one minute to release the aroma. Add the pork pieces and stir until the juices start to come out. Add the tablespoon of *paa-dek* water.

Now add a teacup of water to the pan, enough so that the meat is not quite covered. After 5 minutes add the aubergine quarters and the whole lime leaves. After another 5 minutes add the beans.

In the countryside around Vientiane, three more whole chillies might be added at this stage, but they are not essential to the recipe.

Leave the *or* to boil for 10 to 20 minutes until the meat is tender and the vegetables are still firm. It is very important not to overcook the vegetables. The aubergine should be solid and the beans crunchy.

At this point, Soun's mother would have added some soaked sticky rice to the mortar, pounded it into a paste and then added a little water. This would be used to make the stew thicker and have the added benefit of cleaning every tasty bit from the mortar. You can use cornflour to thicken the stew instead, but personally I'd just leave it liquid.

Remove from the heat and sprinkle some sweet basil leaves and chopped spring onion on top. Serve with sticky rice and a plate of salad vegetables.

Bon Paa Vientiane-Style, Made with Cod

Bon paa is usually eaten with plain rice rather than the sticky variety, and a large plate of fresh and lightly steamed vegetables such as green beans, cucumber and carrots. It can be eaten as a dish in itself or pounded more finely and used as a dip for the steamed vegetables.

1 tablespoon *paa-dek* water, or 2 tablespoons fish sauce

1 large shallot or half a red onion

2 cloves garlic

4 small chillies

3 golfball-sized green/white aubergines, cut into four

20 cm (8 inch) portion of cod with the skin

some people add green beans or other vegetables that
    happen to be lying around

Put half a litre of water in a pan to boil, and add the *paa-dek* (Soun's mother used a mesh ladle to contain the *paa-dek*, which was removed later) or English *paa-dek* water and add to the water. Boil for 5 minutes.

Meanwhile, take the shallot, garlic and chillies and spear them on to a skewer. These ingredients need to be seared black over the gas ring or under a grill (a charcoal barbeque would be the ideal). Once these are blackened all over, remove the skin from the garlic and shallot and the stalks from the chillies and place them in a pestle and mortar. Pound them to a rough paste, not too fine.

When the water has boiled for 5 minutes, sieve out the *paa-dek* lumps and add the aubergines. Simmer them for 3 minutes or so and then add the fish fillet, skin side up. Poach gently, adding more fish sauce to taste. It should cook through in a few minutes.

Remove the fillet and set it aside on a plate.

The aubergines will now be soft – remove them from the liquid and add them to the mortar with the other ingredients. Pound everything together about 3 times and add some of the cooking water. Finally add the fish and pound a couple more times, adding a little more of the cooking liquid. The result should be a loose mash and taste delicious.

Serve immediately with plain rice and a plate of steamed vegetables.

TWELVE
FERMENTED FISH AND WATERFALLS

A few days later I had another shock at breakfast when I heard the news that an aeroplane had crashed in the mountains of the north, killing eight people. On further investigation, I discovered it was a Y-12, maybe even the very one I had flown in to Phonsovan. I had planned to take a plane to Savannakhet down in the south because I'd heard it was an attractive riverside town and a good stop-off on the way to Pakse, a place with a reputation for the best Lao coffee and a market bounteous with fresh fish. Now I decided to take the bus instead.

This meant an eight-hour journey, so I was ecstatic when a luxurious coach rolled into the station. The seats were padded and, to my amazement, a James Bond film, *Tomorrow Never Dies* (dubbed into Thai) was put on for our entertainment on an old TV and video rigged up above the driver. Even better was the revelation that the road was brand new and smooth as lacquer.

I arrived at Savannakhet bus station at four in the afternoon, found a plain clean guest house, and, after dumping my bags, went for a walk in the late afternoon sunshine. The streets around the main road were modern, but like most towns in Laos, the tatty modern frontage belied an older, sensuous heart. I soon found myself in a French quarter of palm-leafy avenues lined with colonial villas. Many of the houses were listing to one side, their pastel walls streaked with mildew, but the pale shutters and pillared doorways still looked majestic in their decay, and were surrounded by carefully tended gardens covered in luxuriant sprawls of flowers. I passed tennis courts filled with enthusiastic young girls in smart school uniforms, and more sunny children were playing badminton in the road along the river. At the waterfront, I stopped for a beer and peered across at the Thai town, Mukdahan, on the other side of the Mekong. My view was of cheap high-rise blocks and something that looked like a concrete bunker, a daily reminder to the people on the Lao side to appreciate what they have got, even if it is a little dilapidated.

Savannakhet is a busy commercial centre for cross-river trade. It lies on a primary route to south Vietnam, and there are plans to build a bridge across the Mekong to form an east–west trading corridor from Thailand, through Laos to Vietnam. Already there is a large Vietnamese presence in the town that makes itself very evident in the restaurants. I found it almost impossible to find proper Lao food (noodles excepted) for dinner, and I ended up in the Lao-Paris Restaurant, its welcoming wicker bar laden with piles of old French magazines for the customers' perusal. At least here they had some traditional food alongside the French dishes and the staff were friendly. They made me an excellent fish *laap*.

Sitting at the next table were three NGOs. I could tell they were NGOs by their clothes. The two girls looked almost identical with their T-shirts tucked inside their flared floral skirts and Jesus sandals. One wore plastic glasses and could have belonged to a fanatical missionary group. The man was dressed equally blandly. They were all humourless and had greasy hair.

I overheard them talking about the growing problem of *ya ba* use among the disaffected youth of Laos. *Ya ba* (crazy drug) is a highly addictive methamphetamine – speed in tablet form.

Across the river in Thailand, speed is already a huge problem. The United Nations Drug Control Agency investigated the trend in 2001 and reported that sixty-two million Thais aged fifteen and above (as many as one in seventeen people) are believed to be abusers of *ya ba*. The effects of methamphetamine are stronger than amphetamine, and the tablets are churned out of factories in Myanmar by the ton, so it makes them very cheap to buy. I naïvely assumed the problem had yet to reach the backwaters of Laos, but apparently you could buy them over the counter at local noodle shops.

Seeing my obvious interest in their conversation, Sarah, Jane and John invited me to sit with them with the condescending manner of those who think they have a supreme knowledge of the culture they are working within; I on the other hand, was just a tourist.

John was setting up a youth club-cum-drop-in centre in Pakse, further south. 'A place with a bar and a disco where they can ask questions about birth control and AIDS and drugs and stuff. Of course all those are taboo subjects in Laos.' He said the word 'taboo' while looking down his nose at me.

'Yes,' stuttered Jane, adjusting her glasses to look at John with adoration. 'Bad speed from Thailand is flooding into Laos. It's terrible.'

'There is no youth law system here, you know. Children are just thrown into jail with the adults.'

'Well!' snorted the other girl, Sarah. 'Some parents actually pay the police to take their children. They're so out of control.'

They were all very concerned and angry about everything. They wanted to help the situation using the old village legal system, but, as they all kept saying, 'everything must be implemented through the *proper* procedures'. They were all so awkward, stilted and unrelaxed it made me feel uncomfortable. I took out my cigarettes and lit one.

If they had been vampires and I had just taken out a bulb of garlic, a cross and a wooden stake I would have had a milder reaction. They all jumped back like they had been stung.

'God, don't smoke that,' said John, taking the cigarette from my mouth and stamping it out on the floor viciously. 'Lao cigarettes are lethal! Full of tar! Uggh!' I was left with my mouth agape.

I narrowed my eyes. 'So are you going to allow people to smoke at the youth club?'

'Absolutely not, we're going to have a no-smoking policy. They can smoke outside but they have to learn that it is *not* OK to smoke.'

I almost laughed out loud. 'But aren't you trying to attract difficult rebellious teenagers?' I'd seen these kids in the riverside bars of Vientiane – cool dudes with attitude, all quiffs and leather jackets, cigarettes permanently hanging from their lower lips.

'Yes, but they will realise!' said Sarah vehemently. 'Smoking's a killer!'

Everyone agreed. 'We'll make it so they want to come. It will be a really good place and they'll learn a lot.'

Yeah, right. Given a choice between a river disco bar where you hang out by your moped smoking like a fifties film star and a drop-in-centre full of earnest volunteers, I know which one I would have chosen as a teenager. I felt like I had gone back to school and was sitting with the unpopular teacher's pets, the ones who told on you for smoking behind the bike sheds and always handed their homework in on time.

We really began to argue as the evening wore on, and I insisted on buying them beer, which helped. We talked of developmental aid and I mentioned the Vientiane Library – a place desperately in need of more books and full of aimless students looking for them. Considering they all worked in education, I was surprised to discover that none of them had been to the library, and said as much. This did not go down very well. Sarah almost spat when she referred to a charity started by 'middle-class do-gooders, who, unlike us,' she pronounced the 'us' with force, 'didn't want a salary or have proper training.' I retorted, 'Don't you think there might be people with other useful skills who perhaps may not have a degree in resource management or technical engineering or whatever?' She snorted. Then I mentioned that I was surprised that the International School, where NGOs sent their children, didn't teach Lao language as an option and drew bursts of hollow laughter from around the table. 'Well, most people are only here for two years,' said Jane, as if this justified it.

Throughout the evening little comments would escape that made me feel as though they didn't even like Laotians (they picked at the food, too). Maybe they were too blinded by their superior attitude to notice. I admire aid workers highly and have met many worthy NGOs, but sometimes there is a certain type of blinkered self-righteous ideologue attracted to the job who hinders rather than helps. They come, they go, they write endless and extremely expensive reports and then they return to the Home Counties with a smug sense of self-worth. The maddening thing is that these people hold a lot of power, and with it they waste time and money. Two years after this meeting I asked my friends in Pakse about the youth club, and no one had ever heard of such a place. It didn't surprise me.

I have to admit that, even though I love coffee, before going to Laos I knew virtually nothing about what goes into a good cup. Coffee is similar to wine in its variety, complexity and cultivation. There are two commercial species: arabica, which produces complex quality coffee, and robusta, the astringent, high-caffeine junk used in 'instant' coffee. The bean variety, elevation, the type of soil and even the year in which it is grown affect the taste and aroma of every single bag.

I had heard that Laotian Arabica coffee was gaining a reputation as one of the best and rarest in the world, on a par with the celebrated Jamaican Blue Mountain, and was being hailed as the crop that was going to 'revolutionise the economy' of the south. I was interested to try the 'best coffee in the world', though I had my doubts that the coffee industry was going to be the champion of the Lao economy, as signs of the global coffee crisis were already apparent. Rapid expansion in

Vietnam and Brazil were causing a glut in the market and prices were plummeting.

Thus, in search of a unique hit of caffeine I spent seven and a half hours bouncing over potholes on the old road to Pakse, looking out of the cramped bus window at the tantalising flat black tarmac of the 'new road' we were not yet allowed to travel upon. The landscape was drier, flatter, and instead of bamboo, some of the stilted houses had unbelievably fragile walls woven from desiccated leaves. I arrived covered from head to foot in the fine, and now familiar, red dust.

Pakse was founded by the French in 1905 as an administrative post, on a confluence of the Mekong. It is not wildly attractive but it has a vital energy about it, and it lies on the edge of the fertile Bolaven Plateau, the home of the Lao coffee plantations.

I had arranged to stay with some 'coffee men' – Rattaprasued Nhouyvanisvong and his father Bounlap, president of the Lao Coffee Exporters Association. They owned an old villa with a wide garden inclining towards the river where a pretty breakfast pavilion was built on stilts over the water.

I could smell coffee as I was ushered into a wicker seat overlooking the Mekong.

Rattaprasued worked for the French-financed Rural Development Project for the Bolavens Plateau, an aid project designed to help farmers expand the agricultural potential of the area, including improving the quality of Lao coffee. He had a square face and wore round glasses and a serious, slightly fretful expression. His father looked very similar but had laughing eyes and bushier eyebrows that rose when he spoke. During the royal regime he had been an ambassador in Paris, and that gave him a certain relaxed style. Both men spoke fluent French.

They greeted me warmly and handed me a cup of the famous brew along with a little jug of fresh milk. First I tried it straight and black. It was extremely good – earthy, rich, spicy and smooth. I like peat in my whisky and earth in my coffee, so Laotian Arabica was just the one for me. It left a rounded aftertaste that lingered on my palette and lacked the citrus or bitter grapefruit flavours found in some coffees that I find too acid for my taste.

'It is good, is it not?' said Rattaprasued, watching my face. 'Not like your Starbucks coffee milkshakes!' He'd been to London and knew all about the high street coffee shop boom.

'This is fantastic. I can't bear Starbucks! Insipid coffee corrupted to a cup of froth to be drunk on the run. When I try something like this, there is just no comparison. They might as well be different drinks.' I could distinguish that this was not the 'best in the world', but it was a great cup of coffee with a flavour distinctive enough to be held in high regard.

'Paaa! Those companies are not interested at all in quality and flavour. They buy in bulk for as little money and as much profit as possible,' said Rattaprasued. 'It makes it much harder for us.'

'Yes, everything is difficult for us,' agreed Bounlap. 'Our coffee is organic, but it is so difficult to get the organic label. We need to have access to the sea to ship it abroad. We have to go through Thailand and transport is expensive. Maybe we could export by plane but we need aeroplanes to transport! We need refrigerated warehouses! Everything! But we try. We try. But we have found a retailer in London now.' He grinned, and poured me another cup. 'So you can drink it when you get home and remember Lao!'

Coffee is Laos's biggest agricultural export, but until now the bulk of the beans had been the poorer quality robusta and earned the country relatively little. The plan was to change all that and switch to profitable arabica, starting from the bottom up. There was a lot of faith in the project and I really hoped it would work for them.

They had to leave for meetings and suggested we meet for lunch at a restaurant in town known for its fish. After two huge cups of coffee I needed to get rid of some excess energy, so I pinged off into Pakse's labyrinthine market like a pinball.

I was definitely in *paa-dek* country: there were huge vats of fermented fish all over the place which looked like grey silty mud full of old fish heads and, I had to admit, not very appealing. However, after several months in Laos I had become a big fan of the condiment. Again, the pungent aroma arising from the mixtures reminded me of cheese, each one uniquely complex and dependent on the personal recipe of the maker. It gave me a craving and I had to find some for a snack.

I stopped at a stall of home-made condiments run by Nye, a sturdy woman with the arms of a wrestler who served her pickles and relishes from bright plastic bowls with pride. I expressed my craving in Pidgin Laotian, and she insisted that I sit at the bench before her table and try her recipe. She handed me a tin plate of raw vegetables and scooped a blob of her pure *paa-dek*, chilli and sugar into a dipping bowl. It was forceful stuff – my face bloomed like a ripe peony bud and the chilli had my blood racing.

Refreshed, I continued through the market until I was stopped by a striking sight. Hundreds of shimmering fish were draped over tables and laid out on sacks with artistic flair in glittering patterns of swirls, waves, twirls and whirls.

The Mekong carries an extraordinary number of edible fish in its waters, and as many as fifty varieties can be caught in one go at the right time of year, though numbers are falling due to overfishing and environmental factors.

Fish are the major source of protein for the majority of people in Laos and the mainstay of the everyday Lao diet. Villagers will tell you that they eat fish not only every day, but, in some form, at every meal! And since *paa-dek* is the principal condiment of Laos this could be said to be true of even the poorest individuals.

I paused by the weird *paa tong* (featherback fish), a large silver creature whose body rises archly behind the head, giving it the appearance of a hunchback. The fins of the *paa tong* lie underneath like the plume of a long goose feather, so they look upside down. Each fish species in Laos is prized for its unique qualities, and many are made into specific dishes, like this one, which is a favourite for Luang Prabang-style pounded *laap*, as the flesh fluffs up perfectly for that particular recipe. The most valued fish in Laos, however, is the legendary *paa beuk*, the largest freshwater fish in the world.

The *paa beuk*, or giant catfish (*Pangasianodon gigas*) is only found in the Mekong and can grow as long as twelve feet, and as heavy as twenty stone. They are scaleless, vegetarian and threatened in the wild. They are found from Cambodia to China, but there is still little information on their life cycle, population or even whether they migrate all the way up the river or live in separate populations along it. The flesh is supposed to be exceptional, and I had heard that, within half an hour of arriving at the market, there would not be a scrap to be had for love nor money so I was unlikely to see it.

I met Rattaprasued and his father for lunch at the Toune Phao Khou restaurant. It was a tatty modern room painted the exact pink of sugar-mice. The walls were decorated with a poster of a white New England mansion set in acres of pristine lawn and another of a baroque fountain surrounded by waxen red tulips. Six of the seven silk-clothed tables were occupied and there was a sink to wash your hands by the door, so I felt eager for my meal.

The owners had been warned of my visit, and freshly caught fish were brought on a tray for my perusal. Two silver catfish with yellow fins lay there about two foot long with trailing whiskers.

'These are called *paa khao*,' said Rattaprasued. 'It is the most popular catfish in Lao, it grows big just now,' he stretched his hands out to about a metre. 'We say it is like a shark.'

I couldn't wait to try it.

'I have ordered *mok paa* for you as it is very good in Pakse. Here we make it with lemon grass, lime leaf and dill,' he explained. '*Mok* means to sear or cook something directly in the embers of the fire. First we wrap in banana leaf and sometimes steam too. It is my father's favourite.'

Bounlap nodded enthusiastically. 'These we often make for the monks on festival days as they are easy to serve and keep for a day or so. Or they make in restaurants. We don't make every day but at home we make a big batch of them at one time on weekend for family and friends.'

The meal arrived: *mok paa* (wrapped exquisitely in leaf envelopes), fish soup, stir-fried wild mushrooms with garlic and sticky rice.

Rattaprasued unfurled a leaf packet with expertise and offered it to me first, as the guest. A wonderful waft of dill, super-fresh fish and the complex undertone of *paa-dek* filled my nostrils. It is a particularly delicious dish and a family favourite at home, where I make it with wild trout. He served his father next, who encouraged me to try the soup in between mouthfuls of *mok paa*.

The food was excellent home-cooked Lao fare, made with fresh ingredients, gathered and caught locally. We enjoyed the *mok paa* so much we had to order more.

This was the kind of Lao meal that I would yearn for when I returned home. The fusion of fragrant lemon grass with dill, sweet shallots and salty fish in the *mok paa* made my taste buds tingle; the mixture caramelised at the bottom of the packet in the flame of the barbecue and the banana leaves infused the fish appetisingly with their particular earthy perfume. The soup, which contained roasted shallots, lemon grass, galangal, chopped egg white, lumps of sour tamarind and local leaves chopped in at the last minute had that smoky-tangy flavour I found so delicious and prolific in Lao food; and the wild mushrooms with garlic were better than black truffles in Tuscany.

The scope of Lao dishes might be small, but the cuisine was exquisite and full of thrilling flavours. Critics who claim it is a poor relation to the broader Thai cuisine have never bothered to discover its complexities. I commented on the delectable but simple meal and mentioned my interest in trying the giant catfish.

'Bahh!' exclaimed Bounlap. 'This meal is nothing compared to the taste of *paa beuk*! It is the best fish in the world. But they are so rare now, you will not find to eat.'

Alan Davidson has tasted it and found that the flesh had 'an admirable texture and unmatched flavour. Like the flesh of a sturgeon', he wrote in *Fish and Fish Dishes of Laos*, his excellent book which was reprinted in 2003. He thought it bore some resemblance to veal, yet it was fishy in a 'subtle and majestic way'. He was also served pickled *paa beuk* eggs at the palace 'on a bed of spring onion tops and decorated with tiny red chilli peppers stuck upright in it like little tongues of flame', which he found very tasty.

He told me he had eaten it prepared in many ways in the seventies and once bought a fifty-kilo head in Ban Houy Xai to make an 'excellent soup', but then realised he would have to invite one hundred and fifty guests to eat it. Instead, he had the head flown to Vientiane by helicopter where its arrival at the British Embassy rudely interrupted a display of Lao traditional ballet that happened to be taking place in the courtyard. His wife Jane was then instructed to empty the freezer to place the prize within. A few days later, the head was packed in dry ice and chauffeur-driven to Bangkok in Alan's 1963 Bentley, whence it flew to London courtesy of British Airways. From there it was taken to the Natural History Museum for their collection as a scientific novelty, and remains, hidden in the vaults, as the only specimen – number BMNH 1977.4.21.2.

'I never see *paa beuk* again, I think,' continued Bounlap with a sigh.

Indeed, I later discovered that they're included in the International Union for Conservation of Nature and Natural Resources 'red list' of endangered species. It is now prohibited to catch *paa beuk* in Laos due to their scarcity, and it is hard to know if there are any giant catfish left at all as when they are caught (there have been rumours of the odd fish trapped illegally in the Khone falls) people sell them secretly. No one I spoke to had seen one for years, and no one really seemed to know why.

However, the biggest threat to all the fish in the Mekong, according to the IUCN, is dams.

China is planning to build six more hydroelectric dams on the Mekong river despite concerns from the five countries downstream that they will wreak untold environmental and economic damage. China claims the dams will ease flooding in the monsoon and provide water during drought, but the main reason is to boost the sagging economy of its own south-western region.

The consequences on the region's fish and fauna would be catastrophic. It is doubtful that the giant catfish would survive the change, and, more heinous, hundreds or even thousands of other aquatic species would disappear along with them. The natural cycles of the river would be transformed permanently, destroying the natural ecology and age-old traditional farming and fishing practices. Nearly half the two thousand, six hundred miles of the Mekong are in Laos; a whole way of life could be lost forever.

Laos, though landlocked, is quintessentially a land of water, a place of rivers, cascades, lakes, steams and monsoon showers; you cannot take a step without splashing through some kind of aqueous conduit, but it was the abundance of beautiful and mysterious waterfalls secreted in the jungles that really enchanted me.

Later that week the coffee men insisted that I stay at Tad Fane, a brand new eco-lodge near dramatic twin waterfalls close to the coffee station. I arrived to find traditional timber huts and an open-air restaurant with dramatic views down the Houay Ban Lieng gorge.

The owner, Chakard, was Thai. He had another guest house in Chiang Mai and had been a trekking guide, but he had always dreamt of having his own resort in unspoilt countryside. He had a cheery disposition and his speech was peppered with personal mottos like, 'My grandfather say you have to smile every day'. He loved Laos like a native; as he said, 'When I crossed the border I kissed the ground!' He was running the place with five staff and, like Robin Hood with his merry band of men, believed in improving the lot of the poor and saving the forest. That week I was the only guest.

When I arrived they took my bags and sent me straight into the jungle to see the falls. 'You get the best view from down there,' he said, pointing to a vertical trail leading into the undergrowth. 'I could have built the restaurant in that place but it would have meant cutting down very old rare tree, so I did not.'

I followed his instructions and found myself looking down at a six-hundred-foot-deep gorge surrounded by green jungle. It was as though a giant apple corer had been plunged into the earth and cracked the landscape open like a ripe fruit. Twin waterfalls, fifty foot apart, crashed down the long drop, spurting, spraying and shattering into a running mist that boiled at the bottom like a vat of dry ice. I stood clinging to tree roots, transfixed. The sun grew hazy, and a cool breeze rattled the bamboo leaves and set the hanging twists of vines aswinging. Butterflies twirled around me and the air was filled with the roar of the water and the whispered mantra of cicadas. I almost swooned at the magnificence of the vision before me.

At that moment a gust of wind brushed through the trees, branches cracked and something heavy rustled away, unseen. I took flight scrabbling up the treacherous earth-steps, made smooth by the past rainy season, clinging to the mossy wall of the mountain and slipping on dry bamboo leaves.

The year before, a man had been killed by a tiger at the bottom of the gorge.

That evening forty teachers were stopping by for an early supper at the restaurant, and I joined the merry band – Peng, Joy, Kiat,

Kiow and Tia – to help and watch them cook the meal. Peng, a bright and beautiful girl with sensual bee-stung lips, was head chef, but everyone was involved. The kitchen was well equipped and brand-shiny-new with a couple of gas stoves and a surprising technical addition.

'You have a microwave. That's the first one I've seen in Laos.'

'Oh yes,' laughed Chakard, 'probably the only one in the province! I always say you need a microwave if you have a restaurant. At first they did not know how to use it, now very easy. They like a lot.'

A large preparation table stood in the centre of the room and everyone was working hard to get supper ready on time. It was hard to keep up with what they were cooking in the flurry – fish soup, pumpkin soup, steamed fish with preserved lime, pineapple-chicken, pork with pumpkin, greens, sticky rice, *jaew* and I don't know what else. I concentrated on Peng who was preparing three eighteen-inch-long snakehead fish by cutting them horizontally across the body into round steaks, bones and all.

'She is making fish steam with preserved lime.' Chakard produced a glass jar of the home-made pickled fruits and a white cabbage from under the table. 'We call the fish "*paa do*", the flesh taste very good.'

According to Alan Davidson's book on the fish species of Laos, this *paa do* has a nasty character. It has been known to attack isolated fishermen (they can grow to three or four foot long) and it eats its own young if they don't leave the nest fast enough. They have an accessory respiratory organ in a space above the gills from which they can take oxygen directly from the air, and as long as their gills remain moist they can survive up to three days out of water. Curiously, this ability to stay alive without being submerged and wiggle over land to find new hunting grounds has caused havoc in America, where the fish was imported live to feed the culinary whims of the Asian community. Somehow they escaped into the wild and were nicknamed 'Frankenfish' in reference to their belligerent behaviour, voracious appetite and weird ability to 'walk' from ponds to rivers. Fears that the alien species could alter the food chain and devastate local ecosystems have called for desperate measures – mugshots of the snakehead have been printed on posters asking 'Have You Seen This Fish?' and offering a $100 reward for every one captured. The US government has even commissioned a team to develop a poison to wipe the species out totally. (It has now been listed as an injurious species and live importation is prohibited.)

They looked pretty innocuous, cut up on the table, and I can attest that they do taste good (a bit like bass), as I ate them all over Laos.

Peng took the inner leaves of the heart of a white cabbage and placed them on a large plate.

'We use only heart of the cabbage. It is sweet, it has a good smell.'

She laid the snakehead fish steaks carefully over the leaves, their heads and tails sticking out at either end for decorative effect. Next she mixed together a small handful of sticky rice, various condiments and lashings of fermented soya bean paste (*tua noi*) and spread it over the fish. Then she added ginger, carrot, chopped garlic, half a pickled lime and poured the liquid from the lime jar over the entire dish. She finished it off with five long green chillies. The plate was then placed in a sizeable pot filled with an inch of water, on another upturned plate and steamed.

'Do not open the lid for twenty minutes! Or all the smell will escape,' warned Chakard. 'Maybe then you can look. If not cooked enough you give another ten minutes.'

Meanwhile, the others were getting frantic. Fish pieces were fried for the soup, boiled pumpkin was being added to the inadequately small blender in batches and they had run out of rice. Noodles had to be found to compensate. Peng kept a cool head amongst the chaos and started on the pineapple-chicken.

Pineapples grow well in southern Laos and are an important commercial crop, and so they turn up in many southern dishes. It is most often used in savoury meat dishes (rather than as a dessert, like in the West) as a balance to sour flavours, or it is eaten as a snack with chilli and salt, a mixture that brings out extra sweetness in the fruit.

Peng flashed together a quick stir-fry dish of chicken, garlic and onion with barely cooked pineapple, cucumber and tomato held together in a sticky sauce.

I tried a little. It was salty, crunchy, tangy, sweet and savoury. Interestingly it was the tomato that made the dish, as it added a tang needed to counter the sweetness of the pineapple.

Now it was all hands on deck as we served everything at once in the Lao manner. I obviously wanted to help, and forty hungry teachers' heads swivelled towards me in amazement as I climbed the steps to the restaurant laden with plates. They thought it was hilarious that they were being served by a *felang* and I clowned around to entertain them. By seven they were gone and we were cleaned out of food, so it was lucky we'd set some aside.

Chakard beamed at our hard work. 'As you are only guest you can have dinner with me and all the staff if you like?' I did, and it set a precedent for the rest of my stay. They were a lovely bunch of people, and as I have often found before, language barriers melt away when you muck in and join people's everyday routines.

The next morning, after an early breakfast of coffee, papaya and pineapple, I was invited to go with Chakard and Kiat on a trek to the twin waterfall. The falls are in the Dong Hua Sao Biodiversity Conservation Area, and this part of the region had escaped the loggers. We would have to walk through the coffee smallholdings of the local village and on into the forest in a horseshoe curve around the end of the gorge to reach the waterfall on the other side. Chakard arrived wearing an eccentrically large white pith helmet.

'We want to start eco-tourism here and develop more things for people to do here, in nature,' Chakard shouted back to me as he sprung down the steep forested escarpment. 'It means jobs for local people instead of hunting or clearing land. I want to start nature trails, start right at the lodge. You know, even since we built the resort birds have started coming. They know it's safe around the resort.' He used his hat rim like a gun site. 'Won't get shot.'

The villagers were growing robusta coffee trees that were ten foot high and had trunks as thick as weightlifters' arms. The ground was thick with fallen leaves and the earth loose and damp from an unexpected shower in the night. It was hot, and the incline was mounting sharply.

Chakard picked up a ripe red coffee fruit and split it open to reveal two beans fitted snugly together like yin and yang. It smelt of plant sap. 'In tradition, the soil of newly cleared forest is considered best for new coffee plants, so they used to cut down primary forest. Now there are lots of people here trying to help with management plans and thing. This is an old plantation. These trees, ten years at least.'

In between the little coffee plantations the natural forest flourished: trees, bushes, weeds, ferns and tiny fuzzy purple balls of flowers like violet mimosa carpeted the forest floor. There was so much growing in between the coffee it was hard to tell where the plots ended and the jungle began.

We walked for an hour without seeing another soul. Then I heard the sound of rushing water and the landscape began to dip down again sharply. We hacked our way down and pushed through the trees to a hollow where a wide stream emerged from the jungle. I stepped into the shallow pools leading to the rim of the gorge. Many flat rocks, made smooth by the flow, jutted from the water and I hopped from rock to rock until suddenly I was at the edge of the waterfall, looking down one thousand, one hundred and sixty-one feet to the bottom of a gaping cavern five hundred foot across. I almost lost my footing as my sense of perspective disappeared down the hole in the landscape. Kiat pulled me back just in time and I retreated to a safer distance before smacking down on a stone with a fast-beating heart.

Surprisingly the water flow was almost sluggish until it reached the edge of the falls and the sound of the gush was carried away to the other side of the canyon where the resort lay buried in the trees. We all sat for a while in wonder. Chakard had a genuine look of joyous contentment on his face, and so, I presume, did I. Kiat, having grown up with this place, peeled a grapefruit with nonchalant lack of interest. He said something to Chakard, who nodded.

'There's another waterfall back there, it comes before this one. If you like we can go swim.'

We shinned back up the hillside, walked a while and then came suddenly to another basin, hidden in the thick under-growth, where a dazzling two-hundred-foot waterfall dropped into a dell with a deep round pool below. The air was thick with spray and the walls of rock were almost fluorescent green with a carpet of minty herbs whose heady aroma was enough to make me want to plunge my nose in.

I tried to climb down carefully, but it was so steep that I shot down on my bottom instead, leaving a red trail of mud and two men in an apoplexy of mirth behind me. Picking myself up with as much dignity as I could muster, I ripped off my clothes to my swimsuit and dived into the fresh water.

The falls above me cascaded over smoothed rolls of lava rock before cracking down into thousands of rivulets to form a diaphanous flounce of foam at its base; from there, the froth spread out like lace and drifted towards me on radiating circles of wavelets that quavered over my shoulders, leaving a cloak of bubbles that shimmered in the sunlight. The walls of jungle rose around us in a protective cup, delicate hands of bamboo waltzed together in the wind and the sky was that rare violet of pure ozone. The landscape was celestial in its beauty and untouched by man.

I felt as though I had reached the mythical Mount Meru, a place represented in temples throughout South-east Asia – home of Indra, King of Hindu gods, and a realm of perfection and transcendence.

There was something wooing in the atmosphere, a mellow har-mony that washed over one like cool water and swept one's cares away. I was overtaken with a state of wondrous rhapsody. There was honesty, an integrity and real goodness about this country that melted my jaded and cynical heart. Maybe it was the high altitude, but at that moment I felt at one with the earth, with humanity, with life: with Laos. And I've never been the same since.

A Perfect Cup of Lao Coffee

Stephan Hurst, managing director of Mercanta coffee importers, is evangelical about coffee drinking and is the only importer of Lao coffee in the UK (see suppliers on p. 336). I spent a tasting afternoon at his Coffee School, and here are some tips on how to get the best out of your cup.

- Don't bother roasting your own beans at home unless you have the right machine (which is extremely expensive).
- Buy your coffee in whole bean form, half a kilo (one pound) at a time, as once you open the bag it starts to oxidise and degrade.
- Keep the beans in an airtight jar with a good seal. You can keep them in the freezer, but it tends to make the coffee damp when you remove it so I wouldn't bother. In Stephan's opinion, ground coffee only lasts a week once opened; beans last longer, about a month.
- Grind your own beans in a coffee grinder.
- Use a ratio of one-third ground coffee to two-thirds water (British people tend to drink their coffee too weak).
- Use either a one- or two-cup filter with paper insert on the top of your cup (available at coffee shops), or an espresso machine, or a Braun home brewing machine. He believes that cafetières filter out some of the subtler flavours in the coffee.
- Drink black or with milk. Stephan uses honey rather than sugar, which adds an extra dimension to the cup if you like it sweet.
- Finally, if you make a large quantity, keep it in a thermos once it has brewed rather than reheating it.

For information on his coffee-tasting classes, email: *mercanta@aol.com* or telephone 01932 784905 for details.

Mok Paa or *Paa Fok*

Mok means to 'sear' or cook something directly in the embers of the fire. In this case the fish mixture would be wrapped in banana leaves and grilled, but you can also steam them. It is quite easy to make the banana leaf packets and secure them with toothpicks, but I have also tried lining little ramekins with the leaves and it works just as well. It can be made in foil, but in my opinion to its detriment – the leaves add a certain perfume to the dish.

2 sticks lemon grass, chopped
2 small shallots, roughly chopped
1 chilli
a pinch of salt
1 tablespoon *paa-dek* water or fish sauce
1 tablespoon soaked sticky rice or cornflour
450 g (1 lb) catfish (or trout, salmon, cod fillet or monkfish tail), cut into 2.5 cm (1 inch) square chunks
3 lime leaves, very finely shredded
2 tablespoons fresh dill, roughly chopped
banana leaves for wrapping

Take a pestle and mortar and pound the lemon grass, shallots, chilli and salt until you have a paste. I like it quite rough, others pound until it is a fine paste.

Add the *paa-dek* or fish sauce and mix around. Now take the soaked sticky rice or cornflour and pound it into the paste until you get a thick mixture the consistency of cream.

In a separate bowl, add the fish chunks, shredded lime leaves and pieces of dill and mix around. Add the pounded paste and coat the herbed fish.

Take an 18 cm (7 inch) square of banana leaf. Soften it in the steam of a kettle so it doesn't split. Place about four chunks of fish in the centre and pinch the sides together, securing with a toothpick.

When you've wrapped them all, place on a steaming rack above a big pan of briskly boiling water. Close the steamer lid and cook for 15 to 20 minutes until the flesh of the fish is cooked through.

The banana leaves should still have some of their green colour. If they have gone all brown you have probably steamed them too long.

Tad Fane Pineapple-Chicken

You need to use fresh, ripe pineapple for this dish – tinned will not do. You can tell if they are ripe by pulling out a leaf close to the core: it should come out with ease. The bottom should also smell sweet. Pineapples contain an enzyme called bromelin which tenderises meat (cannery workers have to wear special gloves to prevent their hands being eaten away), so prepare and eat it immediately.

The key to this dish, surprisingly, is the tomato, which adds a tang necessary to counterbalance the pineapple. You must use fresh, flavourful tomatoes or it will not taste right.

½ white onion, finely sliced
2 cloves garlic, smashed and sliced finely
2 chicken breasts, cut into slivers or small pieces

ANT EGG SOUP

1 tablespoon fish sauce

1 tablespoon tomato sauce

1 tablespoon oyster sauce

1 level teaspoon salt

1 round of pineapple, cut into 2.5 cm (1 inch) cubes

2 plum (or vine) tomatoes, cut into eighths

7 cm (3 inch) length of cucumber, peeled, seeded and
    chopped into 2.5 cm (1 inch) pieces

a splash of light soy sauce

In a wok, fry the sliced onion and chopped garlic on a medium high heat for 30 seconds or until they start to turn golden at the edges. Add the chicken pieces and stir for two minutes.

Now add the fish, tomato and oyster sauces and salt, and stir to coat everything. Immediately add the fresh pineapple, tomato and cucumber and stir to coat.

Cook a little longer, stirring continuously, and add a splash of light soy sauce to taste. The chicken should be cooked through, but the vegetables and fruit must still be firm. Do not overcook the tomato. Serve with rice.

THIRTEEN

A LEGENDARY LINGAM

Down south, the Mekong ceases to be the border between Laos and Thailand – for a hundred miles or so, Lao land lies on both sides of the river. I was on the west side for the first time, in Champasak town.

Champasak is a small place with a big history. The area has been inhabited by some of the greatest civilisations in South-east Asia and even had a separate royal family that governed it as an independent province for two centuries before Laos officially became united in 1946. As a result, people of Champasak have a fervent sense of their heritage, and this is symbolically embodied in a natural phenomenon of gigantic proportions – Phu Pasak, or as the locals informally refer to it, 'Mount Penis'.

The mountain summit ends in a narrow stone pillar that resembles a holy Siva lingam (phallus), and below, on a natural terrace at the foot of the mountain, stands the ruins of Wat Phu, an outstanding temple complex dedicated to the Hindu god Siva. The shrine is on a par with Angkor Wat in Cambodia (though much smaller) and is a reminder of Laos's Hindu past. Siva was originally the third deity in a trinity of gods that then developed into one supreme holy being representing the two aspects of life: creation and destruction. His symbol is the male organ, and it is usually portrayed as a stone column with a rounded tip – a lingam.

The area has been sacred to three cultures since the sixth century or earlier: the Chenla empire (part of pre-Khmer Cambodia) worshipped at the site from the sixth to eighth centuries. The

Khmer empire built the surviving sanctuary there from the ninth to thirteenth centuries and then the Buddhist kingdom of Lan Xang converted the Khmer structures, in the fourteenth century, to honour their own deities which are still used today. The site includes two walled cities, several other related temples, watercourses, thoroughfares, field systems, quarries, kilns and an ancient road leading to Angkor. In 1997 archaeologists found a carved sandstone lingam lying in temple foundations at the top of the summit that confirmed its identification as the famous ancient location once known as Lingaparavata. The entire area is now listed as a World Heritage Site.

The town of Champasak, eight kilometres south-east of the temple, is a shadow of its former self and consists of a few crumbling French colonial villas sprinkled among traditional houses on a road that runs along the river. The town has few streets and is bisected by a grand circular fountain that ran dry decades ago. I had come to visit the Wat Phu Champasak Festival held on the full moon of the third lunar month, a three-day affair when thousands of both Hindu and Buddhist pilgrims come to worship at the mountain temple. It was no longer the season for novice rice and I doubted they had a cultural food tent, so I was interested to see what they would eat, down south, at such a huge event.

I arrived at Mr Bountiem's guest house, pungent from the poultry-filled bus, and climbed the rickety, vertical ladder to my bed for the night. The room was six foot by four and made of woven bamboo with a granite-hard bed pushed up into the corner. Little chinks of hot sunlight filtered through the walls and scattered on to the rush-mat floor. The roof was made of corrugated iron and acted as a heat conductor. Later, rats would dance upon it, keeping me bright-eyed and wide awake until the dawn chorus of phlegm-spitting finally shooed them away.

The next day I took a *tuk-tuk* to the Wat Phu festival to find that it had not yet begun. I didn't care; the place was magnificent, like a lost city. The site is built on three levels, leading the eye across a vast vista and up to the temple with the silhouette of Mount Pasak framed behind.

The lost city was once surrounded by water and I had to walk past a reservoir before I even entered the complex, past an incongruously hideous and, thankfully, ruined sixties pavilion built by the Champasak royal family and on to a processional causeway flanked on either side by enormous Khmer ritual bathing ponds. One had dried up and the other was in reality a large puddle but I got the idea.

The promenade ended with irregular stone stairs leading to two large pavilions surrounded by quadrangles of ceremonial rooms. They were built between 10,000 and 11,000 CE, and, judging by the deities carved into the stone, the left was used for female worshippers and the right for male. The pavilions, like everything else, were made from carved latterite – a reddish-grey stone that weathers into an attractive patina. These were splendid buildings – majestic halls with doorways engraved with symbolic designs and topped with elaborate triangular layered corbels. The walls were delicately carved and the windows barred with barley twists reminiscent of Angkor.

They were, however, in a state of semi-collapse, and the fact that tourists were sitting all over them taking photographs probably didn't help. There was no sign of the festival, but the preparations had begun. Behind one of the buildings, in an electric-orange tent, the inevitable tannoy system (the louder and more echoey, it seemed, the better) was being hastily set up by several monks preparing for the ceremonial rites of the festival.

I shot through the middle level, as I had read in a guidebook that human sacrifices had taken place on the top terrace. I raced up a series of treacherously crumbling steps, past the 'sanctuary' and the sacred spring, to reach the most interesting part – the crocodile stone, the table of human sacrifice. To find it, I had to locate some tiny carved steps, easily overlooked, that led between two enormous boulders. On the other side was a most gripping sight, a large, flat rock with a beautiful silhouette of a crocodile carved deeply into it. It was primitive and stylised with legs outstretched and a bottle-shaped nose. A groove led from the crocodile (for blood to flow?), and beside it several circular bowls had been gouged out of the stone (for organs?). It is described as a 'sacrificial table' and was thought to have been used for Chenla human sacrifice between the fourth and eighth centuries but may even have been used by an earlier civilization, the Chams, one of the first colonisers of South-east Asia (originally from the coast of Vietnam).

The historians Peter and Sanda Simms argue that there was probably a Cham kingdom based at the Wat Phu site in the centuries before CE predating the Mon-Khmer, though no exact archaeological evidence has turned up in the UNESO digs so far. The history of human sacrifice at Wat Phu by the Chenla civilisation, however, is still told in the oral myths of Champasak today, and the Simms were told this story in the fifties by Prince Siromé of Champasak:

> It was in the times before Buddhism . . . The king of Chenla used to mount the great causeway, flanked by a thousand brilliantly dressed soldiers, up the steep side of the mountain and enter the temple of Wat Phu. Two virgins were awaiting him clothed in the finest silks and cloth of gold, perfumed with precious unguents, powdered, and immaculate . . . a blazing red flower with its stalk twisted into their hair behind their ears: the final happy symbol of a maid going to her marriage.
>
> Then, to these two shy and radiantly beautiful girls, he would offer some rice spirit. Hardly had their lips touched it than swords fell upon them and they were hacked to pieces at the feet of their god: their gorgeous costumes and perfumed bodies, were all soaked and spoiled in their own blood. The sacrifice of the two maidens was the price people paid for one more year of prosperity and for the glory and continuation of their king's reign.

Chilling stuff. Until a few years ago, a buffalo was still ritually slaughtered at this festival, a tradition which may have its roots in the original human sacrifice, but when I asked around no one seemed to know whether it happened any more. I was told, 'Some years yes, some years no.'

There were other carved boulders nearby depicting *naga*, snake spirits, which were fed the sacrificial blood, and an elephant probably of a later date. Further on I found a primitive stone building, about fifteen foot square, carved directly from five slabs of the rock. It had imploded, leaving a raised floor covered with debris, and I wondered if it might have been the original temple. It was a fascinating place, but no one else seemed to be bothered with it. None of the shrines was venerated with offerings and I explored for an hour without seeing another soul. The association of these artefacts with ancient and unknown civilisations enthralled me.

After that, the main Khmer sanctuary, though exquisite, could only be disappointing. I examined the rare bas-relief of the sacred trinity of Siva, Vishnu and Brahma and visited the sacred underground spring that flows from a small cave behind the temple. The water once fed through stone pipes to bathe a lingam, like a water feature, within the sanctuary and led to an irrigation system that would have guaranteed a bounteous harvest for the surrounding civilisation. Now, a blue plastic spout directs a jet from the spring and the missing lingam has been replaced by weird Buddha statues with comical smiling faces and triangular eyes like jack-o'-lanterns.

It was still a remarkable place. Behind me, on the slopes of the mountain, lay dozens of meditation caves used by devotees for millennia, their mysterious inscriptions carved into the rock face. Before me, I gazed upon a landscape that had been shaped to reflect the ancient Khmer interpretation of the cosmic world. Now, dozens of tiny tents were popping up among the ancient stones and I stood observing a continuity of worship which stretched back into prehistory. People had been here for a long, long time.

I returned to the central stairway and the buzz of international tourism. I wanted to find the stone yoni, the Hindu symbol of the female sexual organ, which I found by following the smell of incense. It was lying, unromantically, like a millstone on the weed-strewn ground, but was covered with the flowers left by worshippers in the hope of conception. Beside it, the headless statues of two men lay spent and broken.

Back at the festival, pilgrims were arriving from all over the country and setting up camp. Food stalls were appearing in ever-increasing rows, with stalls in between selling everything from traditional textiles to plastic buckets. Every day, I would find it had grown a little larger. One morning a funfair appeared, complete with Ferris wheel. The place was teeming, but still no religious festival.

The food sold at the stalls was snacky, like festival food all over the world, but instead of pasties and toffee apples, these sold spring rolls and fresh bamboo shoots. I also ate taro fried in sugary dough, hard-boiled eggs, peanuts, baked sweet potato and white turnips which I devoured raw like fruit. There was one unusual speciality – steamed baby chicks still in the egg. These were helpfully displayed with dainty holes carved into the shell so you could see the little face of your prospective lunch. I got used to seeing people crunching and talking with a tiny foot hanging out of the corner of their mouth, but never quite got around to trying one myself. I stuck to green papaya salad and my favourite snack, raw spring rolls, the South-east Asian equivalent of the sandwich. This consisted of shredded carrot, turnip, banana flower and mint rolled in a rice paper sheet, then dipped in a tiny bag of fish sauce and lime juice with peanut and chilli.

A PAPAYA SALAD AND A 'BEER LAO'

There was something medieval about the festival: the makeshift stalls, the hotchpotch of food and farming items, maidens with flowers in their hair, gaming stands and spontaneous sports matches. Pilgrims queued to fill plastic drinking bottles with the holy water from the sacred spring and laid flowers at the feet of Khmer sculptures in a confusion of faiths, illustrating how the power of the ancient pagan symbols continues even among today's Buddhist Lao.

By day three, there must have been five thousand people or more visiting the site. I was fascinated to see how the landscape could cope with such an influx, and part of my investigation was realised when I needed to find a loo, as there was nowhere private to go in the bushes.

English people are obsessed with toilets, and one of the first questions I'm asked when I return from trips to the East is how I possibly coped without sit-down loos and loo paper. 'Squat toilets, how revolting.' Personally, I don't have a problem with them. For a start, squatting is much better for you, as the body is in the correct position to release the bowel, bum resting on calves, and it is much more hygienic to wash your bottom than scrape it with a bit of tissue. The Khamu with whom I stayed in Luang Nam Tha were asked if they would like a cesspit loo built in their village, and they were horrified. They thought the idea utterly disgusting – to have a toilet in a single place that the entire village uses as their own was anathema to them.

I hadn't seen any public loos at the festival and Portakabins haven't reached Laos yet. I managed to get my wish across to a girl at a soup stand. She grabbed my hand and led me across four fields, to what was the ladies-loo-field. Adjacent to it was the gentlemen's-loo-field, and no men ever looked our way; it would have been impolite. We peed still holding hands and I mused that this was a very ecological way to deal with a simple problem, keeping sewage far away from the festival and fertilising the field at the same time. After dark, the holding hands thing became strings of women, the leader holding a torch. You just joined hands at the end of a line when you saw a light bobbing off in the right direction.

Loos seemed to be taking up a lot of my time, as my sleep had been severely interrupted, not only by the dancing rats, but by Mr B. and his intoxicated friends, who decided to construct the new 'foreign' toilet for his guest house in the middle of the night – every night. The festival still had not begun, and I was getting worried as I had an appointment to meet the relative of a friend in Sekong town in a couple of days. The appointment had been carefully arranged and it would be impolite to miss it.

The festival might not have started but the games certainly had, particularly football. On my last day I sat down by a dusty field to watch with a bunch of children who had found me whenever I arrived and stuck like glue. Lovely glue. It took about four hours for anything to happen, and in the meantime the single festival fire engine rattled around the pitch spraying water to keep down the dust. The team all looked very young and sometimes a bit bored. I was told that this was the back-up squad.

The game lasted hours and on into the night with much cheering and drinking all around. I hooked up with an English girl called Lizzie who looked like a model-gone-feral and had an amusingly lateral sense of humour. She taught the kids how to count to ten in English and we learnt football terms in Lao. So I didn't get to see the famous Wat Phu festival and I didn't get a whiff of a buffalo sacrifice but I was having a fantastic time at the football match. The next morning I had to leave at dawn – it was a bit like going to Woodstock without seeing the bands – but I really didn't feel I'd missed a thing.

I arrived in Sekong in South-eastern Laos in the evening. The town was created in 1986 when the province of Attapeu was split in two for municipal reasons. There was a choice of two hotels but I was only allowed to stay in one of them as the other was reserved for government officials only – so much for Communist equality. Mine was horrible and modern, an echoing chamber of empty rooms with a closed restaurant. My room was unusually expensive and for the price of six good meals I got a bare, sloppily painted blue cell with grey furniture and an ear-splitting air conditioner. The designer had obviously done his apprenticeship in a Soviet prison. I took an evening constitutional to the river.

The town is encircled by logged mountains and is dominated by a very large government building and a wedding cake-style monument built for a dead Communist. It consisted of three flat streets, one of which was lined with market stalls selling modern things like batteries. The sound of a pop ballad broadcast over a public tannoy system forebode a vociferous start to my morning. There seemed to be lots of empty restaurants and cafés, and when I asked in some of them if I could get some food later, they said no, they were closed. It wasn't always easy to find good restaurants in Laos, particularly in remote towns.

Further from the centre of town the modern pebble-dashed houses gave way to wooden ones with succulent gardens of fruit trees, palms and coconuts. It felt affluent. I walked for some time and then followed a forested side road to the river. There was one fisherman on the water and an old lady cleaning her boat watched by her pet cockerel. It was very quiet and the humid air smelt of fresh earth. I could have been in the middle of nowhere had my view not been marred by the building site of the giant palace-in-progress, a half-built concrete mansion of at least sixty rooms. It looked like a Lao version of a stately home and, somehow, I doubted that they were building the new 'Lao People's Workers' Club'.

Back in town I searched for an open restaurant and could only find *pho* (I was bored of *pho* – there is only so much noodles in broth you can eat), so I slurped one down quickly and went to bed.

I awoke to the tannoy broadcast barking speeches. I heard the word '*felang*' and in a fit of paranoia wondered if it was mentioning me, the only tourist in town. I was due for lunch today with Mr P., the relative of my Lao friend in London, and through a series of hard-to-interpret telephone conversations we had arranged to meet at a restaurant called Vieng Thong, which I hadn't spotted the night before.

I arrived promptly at twelve to find a simple veranda-style restaurant with an enticing bowl of water standing by the gate. It was empty, but a table for twenty people had been laid with a cherry-red paper cloth and festive rice baskets. The Financial Department was having a lunch party. The owner's sister, Vieng Savanh, came and sat with me while I waited for Mr P. She was an extraordinary beauty with a swathe of glossy hair and a pretty way of lilting her delicate head when she spoke. She smiled so often that, at only twenty, she already had laugh lines around her eyes, which only added to her charm. Her T-shirt read 'Wonderful Moments!'

Vieng Savanh spoke perfect English, which she had learnt in three years at Pakse College. She worked as an interpreter for the local bomb disposal unit and was engaged to her boss, a bomb diffusal expert from Manchester.

'Yes, we destroyed one hundred bombs today, mostly bombies,' she said casually. 'We blow them up behind there.' She pointed to a hill in the distance. 'If they are small we transport them to the detonation area and destroy them, but sometimes they are too big to move. Today we found two big ones, one maybe two hundred pound and the other about five hundred.'

'God, what do you do with those?'

'Oh, the team detonates them, the big one had two fuses. They had to dig into it to find the explosive.'

'How many do you find a day?'

'Oh, fifty, a hundred.' It was a surreal quantity to contemplate. 'We go to villages and do a survey, draw a map from what they say. If they are going to build something they do the area square foot by square foot. But in two months the Norwegian funding runs out and they all go home.' Yet again, my heart sank at the thought of all those bombs that would be left in the ground once they had gone. The scourge of Laos. I could not imagine that this beleaguered country would ever be rid of them.

The Financial Department had arrived on their mopeds, and Vieng Savanh went to help her sister in the kitchen. Then she popped her head out of the kitchen door and said, 'My sister is a good cook, you must try her deer *koi*. Venison, it's very special here.' I was greatly relieved to hear there was more to Sekong than *pho* soup.

Mr P. was late and I was starving, so I ordered some. He arrived at the same time as my food, and he looked embarrassed. He was a stringy man of about forty, with buck-teeth and trembling hands. Deep lines crossed his forehead and his shoulders were bent with the weight of worry.

He greeted me and sat down, apologising for not being able to speak English very well. I apologised more profusely for not speaking Lao and dug out battered gifts from his cousin in

England that I had carried all over Laos until that moment. I invited him to have lunch and a beer and we spent the next five minutes in a state of language-related confusion. I wanted to invite him to eat, he wanted to invite me, he had already eaten, or maybe he hadn't, we were supposed to be somewhere else, or not, I had no idea what was going on. Then suddenly Mr P. rushed off on his moped and I was left alone with my *koi*.

Koi is not unlike *laap*, that is, a meat or fish salad, but it is not finely minced and the meat (or fish) is cooked very lightly or used raw. It is called *soua* in the north. Sometimes other vegetables are added to the salad, such as raw sliced aubergine or green beans. I tried it prepared with raw fish, *paa-dek* and banana flower, and it's a dish that translates very well using raw salmon or cooked fillet steak, but deer is still my favourite.

In this recipe the venison fillet was sliced finely, marinated in fish sauce, chopped lemon grass and the white part of two spring onions, then tossed in a very hot wok with sliced garlic and the green part of spring onions. Whole mint leaves were thrown in with a dash of soy at the last moment to give perfume and to cool the heat. It was served with a plate of salad leaves for wrapping. It was truly divine. The meat was so tender it just melted away in my mouth and the flavours mixed fabulously.

The party behind me were having deer steaks complemented with chicken soup, vegetable dishes, *jaew* and sticky rice. They were not a very raucous lot, the finance men (like accountants everywhere, a bit careful), and I noticed that they drank only one beer each over their entire lunch.

I'd just finished when Mr P. came back on his moped, followed by the flashiest silver 4x4 I had seen in Laos. It shone like a bar of bullion and was balanced on those ridiculously high wheels designed to raise the driver above the hoi polloi. It must have cost a fortune.

Out of this monstrosity stepped a chubby man with a shiny face. He strode up to my table and introduced himself (I'll call him Fat Man), while Mr P. followed meekly behind. This was Mr P.'s boss, and he was to be our translator. He pulled up a chair with a swagger and placed a state-of-the-art mobile phone ostentatiously on the table. The Finance Department stirred behind me.

'*Sabaii dii!* How nice for you to visit Sekong. Why you visit Mr P.? You must have some more beer. Now celebrate, we need whisky.' He stood up with arms raised to get attention and I noticed he was wearing a gold watch with diamonds for numbers. 'So, what you doing in Lao? Where you been? Where you going? What you think of our countreeee?' He grilled me for details, pronouncing elongated eeee sounds through a permanently self-satisfied grin. He totally ignored Mr P., who was behaving obsequiously to the point of slavery.

I was livid. I could hardly speak to Mr P. Every time I tried, Fat Man butted in with stories of his own aggrandisement.

'I have much moneee, much moneee, one million dollar, one million dollar in the bank.' And I believed him. He was a director of some sort of construction business and his brother was high up in the government oligarchy.

'I train in Russia for six year and now I am business man. Very successful. I travel a lot – Holland, Germany and Japan.' He swigged back his Beer Lao followed by a whisky chaser. 'I no like Japan, too expensive. Nine dollar! Nine dollar for a glass of beer!' He was trying to force whisky down me, but, much to his annoyance, I refused.

'My brother, very high in government, very high.'

'A minister?' I asked.

'No, no, high, head of department. So very easeee for me. Very easeee. Any problem I just call my brother, then no problem.' He laughed heartily, rubbing his thumb and forefinger together. 'Much monee!'

Mr P. had been trying to say something for several minutes and finally managed to get a word in edgeways. Fat Man sneered and translated. 'He say, would you like to go to his house and meet his famileeee?' At last! I was going to be able to get away. I felt like I'd been kidnapped by this loud, aggressive bastard.

'Oh yes, I'd like that very much.' With that, Mr P. zoomed away on his moped leaving me stranded with Fat Man.

'He go and get his house ready, we follow in ten minute.' How irritating, he was coming too. Fat Man went on and on and on about the wonders of himself.

'There is so much moneee in Lao. Foreigner give much, aid projects. It so easee. We tell them we pay workers ten dollar a week but we give them one dollar a week. Keep nine! Ha ha ha.' He laughed triumphantly. 'They never check!' This was vile. Obviously I knew about corruption in Laos, but travelling as a tourist I hadn't come across it face to face. It was there before the Communists, and it will be there afterwards, but seeing it sitting next to me was hard to endure. At last the ten minutes was up, and I insisted on leaving by asking for the bill.

Interestingly, and against Lao etiquette, Fat Man sat by without offering to pay it (even though he'd drunk three beers and two very expensive whiskies). I noticed that before he decided not to offer, he checked to see if anyone was watching. He might be stealing people's hard-earned money, but he wasn't going to waste it on me unless there was someone to see it.

We got into his stupid car and drove to Mr P.'s house. It was a concrete box of half-plastered breeze blocks, and though set in a beautifully tended garden it was still pretty grim. The whole family were waiting outside and someone was sweeping frantically as I arrived. Fat Man took a litre bottle of Johnnie Walker Black Label whisky from the back seat and leapt out, brandishing it like a prize. I followed him into the house.

Inside, the furnishings were simple: a plastic sofa, some stools, a low coffee table and a plastic woven rug. A large grilled fish lay ceremoniously on the table surrounded by bowls of greens, bamboo shoots and steamed marrow. The party consisted of two maiden aunts, a grandfather, a young couple, three children and the next-door neighbour, but I hardly had a chance to speak to them as Fat Man dominated the conversation completely. *Lao-lao* was brought out, whisky was poured and everyone kept putting morsels of food in my mouth.

As far as Fat Man was concerned, I had become his guest, not my friend's family's. He pushed everyone out of the way to sit next to me and touched me at every opportunity. I moved away constantly, spoke to him grimly, smiled only at the relatives and ignored what he was saying, but he didn't notice. Shots of *lao-lao* were held to my lips and I struggled to refuse them. We had a *baci* ceremony and I tried desperately to chat to the family whilst becoming inordinately interested in their photo albums. After an hour I felt I had been there long enough to leave politely. I had got away with only four shots of *lao-lao*, but when I stood up I felt woozy and the blood rushed to my face. It must have been strong, and I hadn't drunk anything more than a few beers for about four months. I just wanted to go back to my hotel and sleep.

Fat Man insisted on driving me there and there was no way I could refuse such a 'bountiful' offer from the boss without embarrassing Mr P., so I got in the car with reluctance. We drove to the hotel with me plastered to the side door as far away from Fat Man as possible. Once there, I flew out of the car, shouted bye-bye without looking back and raced into my room with relief. Thank God that was over.

I went into the bathroom, took a swig of water from a bottle I'd left by the sink and realised that I felt really drunk. When I came out I walked right into Fat Man.

He must have followed me into the hotel without my noticing. I hadn't thought to bolt my door – it just hadn't occurred to me that I'd be followed. I shouted at him, 'What do you think you are doing? NO! NO! NO!', pushed him out and slammed the door, then reeled back in shock for a moment before he pushed his way back in again. This time he grabbed me with one hand and shut the lock closed with the other. By this time I was really screaming with anger, but the hotel was empty. He grabbed me by the upper arms, pushed me across the room towards the bed and shoved me down.

Now my adrenalin kicked in. With Superwoman strength I flipped both of us off the bed, grabbed him under the armpits and physically lifted him six inches off the floor. I carried the fat oaf across the room and slammed him against the door. Then I undid the lock with one hand while I pinned him immobile with the other. I shoved him out so hard that he shot eight foot across the corridor and smashed into the wall.

I bolted my door, and sat on the floor leaning against it, nearly exploding with anger.

He got the message. I stayed there for fifteen minutes to make sure he was gone and then tentatively went out to check. There was still no one in the hotel and a wave of fear swept over me at the thought of what might have happened, though I probably would have killed him first. I locked my door and fell into an exhausted sleep, longing to be back at home with my boyfriend Giles.

The next day I felt better and ready to face the world, even with my bruised upper arms. What really got to me, though, was the fact that, just by being a woman, I was always going to be vulnerable to that kind of attack. That really enrages me still.

Raw Spring Rolls

This is a Vietnamese import that is eaten all over South-east Asia as a snack. I usually serve this as a starter with all the ingredients laid out on a platter. I put a wet napkin on everyone's plate and a bowl of hot water on the table. Guests dip a rice paper into a bowl and make their own – it's messy but fun. When I'm alone I make vegetarian ones for lunch, but you can add cooked meat or prawns as I've suggested below.

    4 oz dried vermicelli noodles
    15 circular rice papers
    1 handful bean sprouts
    3 carrots, shredded into matchsticks
    3 spring onions, shredded into matchsticks
    $\frac{1}{2}$ cucumber, deseeded and shredded into match-
        sticks (hard part and skin only)
    1 handful cooked prawns, shredded chicken or pork
        (optional)
    1 big handful mint leaves
    1 handful coriander leaves

    DIPPING SAUCE
    2 tablespoons fish sauce
    2 tablespoons lime juice or rice vinegar
    2 tablespoons water
    1 teaspoon caster sugar
    1 bird's-eye chilli, chopped into fine rings
    1 tablespoon peanuts, crushed

Boil a pan of water and drop in the vermicelli noodles, cook for two minutes, drain and rinse with cold water. Set aside.

Wet a large clean tea towel, squeeze out the excess water, fold it in half and lay it on the work surface beside you. Fill a large bowl with boiling water from the kettle, drop in a rice paper for 30 seconds or less and remove with chopsticks on to the tea towel. Place one teaspoon of cooked noodles two-thirds of the way down the circle, and spread them out into a horizontal line. Now take a pinch of beansprouts and lay them on top, then do the same with the carrot, spring onion and cucumber. (If you are adding prawns, chicken or pork, shred it first and add a pinch at this point.) Lay some mint leaves and a little coriander along the top.

Now take the nearest edge of the rice paper and part-roll it over the filling to form a tube. Lift the left side and fold it inwards to join the centre of the tube and do the same on the other side. At this point it should look like an open envelope. Gently roll it away from you to form a sealed package. Place on a serving plate under a damp cloth. (They last about two hours like this.) Repeat until you've run out of ingredients. Serve immediately with little bowls of dipping sauce for each guest.

Beef/Venison *Koi Saa*

This recipe is speedy and healthy and the ingredients are easy to find in a good supermarket. If you want to make it quickly for supper you can marinate the meat for just half an hour. It is a great dish with which to introduce your friends to Lao food – they'll love it.

½ lb beef sirloin, rib-eye steak or venison fillet, very
    thinly sliced in 2.5 cm (1 inch) pieces
1 tablespoon fish sauce

2 stalks lemon grass, finely chopped

2 spring onions, green bits only, finely chopped
  (reserve half for later)

1 dash of oil

1 clove garlic, peeled and finely sliced

a dash or two of light soy sauce

1 large handful mint leaves

Marinate the beef with the fish sauce, lemon grass and half the chopped spring onions for $\frac{1}{2}$ hour – 24 hours. (If using venison fillet, marinate for a couple of days.)

Heat the oil in the wok on a high heat and fry the sliced garlic until golden and just crispy. Remove and reserve.

Add the marinated beef or venison and the soy sauce and toss for 1–3 minutes on the highest heat. The wok must be very hot. The meat should be seared brown on the outside and very rare on the inside and there should be some juice.

Remove from the wok and toss with the fried garlic, mint leaves and remaining spring onions. Serve immediately with rice.

FOURTEEN
ANT EGG SOUP

The bus driver dropped me on the road and I walked the two kilometres into Salavan with my rucksack. The lush plantations of the Bolaven Plateau had petered out to be replaced by a landscape of dry bush that reminded me of an African savannah, and the sun beat down on my sunblock-slathered feet with blistering intensity.

I was on my way to meet Rachel Dechaineux, a young Australian aid worker I had met in Vientiane. She was involved in a study in Salavan that would help villagers use their local food resources without damaging the forest and sell the surplus at a profit. The study was part of a global forest conservation project, dealing with 'non-timber forest products' (i.e., not wood but food, medicine and craft materials). Supported by the IUCN and funded by the Dutch, the idea is to develop realistic projects with local people to maintain their environment whilst protecting their cultural heritage. I was just enthralled to find out more about everyday country-style food.

Over lunch in Vientiane, Rachel and her manager, Joost Foppes, had dazzled me with their enthusiasm for Lao culture as we feasted on roast fish roe, venison *laap* and steamed, stuffed *khae* flowers. Lunch had lasted three hours and I had filled my notebook with little sketches of edible mushrooms and descriptions of the medicinal uses of forest leaves. It was fascinating stuff and their passion for the project was palpable.

Rachel, in particular, was a true Laophile: fluent in the language and married to a Laotian, Somphan. She was a delicate, alabaster-skinned brunette, with huge chestnut eyes and a soft-spoken voice, but her eyes widened with an energetic zeal when she spoke of her work. This was a woman who made things happen – quietly and with respect.

She had done a BA in Asian Studies at the Australian National University and spent a year of her course learning Lao language, literature and history at Dong Doc University in Vientiane. The students had the afternoons off, and while the others went home to tend their rice paddies, Rachel sought out jobs with the NGOs and quickly learnt the politics of developmental aid work. Hardly any foreigners spoke Lao in the early nineties, so she was handy to have around. After she finished her studies in Australia she couldn't get back to Laos fast enough.

'The NTFP has already done two studies on which forest foods are central to the local Lao diet,' she had told me, her eyes shining with excitement. 'What is eaten at home? What is used for ceremonial or medicinal purposes? What were the sought-after delicacies? I think you would find it really interesting. Me and Somphan are living in Salavan right now. When you come down south, give me a ring and we'll show you around.' I had jumped at the invitation.

Salavan is an agricultural town on the northern edge of the Bolaven Plateau, and a distribution centre for local farmers. Built along the Xe Don river, it was severely damaged in the war, but it has been there a long time and it has a comfortable, provincial feel. The town, and in fact the whole province, has a reputation for sorcery and magic, and some Laotians fear to visit for more than a short period for risk of bewitchment.

All the guest houses in Salavan were modern so I picked one at random. It looked reasonable, but on closer inspection my grey concrete room had no window, and pulling back the towelling coverlet from the bed I discovered the sheet and pillowcase were made from a dark grey striped material that looked like the remnants of a roll destined for 1930s prison uniforms. It smelt, too. I replaced the coverlet and laid my sleeping-sock on top, then bored a large (and bad-tempered) hole in the wall to fix up my mosquito net.

The bathroom had not been cleaned and there were eight used sachets of shampoo screwed up in the soap dish (making me wonder if it had ever been washed). I emptied the red plastic wash bucket on to the floor, refilled it (cold tap only), and gave the place a rinse-over. On the plus side it had air conditioning (as it was getting hotter by the day), a big green fridge for my one water bottle and a narrow door which, I discovered, opened on to a slim balcony overlooking the market. I opened it with some difficulty, stepping over a pile of used cottonbuds, and let out a yelp of joy as I surveyed my bird's-eye view over the late evening commerce below. I decided to stay.

I rang Rachel and we arranged to meet at the market the next morning.

At dawn, the farmers' market of Salavan looked like a tatty wasteland with its dilapidated trestle tables and the customary plastic bags caught in the ruts of the dried, trampled earth. The rusty corrugated iron storage sheds that surrounded the market-place had yet to open their doors, but the people were coming thick and fast and I went down to join them.

Women were unfolding their parcels of produce, dumping their bright plastic-mesh baskets and opening their sun umbrellas with such speed it was almost a blur. One minute a strip of earth was bare; I'd look away for a moment, and when I looked back a line of women would have appeared from nowhere to unload their goods on to pastel-coloured groundsheets. Strange plants lay in lush bunches on sugar-pink plastic next to handfuls of tiny little fishes on violet sacking by creamy eggs nestled in lemon and lavender baskets. These were the very poor; they had little to sell, and what they did have would be sold or bartered within the half-hour.

The everyday traders were also unloading their gourds and aubergines, their bananas and maize and beans and sweet potato, their chilli and garlic and mint, their little heaps of knotty galangal, leggy spring onions and tufts of petite-leafed coriander, and their piles and piles of unidentified wild forest leaves, all the more fascinating for their mystery. Were these shrubs to be savoured in soups, were those pods to be pounded into pastes, their sacred saps to be used to soothe the sick? I was dying to know.

Rachel tapped me on the shoulder.

'Hi, Natacha, this is my husband Somphan.' Her eyes shone as she said his name. He stood beside her, his fingertips just touching hers. He was a big man with a square jaw and a thick thatch of hair parted to one side. He had a kindly face, a gleaming smile and looked much younger than his thirty-eight years.

' *Sabaii dii.*' He put his hands together in greeting. 'How do you like our market?'

'It looks wonderful.'

By now the ground was covered, the tables laden and the air fragrant with the smoke of little cooking fires.

'There are so many things I've never seen before. And that wonderful, wonderful smell.' I was referring to the sweet-musky scent of some kind of incense. Not that heavy joss stick smell mixed with rotting fruit and wet earth that I associate with India, but a much lighter, amberous vapour. This delicious perfume had been the first thing to hit me when I initially flew into Vientiane and the cabin door opened on to the smoke-wisped runway. As it curled into my nostrils the smell had begun the start of my love affair with the country. It fills the air of Laos in the morning.

'Oh, that's yang oil,' said Somphan. 'We call it *nam man yang* in Lao. It is a kind of resin.'

'It is one of the main commodities the villagers can sell from the forest,' said Rachel, picking up a bamboo tube packed with fibres. I had assumed the tubes were some kind of food. 'These are firelighters. They're filled with the resin from a special tree,

Dipterocarpus alatus. They harvest it by making a small dip inside the base of the tree large enough to burn a fire. The heat stimulates the resin oil to drip into the basin and then it is scooped out. They leave most of the trunk intact and the process can be repeated. The trees are marked as 'belonging' to family and can last for six generations or more.'

Somphan pulled out some fibrous stuffing to show me. 'We mix the oil with bits of dry wood and grass, to make for fire-lighting.' He glanced at Rachel with tenderness. 'We would like to invite you for lunch and show you some local cooking as you like so much.'

It can be very dull to be with people in love, but Rachel and Somphan were so deliriously happy to have found each other and showed their affection so lightly, that it felt uplifting to be with them. Generous and enthusiastic, they planned the next few days ahead for me.

'Unfortunately,' said Rachel, looking worried, 'I can't take you to the project villages as they won't allow foreign tourists in the countryside down here. It is so stupid because there hasn't been any terrorist activity here for years.'

I hid my disappointment. The night before I had made enquiries about venturing out on a bicycle but had met a brick wall. I would have to get a permit (it would take days) from the district office, etc., etc., and I was conspicuously, again, the only tourist in town.

'We can make it up to you, though, with some good Lao home cooking. And I can show you what we are doing here and what we've learnt about the local diet. They eat a lot of plants they pick from the forest. Things you've probably never seen. Like this . . .'

I had become aware of a new and powerful scent, a perfume so strong that it felt like I had just plunged my nose into a bottle of Chanel No. 5. It was emanating from a table where a toothless old woman in a headscarf sat almost obscured by lush bunches of exotic herbage. There was no commonplace lemon grass on her table; this lady specialised in the foliage of the forest.

Rachel picked up a bouquet of long feathery stems covered in little pointed leaves and tiny purple flowers the colour and shape of violets. The scent of Chanel No. 5 was coming from this. '*Pak an yeng*. It grows in the rice fields only during the rice paddy season. It's in flower right now, taste some.' It tasted exactly how it smelt – strong and heady. 'We dry it and then use it in soups in the dry season. And this is *pak ka*.' She pulled out a plant with compound leaves arranged on the stem like a fish bone; it smelt strong and rather unpleasant. 'It's tangy, slightly astringent, mildly bitter. We only use the new shoots. The smell goes when you cook it and it's great with fish.'

Somphan picked a bit up. 'In Vientiane we call it *pak ka*, in Luang Prabang another name *som pon*, and maybe here a local name, *pak nau*, that is different again. Even Lao people get confused.' I agreed; it seemed impossible to name plants. Just as I learnt to recognise something with one name, I'd move on to find it called something completely different in another town.

Rachel giggled. 'The Lao believe that if you want to plant this shrub you must steal a cutting or it won't grow. So you can't buy the whole plant anywhere.'

The old lady stretched across the faggots of leaves and handed me some fernlike shoots, explaining in Lao how good they were. '*Pak koot*. a shoot from a fern that grows by river. It's really like a green vegetable. You can steam it and eat it with tomato *jaew*,' explained Rachel.

'This is *pak waan*.' Somphan began to pick out bunches to buy. He had chosen some light green soft leaves. 'These are also found in wet places by the river, they taste slightly sweet and at same time sour. I always use in soup.'

I thought of the food writer Betty Fussel, who wrote that one man's weed was another man's salad, 'for those who knew where to look, and how to transform, root, stalk, leaf, pod, fruit, blossom, seed, nut, berry and pollen into foods raw and cooked.' She was referring to the Native American Indians, but it couldn't be more true of the Lao.

We moved on to the next stall selling the (less popular) cultivated *pak hom*, a general term for herbs grown in the garden. Everything was beautifully presented: sprays of spring onions were tied with sprigs of coriander like posies of flowers, and individually washed cherry tomatoes shone on flat wicker baskets. Somphan bought bushels of stuff and gallantly refused to let me pay for anything.

'Now is the high season for frogs. I thought to make *or* frog, southern-style, with young coconut water, *soop pak* with the forest plants and tomato *jaew*. You like, Natacha?'

'That sounds great. I've only ever eaten frog's legs. Do you eat the whole thing?'

Somphan smiled. 'Oh yes, and Lao people are frog connoisseurs! And can tell the difference in taste between wild and farmed.'

We began to weave our way through the shoppers to where the frogs were sold along with the fish at the back of the covered market. Here, the volume increased tenfold as housewives bargained over prices and inspected the piscatorial produce. There were heaps of frogs, baskets of frogs, buckets of frogs, strings of frogs and plaited ropes of frogs, some as small as my thumb, and all alive.

'You've hit the frog high season right now,' said Rachel, 'that's why there are so many.' Somphan was already sifting through a bucket. 'There's been a shortage, but we supported a frog resource management project that was really successful. Frogs were declining rapidly as villagers eat the frog spawn, tadpoles, everything, all year round. One village in our study, Konglunoi,

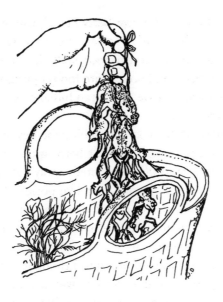

A NECKLACE OF FROGS

designed their own conservation system which involved choosing a breeding area to close in the rainy season and opening it for harvesting in the dry. It is really working, with instant results,' she winked. 'Luckily it was a good first year so they had lots of frogs. Now they've expanded the idea to all the adjacent villages.'

Somphan chose six specimens in combat gear – dappled khaki, dark green and beige. They cost one 1,000 kip each and croaked in the bag all the way back to the house.

Rachel and Somphan were about to move back to Vientiane, so their place was sparsely decorated with a few boxes lying in corners. The two-storey house had been built ten years before, with a carport at the front and a veranda on the top floor. The kitchen was modern for Laos – a big room with a white-tiled work surface, a sink in the corner, and a chocolate-brown enamelled gas stove with its knobs missing. Two windows opened on to an overgrown garden, and their tortoiseshell cat jumped through one of them, greeting us loudly as she began sniffing at the bags.

'Last year we had a wonderful vegetable patch, tomatoes and greens,' Rachel said as she opened the shopping. 'We didn't have to go to the market for weeks, but we've let it go as we're leaving.'

They worked as a team; Rachel washed vegetables while Somphan dealt with the frogs. He emptied them into the sink.

'Look, one is jumping,' he exclaimed with glee, 'I can let it go!' It is common practice in Laos to break a leg of each frog when it is caught to stop it escaping, but one of our frogs had managed to avoid the snap. He lifted the frog tenderly to the window and let it hop out into the wilderness. 'He is not bad, I think he will live.' He was really pleased. 'One for the river.'

'Somphan never likes killing frogs,' said Rachel, 'their little hands freeze up as if in prayer – it is quite traumatic for someone who cares about the lives of small creatures. I can't kill them at all.'

'I have to do it fast, so they don't know.' With that, Somphan took one from the sink and despatched it quickly by hitting it on the head with the heavy handle of his chopper. He then laid it on its back, took a broad knife and made a horizontal slit across the tops of the legs and below the stomach to gut it with a scoop of his finger. Next he made a light vertical cut between the legs and pulled off the skin in one go.

'Some people like to leave the skin on,' he said, throwing it away and cutting the frogs into four pieces. Rachel had laid out the next ingredients ready for him. 'Now I pound the galangal, garlic, lemon grass. If you want it spicy, Natacha, I can put chilli.'

'I'm happy with spicy. I like chilli, it wakes me up.'

I caught Rachel and Somphan glancing at each other over the cooking pans. Somphan grinned as he pounded the herbs into a paste and scraped them into hot oil in the pan. An appetising smell of lemon grass and garlic rose into the air. Rachel, having finished washing the greens, laid them out for the *soop pak* and went to get NTFP project papers for my perusal.

'Later I add aubergine,' continued Somphan, 'dill, a bit of coriander and spring onion and *pak an yeng* – it is good for you, to put in tea, it good for heart to get going. I'll show you how to make properly later.'

Rachel returned with two thick reports which she lay to one side and proceeded to help with the cooking while filling me in on her work there.

The NTFP were working in various ways with twenty-four villages in the Xe Bang Nouan conservation area. Rachel's project covered three typical villages, Ban Khamteuy, Ban Konglunoi and Ban Nongthe, predominantly of the Kathang minority. They had already done two studies on the local Lao diet. Now their aim was to achieve food security for communities with regular food shortages and to help villagers use their local resources without depleting the forest.

Rachel began to assemble the ingredients for Somphan's tomato sauce. 'You see, it's a big issue for Laos. In the past, protected areas have been promoted as wildlife sanctuaries, not cultural, traditional resource areas. There is a problem with the intensity of resource use, so people have been forcibly moved and just left to struggle for themselves. We are trying to train people to be responsible for their own environment. To empower them so *they* are in control.' She pierced a whole head of garlic on to a skewer with animated force. 'Through our work with the villages they've promoted regeneration by defining breeding and reserve areas, and regulating their harvesting patterns. They're establishing fish and frog breeding and they're planting bamboo, rattan and fodder around rice fields and on common land. This all helps to promote intervillage cooperation. The forest products are vital to their existence and they can be managed to benefit everyone.'

Rachel had become impassioned, her eyes wide and her hair flinging about. All the best aid workers I have met are Australian women; their positive attitude is infectious. She inspired with her intensity, which she managed to convey with a lightness of touch.

'You see, rice cultivation is the dominant economic activity but the soil is poor. They only have one planting season per year. In the fifties the three study villages were based inside the protected area along the Xe Bang Nouan River and then they were moved down to the lowlands to plant rice. The land they were given was not so good, sandy soil where once there were trees. Very often they don't have enough to last the year. Besides rice, the rest comes from the forest, to eat or sell. We found very little home-produced foods – pigs, chickens and cows that are mostly raised for ceremonial purposes or sold for cash.'

It was hot and Rachel pulled sticky hair from her face, coiled it into a thick rope and jammed it up with a biro lying on the work surface.

'And each family's food consumption varies according to the amount of labour they have to do in the home; you need time to collect food. If there is a husband and wife and three kids under four, who can't play in the village gang, it is difficult then as one adult has to stay looking after the children. Then, if there is an emergency or they need medicine, they pay with rice, causing more shortages. A catch-22 situation as you don't have time to tend the rice field or produce handicrafts to sell when you have to find food because of those shortages. And areas have become depleted. As one villager said to me last week, 'We can go out all day and not find enough food for one meal.'

'But what do they eat from the forest, exactly? Stuff like this?'

'Yes, but much more rice than anything else. And it depends what they found that day. They subsist mainly on bamboo shoots, rattan, frogs, toads, fish and lots of forest greens. Other seasonal items such as honey in May and June, mushrooms from July through December, grasshoppers, dung beetles, which are collected by kids . . .' She paused and smiled. 'Umm, then there's snails, shrimps, crabs, turtle, squirrel, eels, rats, lizards, bee larvae, rabbits, snakes, tadpoles, algae . . .' She thought for a moment. 'But the most common foods in the dry season right now are frogs, red ant eggs and *pak waan*, that edible green leaf we saw in the market.'

My ears pricked up. 'Ant eggs? I'm dying to try ant eggs. I've been looking for them ever since I arrived.'

'Really?' she exclaimed. 'Ant eggs are the third major resource after frogs and fish!' She flicked open a report. 'Look here, during the dry season the average household gathered between 170 and 800 grams of ant eggs a week.'

'That's nearly a kilo a week! I haven't seen them anywhere!'

'Oh, I'm amazed. In the high season, people around here eat them practically every day,' said Rachel, laughing. 'They're good for you, too. They contain protein, fat and natural nutrients.'

Somphan had finished with lunch and we took it upstairs to the balcony. The food was placed on a traditional wicker tray and we all tucked in. 'You want to try ant eggs? They are very good. We must find some for you.'

'Oh, that would be marvellous,' I said with my mouth full of frog stew. 'This is exquisite!' A wonderful group of flavours was zinging across my tongue. The *pak an yeng* herb gave the stew an interesting aftertaste – a slight dryness in the mouth, making you want more. Eaten with rice, fresh tomato sauce and just-picked greens it made my kind of perfect meal.

Somphan, like all good cooks, was pleased to see his efforts get such an enthusiastic response.

'We'll get some ant eggs with you tomorrow, in the morning market,' he offered, chewing on a frog leg.

'I'm really surprised we didn't see any today. Usually there's heaps. If we find them we can make something with them for dinner. Maybe *kaeng paa kai mot*?' She looked at Somphan for approval, and he nodded. 'An ant egg soup.'

'Oh thank you, I'd love that.' I was thrilled at the thought.

The rest of the day disappeared in a mellow haze. Somphan

went and bought more frogs and showed me how to cook the food we had eaten at lunch, then we supped on barbecued frog, talking late into the evening. I felt like I'd known them for years.

I took the forest food reports back to my hotel and could not resist reading them into the night.

In the study they weighed the forest foods gathered in a week from three households in each village to gauge the average consumption in a village, and then the foods were then analysed for nutritional value. They found that an average of 70 per cent of food eaten every day was glutinous rice, with forest foods making up the rest. The rice diet was low in vitamins A and C, iron, calcium and iodine, so in the poorest households the small amounts of vitamins in forest foods were vital to their health. Nutrition was broken down into 85 per cent carbohydrate, 10 per cent protein and 2 per cent fat. I suspected that the diet of the entire population of Laos was made up of a similar ratio, with a bit more fat consumed by wealthier people in urban areas. Laotians are not fatties, and the weight was dropping off me even though I was eating all day long.

Interestingly, there was little home-grown produce as the villagers complained of soil infertility, unreliable rainfall and lack of labour. Some people did grow fruit and vegetables in field gardens such as cucumber, pumpkin, pineapple, watermelon, ridge gourd, aubergines, beans, corn, taro, spinach and sweet potato, but in Khamteuy, the poorest village, only two or three households grew vegetables. Fruit trees tended to be communal to the whole village, as is often the case throughout Laos, and everyone grew herbs at home such as lemon grass, spring onion, chilli, garlic, mint, and galangal.

What really caught my interest in the reports, however, were the household food records of a typical family's consumption in a day. The food was broken down into the menu, exact ingredients, weight, who ate it and where. As I expected, this was not haute cuisine, and herbs, chilli, monosodium glutamate and *paa-dek* were used to overcome the simplicity of the cooking, or to give it flavouring. Rice, of course, was the main part of every meal.

The family of seven in Khamteuy started their day with rice and four bowls of bamboo shoots and a bowl of *goi* (an unappetising tuber, eaten mainly when rice is short). At midday, six members of the household out working in the fields caught one frog and made a watery soup adding chilli, *paa-dek*, MSG and a plant called *pak samek* which they ate with rice, and then the evening rice was supplemented with a boiled pumpkin, two big bunches of boiled marrow leaves and a chilli *jeow*.

Another large family of seven's non-rice intake in Konglunoi was even more meagre. They began their day with one shared bowl of frog soup and one bowl of grilled dung beetles. Lunch consisted of two and a half bowls of ant egg soup flavoured with chilli, *paa-dek*, basil and two leaves of something named *pak kadohrn*. The evening meal seemed like a feast, with ten grilled and steamed frogs in banana leaves, until I noticed that all ten frogs together weighed only 200 grams – the weight of an average British pear. And this for seven people.

It is easy to imagine Laos as an Eden of sumptuous bounty when you go through the spectacular markets or are fed in villages where people serve you, an honoured guest, as abundantly as possible, but the daily diets of the two families were pretty measly for seven people.

In rural areas, many villages survive at subsistence level, suffering shortages for at least part of the year. In the past these people were used to surviving on what the forest provided, but times have changed due to population growth and deforestation. The NTFP project suggested realistic answers to difficult questions by asking the people what they needed first. They'd set up village rice banks for food shortages and low-interest loan systems for emergency situations. Solutions such as defining wild breeding areas and planting foodstuffs on common land were decided in village workshops, and government involvement was secured by including enthusiastic district officers in the meetings. I felt a little envious of Rachel – she was making a valuable contribution to her adopted country. No wonder she exuded such happiness at having found her vocation.

The next day I woke up excited. Today I was going to eat ant egg soup.

I was at the market at dawn again, fortifying myself with the nuclear Lao coffee. Maybe because it was a rest day, there were fewer people – just a few women with forest produce and home-grown herbs. The covered dry goods area, however, was doing a brisk business. With great self-restraint I stood by a stall and perused the goods for sale while I waited for Rachel and Somphan. To pass the time I bought a cassava cake – a crisp golden patty covered in coconut, soft inside with the consistency and flavour of a macaroon. By the time Rachel and Somphan arrived I'd eaten seven.

I bounded outside into the clear sunshine to embark on our treasure hunt. The produce may have been thin on the ground, but it was freshly picked or caught within the last few hours. I walked eagerly down the rows scanning the produce – but no ant eggs.

Rachel stopped and called me over. She was crouching down by a bundle of green sticks. 'Look, fresh rattan shoots.' She put her hand to her forehead to block the sun and smiled at Somphan. 'Shall we make something with this?'

'Yes, yes.' He beamed at her. 'We could make a *jaew*. With this I usually make *jaew* or an *or* or soup,' he explained to me, but his eyes were still on his wife looking up at him in the sunshine.

'Yes,' said Rachel, 'you only eat the inner part of the rattan shoot and from one shoot like this –' it was about a foot long and as thick as a broom handle – 'you only get a little strand in the centre. Five sticks gives you a very small bowl, but it's a delicacy, like asparagus, you don't eat it every day. It's bitter, though, do you like that?'

But my attention was elsewhere. I raced away down the line. 'Look! Look! Ant eggs!'

There on the ground, on a shiny heart-shaped leaf the size of a serving plate, lay a creamy mound of fresh ant eggs. To me it was like finding a pile of priceless diamonds. And they were fresh – there were live red ants crawling all over them. I was ecstatic.

The woman selling them was also pleased – they were all she had to sell. The basket and long stick she had used to bring the nest down from the tree was still beside her. Like the noodle maker, she had probably walked many kilometres that morning. She was barefoot and wore a tatty shirt, faded *sin* and bamboo hat that had seen better days. The cost of the eggs was piffling. Somphan again refused to let me pay for anything and remunerated her fairly, but when he had walked away I slipped her some more cash. At first she refused to take it, but I persuaded her in the end.

I caught up with the others. 'What do ant eggs taste like, then?' I asked.

'Well,' said Somphan, popping the plastic-bagged eggs into his basket, 'you can eat them raw, when they taste a little bit sour, or when they are cooked they have a nutty taste. I think I make a soup like they would eat in the village. You would like?'

'Yes, please!' And we strode off victoriously to get the other ingredients.

Later that evening Somphan built a fire in the yard outside their house using an archetypal Lao earthenware stove, shaped like a large flowerpot with a rectangular hole on one side and filled with charcoal. He lit the stove using the yang-oiled fibres, and its pleasant smell rose in the evening air.

'I have to start this first, rattan *jaew*, before the soup as it takes time. About half an hour on the fire.' Somphan stripped the green sticks of rattan of their prickles, but they still looked hard and unyielding to me.

Rachel stoked up the fire. 'We encourage this species for domestication in the village. We're doing trials at the moment. It takes five years for it to grow large enough to make furniture, but this edible shoot would be two or three years old and they sell well. We are encouraging people to grow it in their own gardens and in plantations in bare parts of the forest.'

When the fire was ready, Rachel took six rattan sticks and placed them across the top of the stove an inch above the flames. 'We can leave them now and I'll come back and turn them every once in a while.'

Back in the kitchen Somphan had laid out the ingredients for the soup – the bag of ant eggs, two of those 'Frankenfish', the snakeheads, garlic, galangal, lemon grass, a tamarind bean, a bunch of *pak waan*, a bunch of sweet basil, coriander and some tomatoes. A wicker rice steamer and stockpot bubbled on the knobless hob.

First Somphan scaled and gutted the fish, then he washed them under the tap and cut them into pieces.

Meanwhile, Rachel had emptied the bag of ant eggs into a large bowl of water.

'Often they're much bigger than this, these are in their very young stages, they are still laying the eggs.'

I felt a pang of guilt. I have always been fascinated by ants, ever since I was a child while on holiday in the South of France. I observed a red ant colony wage war for three days against a neighbouring black ant hill. The red ants won, enslaved the remaining black ants and amazed me by burying their own dead in communal graves especially dug for the purpose. Now I was about to eat them.

She swished them around in the water. 'You have to wash them to get rid of the earth and sand they accumulate. You see,' she said, showing me the grit in the bowl, 'it drops to the bottom while the eggs float.' A few live red ants were scrambling over the larvae in a desperate attempt to reach dry land, and many drowned ones attested to the difficulty of the task.

Somphan came over and had a look. 'They have some soil in there or something like that. You know the nests are made of twigs and all sorts of things, the leaves all wrapping around so you get other bits in them. To avoid getting stung they get a basket on a long, long pole and shake the nest into it from a distance. The ants pour out.'

Rachel sifted through the floating eggs with her fingers and pulled out bits of twig. 'Sometimes it can be fairly painful if these big red ants come crawling out of the basket and sting you.' Just as she said it one bit her on the arm. She flicked it away. 'They have a nasty sting, but I think this one was too weak to hurt me. There, I think that's done.' She took a sieve, removed the cleaned eggs from the water and rested them over an empty bowl to drain.

'I'm going to use fish stock,' said Somphan, ladling it from the stockpot to another saucepan. 'I have already made.'

He had been chopping garlic, galangal and lemon grass which he now added to the boiling stock. Next he threw in the fish and a sour tamarind, and then stuck his nose in the pot. 'Smells good.' He tasted it and then added salt and a splash or two of fish sauce. 'Oh, the rattan!'

'Don't worry, I'll do it.' The sticks needed turning to roast evenly. Rachel went outside to turn them and I stayed in the kitchen, close to my ant eggs.

'Now you add *pak waan*, basil and tomato, boil for ten minutes. So the flavours mix, yes? We go out and make the *jaew*.' I followed a little reluctantly.

Half an hour had passed and the rattan sticks were totally black with soot. Somphan split them open with a large knife and pulled out the hot soft centre. He gave me some to taste. It was very bitter but strangely moreish. I could see why it was a delicacy.

'Mmmm,' said Rachel, playfully pinching a morsel from Somphan's bowl. 'The charcoal is good too, it makes a difference, you know. They've probably used good wood because there's a sawmill in town that's come back into processing. It's great because the families that live around it have a new income by producing charcoal from the leftovers.'

We took the rattan back to the kitchen and in three minutes Somphan had made the *jaew* with garlic, ginger, chilli and coriander leaves.

Now my beautiful ant eggs were finally added to the soup. They cooked for ten seemingly endless minutes before Somphan threw in some coriander leaves and everything was ready.

It was a balmy evening, so we took some cushions and went outside to eat. The soup smelt heavenly and the ant eggs had gathered in patches on top, bobbing between the fish and herbs. Somphan flamboyantly ladled soup into my bowl, while Rachel scooped on lots of extra eggs. They both watched my face closely to gauge my reaction. I felt a pang of guilt again. Those clever, industrious ants — a species with such a sophisticated social system that even David Attenborough admires them and thinks they're awe-inspiring – and I was about to annihilate the entire progeny of the colony in a few mouthfuls. Ah well, I wanted to know what they tasted like.

I opened my mouth wide and tried a big spoonful. Luckily they tasted delicious, with a mild nutty flavour just as Somphan had told me. They were firm on the tooth, not sticky like the silkworm.

'Yum, they're lovely, really good. I can see why they're popular. You could say this was the caviar of Laos!'

They beamed at me and laughed. 'Oh yes, we think they are very good too,' said Somphan.

I ate some more. 'I mean, they're natural, organic, full of nutrients and they don't crawl around in your mouth! Ant eggs! The ideal wild food!'

In fact they are full of protein and have been found to contain vitamins B_1, B_2 and B_{12} and the trace minerals calcium, phosphorus, iron, selenium, zinc and magnesium. Not bad for something so tiny. Western Europeans these days think it's weird to eat insects, but insect eating is part of our heritage. Locust suppers are mentioned in the Old Testament, and the Ancient Roman foodie, Lucullus, had stag beetle larvae fed for months on wine and bran and then ate the roasted results with gusto.

In the past, insects added valuable nutrition to the Western diet and they still do today, not that we know it. There are loads in our processed food, so much so that in America the amounts are regulated by the 'Food Defect Action Levels'. According to this, insects in our food are seen, not as a health hazard, but, in the exact wording of their report, an 'aesthetic nuisance'. Chocolate can legally contain sixty or fewer insect fragments per hundred grams, flour up to seventy-five fragments, and a can of tomatoes up to ten fly eggs or one maggot. Tomato ketchup is made from all the wormy tomatoes rejected by the canners (keep that in mind when you next splat some on your plate). At least in America the level of creepy-crawlies in food is regulated. In Britain, the Food

Safety Act doesn't even mention insects. We Westerners may think we are not eating insects, but we are. All the time. So why not try ant eggs as a dish? I can recommend them highly.

'You know, the Chinese believe that eating ant egg is good for vital energy and physical strength, strong like the ant,' said Somphan.

Indeed the famous Ming dynasty Chinese herbalist Li Shi-Zen wrote about them in his book on Chinese medicine, *Ben Cao Gang Mu*, published in 1596. Li spent thirty years collecting all types of plant and drug specimens in rural areas and described how ants and their eggs were considered so beneficial that they were served to the chiefs of tribes and noble lords. Until recently, they were also served to Laotian kings – the royal chef Phia Sing includes a recipe for steamed ant eggs in banana leaves (not soup) in his book and must have dished them up at the palace.

'They're also supposed to help combat arthritis and rheumatism. Good for old people. And,' added Rachel, raising her eyebrows, 'are, I believe, renowned for increasing the libido.'

I already knew of this supposed benefit, as my friend Alex had been handed a jar of pickled ants (minus the eggs) in a Marrakesh medicine shop as a sure tonic for sexual empowerment. He still claims to this day that he stuck his nose in the jar and got an instant erection.

'Well, whatever they are supposed to do, they taste great – thank you so much for cooking them for me.'

'I'm glad you had your first taste of them with us. If that isn't a perfect example of Lao forest food, I don't know what is.'

I spent the next few days with Rachel and Somphan, and they took me to Tad Lo, a resort by another waterfall on the edge of the Bolaven Plateau. I had avoided it on the way to them as I had believed it was a Club Med-type complex with piped music and manicured lawns. It was nothing like that. Instead I found simple bungalows built along the edge of the broad-tiered falls and good hospitality. They knew the owner's son, Baii, who came and joined us at the temporary open-air restaurant. The last one burnt down due to a firecracker incident, and I was glad that the splendiferous new building being constructed across the way was not ready yet. A kitchen had been assembled at one end and the family sat beside it on a bamboo sofa watching a battered television which was constantly admired by passers-by.

The waterfall gushed in front of us as we drank Beer Lao and ate pink papaya. Baii had saved two baby otters found in the market, and they played delightfully at our feet. They followed him everywhere and swam with him every morning, catching their breakfast in the water. I had come to the end of my trip and it was about time for a bit of luxury before my return home, so I booked a bungalow with a hot shower for a couple of days. The balcony opened directly on to the falls.

In the early morning I watched fishermen casually throw their nets into the flow and heave them out loaded with fish. I swam in the pools above the cascade, massaged my back in the gush and decided to break my rule of not eating Western-style bread in order to try the local wild honey. I sat on my bougainvillaea-tumbled balcony surrounded by the bobbing Chinese lanterns of its crimson flowers and ceremoniously spread a fresh baguette with butter and lashings of wild honey – thick as caramel and dark as molasses.

I realised then that Laos had bewitched me in a way no other land had ever done. The resplendent verdure of the scenery, the generous, open-hearted people and the bold, wild foods of the land combined to make a place that, for me, was near-paradise. I had totally fallen in love with the place.

Maybe it was the ambience, the flash of the sun on the water, the perfume of wood smoke in the air or the simple rapture of being in such an enchanting place – whatever it was, the taste of that honey was in a different league of sensual pleasure. It was, without doubt, the best honey I have ever eaten, anywhere – so potent as to be almost alcoholic. True Lao nectar.

Somphan's Frog Stew, Country-Style, with Young Coconut Water
Or kop sai nam maphao ohrn

This dish is often made in the cold season in Laos as it is supposed to warm you up. Frogs are delicious, a fact that the French well know, as they eat 3500 tons of frog's legs every year. If you are of an intrepid nature you might want to catch your own. In Britain, the edible frog *Rana esculenta* – a medium-sized spotty fellow – may be found around ponds in the Fens and the south-east of England. Alternatively, use fresh or frozen skinned legs from Simson's Fisheries (see suppliers on p. 337). It can be made with chicken. If so, use flavourful birds and include the bones when cooking.

5 frogs, gutted and skinned, or 500g (1 lb) frog's legs
2.5 cm (1 inch) piece galangal, peeled
3 stems lemon grass, finely sliced
5 small or 3 large cloves garlic
1 bird's-eye chilli (or more to taste)
1 tablespoon vegetable oil
5 golfball-sized green/white aubergines, sliced,
    or $\frac{1}{2}$ a purple aubergine (5 cm/2 inch chunks)
2.5 cm (1 inch) piece ginger, peeled and sliced
300 ml ($\frac{1}{2}$ pint) chicken stock
a pinch of salt
1 dessertspoon fish sauce
$\frac{1}{2}$ litre (1 pint) immature coconut water, or $\frac{1}{2}$ tin
    coconut milk plus $\frac{1}{2}$ tin water
a large handful dill
4 spring onions, chopped
a handful of *pak an yang* plant or sweet basil leaves
1 spring onion, chopped

Despatch your frogs by hitting them on the head with the heavy handle of a chopper. Wash them under the tap and then, one at a time, lay a frog on its back, take a broad knife and make a horizontal slit across the tops of the legs and below the stomach. Gut it with a scoop of your finger and rinse well under the tap again. Next make a light vertical cut between the legs and pull off the skin. Chop into four pieces (you can discard the heads if you prefer).

Take a pestle and mortar. Add the galangal, lemon grass, garlic and chilli and pound to a paste. Heat the oil in a large pot and add the pounded ingredients. Stir for a minute or so until you get 'a good smell', adding a little more oil if it is too dry.

Add the frogs, the aubergine slices and the ginger and stir to coat the frog pieces and brown them a little. Add the chicken stock, salt, fish sauce and coconut water. Cook on a medium flame at a good boil for 10 minutes and then quickly add the dill, spring onion and *pak an yeng*/sweet basil leaves.

Switch off the heat and leave, covered with the lid, to rest for 5 minutes to produce an aromatic dish. Serve immediately, sprinkling some chopped spring onions on the top.

Ant Egg Soup
Kaeng paa sai kai mot daeng

You can buy tinned ant eggs on the Internet (see supplier's, p. 337), and can sometimes find frozen eggs in Asian stores.

> 2 snakehead fish, cut into 2.5 cm (1 inch) pieces
> (or use monkfish tail)
> 2 cups ant eggs
> 1 litre (1 $^3/_4$ pints) fish stock

8 small or 4 large cloves garlic, peeled and cracked with
   the back of a machete
5 cm (2 inch) piece of galangal, peeled
2 stalks of lemon grass, finely chopped
1 sour tamarind bean, peeled and seeds removed,
   or 1 tablespoon bought paste
1–2 tablespoons fish sauce
1 teaspoon salt
1 bunch *pak waan* or the juice of one lime
4 handfuls sweet basil leaves
4 plum tomatoes, chopped in eighths
1 handful coriander

Scale and gut the fish, cut it into 2.5 cm (1 inch) pieces and wash it under the tap. Reserve to one side.

Now prepare the defrosted ant eggs by putting them in a bowl of water. The earth and sand they accumulate will drop to the bottom of the bowl. Scoop out any other floating detritus such as leaves and sticks, and sieve eggs to shake off any excess water.

Bring the fish stock to the boil in a large pan. Add the garlic, galangal and lemon grass and let it boil for 5 minutes. Now add the fish, the sour tamarind, fish sauce and the salt.

Next add the *pak waan* or lime juice. Add the sweet basil leaves and tomatoes and simmer for 10 minutes. Add the ant eggs and simmer for another 10 minutes. Remove from the heat, throw in the coriander leaves and serve with sticky rice.

Somphan's Rattan Shoot *Jaew*

After cooking the rattan, this *jaew* takes about three minutes to make. The result is bitter, but not in a way that gets the back of your throat. Rattan is strangely moreish and quite addictive.

the cooked, soft innards of 5 sticks of rattan
4 cloves garlic, seared black and peeled
2 bird's-eye chillis, seared
2.5 cm (1 inch) piece ginger, peeled, seared and sliced
a pinch of salt
1 handful coriander leaves
1 tablespoon fish sauce

Prepare the rattan by placing the sticks approx 2 cm (one inch) above an open fire for half an hour, remembering to turn them every few minutes. When ready, split the rattan sticks open with a large knife, allow to cool, and remove the soft insides with your fingers. You will have enough to fill a small bowl.

Next, take a pestle and mortar, add the garlic, chilli, ginger and salt and pound to a paste. Add the rattan, a handful of coriander leaves and the fish sauce. Mix together and serve immediately.

EPILOGUE

'On New Year's Day in Laos all the population make for the wats in order to sprinkle the images of the Buddha with lustral water. Men and women beseech the gods to make the New Year propitious in bringing them health, wealth and happiness, visits are paid to relatives and the *baci* ceremony is celebrated. In the subsequent days rejoicing take place in the streets and *phubaos* (boys) and *phusaos* (maidens) sprinkle each other generously with water on the commendable pretext of purification. As those festivals draw to a close, small mounds of sand, shaped like stupa, are erected both in wats and on the banks of the Mekong; they are topped with paper streamers and ornamented with zodiacal signs. Their builders beg the gods to grant them the favour of wonderful days filled with happiness as numerous as the grains of sand. Merriment and general good humour prevail all over Laos during these festivals, where the sacred aspersions extend joyfully to all and sundry in an atmosphere of joy and brotherhood.'

Taken from a special issue of the cultural monthly
France-Asie 1956 *The Kingdom of Laos*

Lao New Year corresponds to sometime in April in the West, which, in Laos, coincides with the first rains and thus the rebirth of nature. In Luang Prabang, the Boun Pimai is particularly spectacular and can last for days. The streets are filled with costumed parades, people deluging each other with water and punting exquisitely decorated boats down the Mekong – the whole town joins the celebrations. The Boun ends with the crowning of Miss Pimai, the most beautiful maiden in Luang Prabang.

Since I was no longer in Laos, I would be celebrating Lao New Year at the VLC (Vietnamese, Lao, Cambodian) Community Centre in Haggerston, East London.

I was still in shock. After the gauzy tranquillity of Laos, London seemed like the cesspit of the earth. It was dirty, dusty, damp and it appeared to be made up of concrete flyovers and tatty billboards. Cars stood still in traffic jams belching fumes, fetid rubbish flew along the streets and every tenth person in the endless seething crowds seemed to be furious or mad.

I drove through drear and grim parts of East London to reach the VLC Centre and found it to be an unprepossessing shedlike building overlooking a council estate, and in some need of repair.

There are only about five hundred Laotian exiles living in England (as opposed to half a million in America, one hundred thousand in France and forty thousand in Australia), so the centre acts as a cultural haven for émigrés from three South-east Asian countries. What they all have in common is that they all had to escape their homelands with nothing but their lives.

I entered what appeared to be a school gym hall lit with strip lights, coloured tape marking out a tennis court on the wooden floor and a little stage at the far end with a hand-painted banner proclaiming Happy New Year in Lao. The room was strewn with balloons and tables covered with festive red paper cloths and bottles of wine.

Below the stage, a space had been cleared for the forthcoming New Year *baci* ceremony. The *phakwan* cone of banana leaves stood three feet high, dotted with flowers and pierced with skewers tied with dozens of white cotton threads. Offerings of candles, incense, hard-boiled eggs and sticky rice surrounded the structure, and people stood in anticipatory groups all around, including my friend Soun and the whole Sisouphanh family of royal cousins.

It was then that I noticed the King.

Well, he would have been King if the Communists hadn't deposed the monarchy and mysteriously made half his family disappear. Sadet Tiao Fa Jaya Sulinger Varman Savangsa, commonly known as Crown Prince Soulivong, is the next in line to the throne. He escaped from Laos secretly in 1981 at the age of eighteen, and now was standing in a run-down community centre south-west of Hackney.

Aged thirty-eight and notorious for refusing interviews, I had been trying to meet him informally since I had first picked up Phia Sing's recipe book in Books for Cooks. This was the Crown Prince of Laos, a man who had grown up in the palace, shared everyday meals with the King and known the royal chef as a friend. I was aching to know what he remembered.

The prince was fourteen in 1977 when the Communists took his grandfather, father and six other members of his family away to the re-education camps. He stayed in Luang Prabang with his mother, and the government controlled his secondary education to include their Marxist-Leninist doctrine. They lived quietly and grew their own rice, but existed under constant scrutiny from the authorities.

In an exceptionally rare interview with the *New York Times*, he explained that even making close friends at school became dangerous, as they started disappearing. The government's paranoia about insurgent groups meant that anyone who showed signs of support for the monarch was taken away for 're-education', and as he grew up and became a stronger and stronger symbol of danger, he heard whispers that he himself was going to be taken away to a Communist country for 'further education'. He realised he had to get out.

The Prince faked an allergy that needed urgent treatment in the capital, Vientiane, then fled across the Mekong to Thailand with his brother and nanny on a raft made of banana palms. Eventually he settled in Paris, where he presently lives with his uncle (who escaped in 1975), Prince Sauryavong. On a rare visit to London, there he was, standing ten foot away from me; but before I could meet him the ceremony began.

We all kneeled on the mat around the *phakwan*, our feet tucked underneath to one side. I touched the rim of the *phakwan* with one hand and raised the other to the side of my face in the traditional stance and listened to the invocations with a growing sense of excitement. I could hardly wait for the strings to be tied on before leaping up from the mat to find Soun to introduce me to the Prince. However, Prince Soulivong was whisked on to the stage to play the *saw-ee* (Lao violin) as part of a Lao orchestra that performed for the next twenty minutes.

Then Lay Sisouphanh's daughter, Keenda, got up to present a traditional Lao ballet, and after that the Lao Committee stepped on to the stage to sing a New Year song. Meanwhile, more people had arrived in little family units, informal and laughing. Several of the women had dressed in their best Lao finery with jewel-coloured silks and the flash of gold filigree. Tiny children ran around chasing balloons, two sultry Lao teenage boys with spiked hair break-danced in the corner and the bottles of wine were popped open all over the room. Within minutes the place was buzzing and people were partying in the wonderful way for which Laotians have been renowned for centuries.

Then it was time for the Lam Wong, a slow and graceful Lao tradition in which couples dance in concentric circles, twisting their hands in graceful curlicues. I, however, dance it like a walrus out of water with paddles for hands; it is painful to watch. Inevitably, I was asked to get up and join the ring and there was no avoiding it.

Now Prince Soulivong was dancing two people away, in front of me. I had still not managed to talk to him. I flapped and clod-hopped around in an increasing state of anxiety until, mercifully, the music stopped and I rushed to Soun to ask him to introduce me to him. A moment later I was sitting at a table asking the Crown Prince, a person I never thought I would meet, about his favourite dishes.

Tall and broad for a Laotian, and strikingly handsome, with lustrous thick hair, he had the strong nose of his grandfather, the late King. He was dressed in the classical navy suit and tie of a French businessman and wore understated glasses. My table quietly emptied as he sat down to talk to me, and we were left alone in a little oasis of space in the packed room.

He regarded me warily as I explained my love of Lao food.

His reticence for publicity is well justified, since every time he has opened his mouth in the past, he seems to have been grossly misrepresented. He has never called for a restoration of a governing monarchy in Laos (only a constitutional one, and only if the people still wish it), but his words have been twisted, journalists have misquoted him when they've never even met him, and the spread of Internet chat rooms seems only to make matters worse. Anti-Communist insurgent groups leap to name him as their figurehead, Communists accuse him of being a pretender to the throne, and every time there's the slightest insurrection in Laos his name pops up as the mastermind behind it all. The fact that he is none of these things and that he repeatedly states this clearly doesn't seem to register. So now he keeps silent, and I don't blame him.

He held himself with dignity and a gentleness of manner, but there was a sadness in his eyes, and I reflected how difficult his position must be. As an absent monarch of a tenuous royal line in a modern world, he is bound, by his position, to be doubly estranged, both politically and socially.

He remembered Phia Sing and described him as part-tutor, part-genius, part-engineer; close to the King, like Leonardo da

Vinci at the court of Francis I of France. The Prince's last recollection of this 'renaissance' man was when he came to his bedside as a child and helped him recover from a bout of sickness using traditional methods of psychic healing.

Lao pop music was pumping out of a stereo and a lady passed by with a bowl of water and a sprig of leaves to dip and flick, spotting us with purifying water. The noise level in the hall had risen and people were greeting each other like long-lost friends. Our table remained empty.

'Regarding food,' he explained, 'Phia Sing only cooked on very special occasions at the palace as usually their meals were prepared by a team of women in the kitchens.'

This didn't surprise me as just as in much of the world, most of the cooking in Laos is done by women.

'When we had big parties, more people were brought in from the country to do the cooking. My grandfather's (the King's) favourite food was made by the Kha (the tribal palace guard) in the old way – *or lam nor kor* and a *jaew kha*.'

I was intrigued. 'Really? What is *nor kor*?'

'It is a type of bird from the jungle. It tastes very strong, you have to hang it for a day or two until it smells and then smoke it. After that, it is ready to be made into *or lam*. The bird is very typical of Luang Prabang. The Kha cooked this in the old way, in a piece of bamboo over the fire, very slow. You know?' He shaped the bamboo tube at an angle in the air and I noticed he had beautiful hands with long, tapering fingers.

'Yes, of course.' Soun had described the method to me at the That Luang festival in Vientiane. 'That was the King's favourite food?'

'Oh yes, and mine also. The King liked very traditional-style Lao food, like *laap* and sun-dried water buffalo meat. His other favourite was a special *jaew* also made by the Kha people.'

As I have mentioned before, the Kha were seen as the original inhabitants of Laos, and, in a strange form of respect, the king traditionally recruited them as his personal guards, keepers of the sacred white elephants and farmers of the royal rice fields. In ancient times, when the new immigrants arrived in Laos, they supposedly asked the Kha to become their brothers, and still refer to the Kha as 'big brother' in respect of their cultural heritage. During the New Year festival in Luang Prabang they held a special place in the ceremonies. Prince Soulivong told me that during the New Year reception at the palace, the Kha would even sit down before the king.

'You make this *jaew* with green chillies,' he continued, 'garlic, shallots and salt, that is all. No *paa-dek* and no fish sauce. You must sear everything first in a charcoal fire and then pound them together. It is very simple, but that is how my grandfather liked it.'

Lay (Prince Soulivong's second cousin) explained that this *or lam* was traditionally served with *som paa pai* (pickled fish mixed with sticky rice) and a simple spinach soup. Lay's father used to make pickled fish by leaving a fresh-washed fish in a plastic bag for a day, then adding salt, crushed garlic, cooked sticky rice and a little water and leaving it to ferment for another four days. The soup was made even more simply with just water, salt, lemon grass, spinach and *paa-dek*. He remembered his father telling him that even he, a member of the family, expected the king to favour elaborate sophisticated food but found that he far preferred to eat simple Lao fare sitting on the floor in the traditional manner like a man of the people.

When I asked Prince Soulivong if he still ate traditional Lao food every day after living in France for twenty years, he said to me with feeling. 'Of course! A plate in a village in Lao, at a party in London, in a Laotian home in Paris, they are all the same! Are they not?' He looked up at his cousin Lay, who had come to fetch him.

'You see,' reiterated Lay grandly, 'it is the royalty, the aristocracy and the poor who understand real Lao food – the simple wild food of our country made the same way for centuries. It is the new middle classes and nouveau riche who turn their back on tradition to eat chicken and Vietnamese imports. We exiles, we are conscious of our rural roots and keep the food traditions alive. But it is not because of nostalgia. It's the food of our ancestors.' The King was whisked away, but my distress at losing him so soon was replaced with a growing excitement as, right on cue, the food arrived.

I smelt it first, and it felt like a reunion with a long-lost friend.

There is a particular fragrance to real Lao food that makes it different from its neighbouring cuisines – more of a perfume than anything else. It is a low note of flavour, something that lasts in the mouth long after the meal, and, once it has gone, leaves a gap. It is a complex, pungent and multilayered something that grows on your tongue and develops there. It's like trying a fecund cheese or a rare vintage for the first time. You need to make space to explore it, develop your taste buds to notice its subtleties, build up a palette of the new aromas, take some time over it. Nothing you have had before is like it; nothing again will taste the same. Then a novel thing happens once it has become ingrained in your senses: that taste, that flavour, that nebulous, pungent, rare, delicious, piquant thing, that Laoness, gives you a craving for more. The real stuff and nothing else will do.

A feast was appearing and it came from all directions. Men and women were opening their bags and pulling out Tupperware. Recycled four-litre containers of soft-scoop vanilla-flavoured ice-cream now spilled out celebratory quantities of mint- and banana flower-infused *laap*; tubs of Flora vegetable spread transformed into chalices for piquant sauces to stimulate the heart; fresh rice noodles appeared from plastic bags; soups were poured from tartan flasks; rare wrapping leaves fluttered from cardboard boxes; bamboo baskets of sticky rice disgorged their contents into the communal tub; and on and on until the Formica buffet table looked in danger of collapsing under the weight of it all – pigeon *laap*, raw beef and lung *laap*, *khao poon* noodles with all the trimmings, three types of *jaew*, tomato, buffalo hide and crab, *poun paa* made with catfish, spring rolls, *paa-dek*, pickled greens, red sweetened rice, platters of fruit, green coconut jelly, steamed pumpkin, raw aubergines, crunchy beans, stews, sauces, soups and savouries. It was all there: the raw, the wild, the cooked and the rotten.

I may not have been in Laos, but Laos had come to me with the scent of the food, and I breathed it in deeply.

Or Lam Nor Kor – Smoked *nor kor* bird stew
A favourite of the King

This is a very ancient stew cooked slowly in a bamboo tube in the traditional way as described on page 234. The Nor Kor is a wild jungle fowl similar in looks to a pheasant, though the meat is dark red. The bird is hung for a day or so to give it flavour before being flattened in the spatchcock style and smoked until almost dry. The result is then made into this *or*.

Crown Prince Soulivong's cousin Lay suggests that pheasant or pigeon could be substituted instead of *nor kor*. He kindly showed me how to make the version with smoked pheasant breast (see suppliers on p. 337). Alternatively you can use plain pheasant that has been hung for four to seven days (we have a cooler climate). Flatten it and grill for a short time on a high heat to bring out the roasted flavour.

4 smoked pheasant breasts (or 1 unsmoked pheasant or
    2 pigeons seared first under a grill)
1 litre water
7 golfball-sized green/white aubergines, de-stalked and
    cut halfway down
7 whole red chillies, stalks removed
5 shallots, peeled and cut halfway down
2 sticks lemon grass, seared and broken in two
2 cm (1 inch) piece galangal, peeled, sliced and seared
    in the flame
5 dried Jew's Ear mushrooms (optional)
½ teaspoon salt
3 pieces dried buffalo skin, soaked for several hours in
    water (optional)
5 cm (2 inch) piece of *sa-khan* (optional)

1 small ball sticky rice, flattened and seared, or a
teaspoon of cornflour
2 dessertspoons *paa-dek* water or anchovy sauce
(optional)
2 handfuls green beans, chopped into 5 cm (2 inch)
pieces
1 handful finely sliced banana flower (optional)
2 spring onions, chopped small
1 handful dill
2 handfuls sweet basil (and *pak tam ning* if available)
4 Szechwan peppercorns (optional)

Place the smoked pheasant under the hottest grill you have
and sear it for 3 minutes, but not long enough to let all the fat
run off. Cut the pheasant breasts into bite-sized pieces.

Place a pot on the stove and fill it with a litre or so of water.
Prepare the aubergines, chillies and shallots. Sear the lemon
grass and galangal and add to the water with the pheasant
pieces, mushrooms and salt (also add the buffalo skin and *sa-
khan* if available). Bring to the boil, lower the heat to a simmer
and cover.

If you want a thicker *or*, take a ball of cooked sticky rice
and squash it flat in your hands, sear it on an open flame until
it puffs a little and blackens, then drop it, little bit, by little bit,
into the stew. Alternatively, you can thicken the stew with a
little cornflour. Add the *paa-dek* water if you wish.

After about twenty to thirty minutes, the aubergines will
be cooked but still hold their shape. At this point remove the
whole chillies with a slotted spoon, place in a mortar and
pound them to a paste. Now do the same with the aubergines
and follow this with the shallots until all the ingredients are
thoroughly mixed. Look at the remaining *or*, you may need to

add some more water if it is too dry. The liquid should just cover the meat.

Usually you would add the pounded mixture back into the *or*, but we found that British pheasant is a bit tough and needs to cook longer, so set the mortar aside and slow-cook the meat for another forty minutes, then add the aubergine, shallot, and chilli mixture back in and bring it back to a simmer.

Now add the green beans and cover for three minutes (the beans must stay bright green or you have overcooked them). Add the banana flower. Add the dill, sweet basil and spring onions and serve immediately. A few Sechuan peppercorns may be added at the last moment for an added zing in the likely event that you have no *sa-kwan*.

Traditionally, at the palace, this was eaten with sticky rice mixed with pickled fish and a light spinach soup. Serve with a plate of fresh salad leaves, cucumber slices, and raw aubergines.

Kha-Style Green Chilli *Jaew* – A favourite of the King

12 small green chillies
4 cloves garlic
3 shallots
salt

Skewer the chillies, garlic cloves and shallots and roast over charcoal until totally blackened. Remove the stalks from the chillies, peel the garlic cloves and shallots and pound to a paste with the salt. Serve in a small bowl.

GENERAL RECIPES

Lao Stocks and Basic Soup

In Laos, nothing is wasted in the kitchen and most people keep a stockpot simmering away in a corner somewhere. These stocks simmer uncovered for hours on end and simply consist of meat or fish bones, galangal or lemon grass (or both together), garlic and sometimes shallots. These are the 'vital' first ingredients as the aromatics counter the 'smell' of the meat (the 'highness' inevitable in a hot climate where there are few fridges). Other herbs and additives tend to be added later to suit a particular recipe when it is being made. Lao stocks are *much lighter* than Western stocks, and this is the key to Lao cooking. The stock is used as a base to enhance other flavours and ingredients. It must not overpower the dish.

Since few of us can stay at home for a whole day to watch a stockpot, you could make a quicker stock in advance and freeze it in bags. In the recipes below I have used meat and fish plus Southeast Asian herbs and vegetables to give them the appropriate perfume, but you can experiment with your own stocks. If you want a really lemony stock, add lime leaves during cooking and squeeze a lime into it at the end.

Laotians often serve extremely simple soups with their meals which consist of water, salt, lemon grass, *paa-dek* and maybe some galangal, simmered together. They then throw in other items such as watercress, tomato or local leaves and herbs at the last moment and serve it in a communal bowl as a refresher of the palette. I leave the concoctions of such soups up to you.

SOUTH-EAST ASIAN CHICKEN/PORK/BEEF STOCK

1 whole chicken, including skin (also feet and head if possible),
   cut into eight pieces
or 1 kg (2 lbs) fish bits including heads, tails and bones
   (trout, bass, catfish)
or pork ribs, not too fatty
or 1.5 kg (3 lbs) beef soup bones
1 medium red onion, chopped roughly, or eight shallots
3 spring onions, trimmed and snapped between your hands
3 cloves garlic, sliced
2 stalks lemon grass, left whole but tied in a knot or snapped
   in two
2 lime leaves, torn (optional)
1 piece galangal or ginger, 2 cm (one inch) long, cracked with
   the heel of your hand (optional)
1 red chilli (optional)
2 tablespoons fish sauce
10 black peppercorns
½ teaspoon salt

For chicken or fish stock, place the chicken or fish in a large pot with all the ingredients except the salt. Cover with water and bring to a fast boil over a high heat. Reduce the heat to a good simmer. After an hour you can remove any large pieces of chicken meat that may be falling from the breast and leg bones to use in another dish; the meat will still have flavour and it is delicious (it is a favourite with my little girl).

If you are making pork or beef stock, cover the meat bones with water and bring to a boil on a high heat, cook for ten minutes then remove. Throw out the water, rinse the meat and clean the pot. Put the rinsed meat and bones back in the pot cover with clean water and add all the other ingredients except the salt. Continue as below.

Let the stock simmer with the lid off, occasionally removing any scum, until the stock has reduced by two-thirds, and then season with salt or fish sauce if necessary. The result should be a tasty broth with a light, dilute flavour; if it is strong and sticky then you have cooked it too long for Lao recipes. Strain the stock and use immediately, or freeze in bags for up to three months.

SOUTH-EAST ASIAN VEGETABLE STOCK

450 g (1 lb) turnips, peeled and chopped into big cubes,
   or Asian white radish
4 medium carrots
2 stalks celery or two leeks, roughly chopped
2 stalks lemon grass, tied in a knot
2 tablespoons Asian coriander roots
1 piece ginger, 2.5 cm (1 inch) long, cracked with the heel
   of your hand
10 peppercorns
$\frac{1}{2}$ teaspoon salt

Place the vegetables in a big pot and cover with water. Bring to the boil and then lower to a simmer, skimming occasionally. Reduce by two-thirds or more, adding salt if needed. Strain the stock and use immediately or freeze in bags for up to three months.

Lay and Khamtoune's Luang Prabang-Style Fish *Laap* made in the traditional manner

This recipe for *laap* was shown to me by my friend Tiao Khamtoun's brother, Tiao Phanouvong Sisouphanh (nicknamed Lay). The Tiao in their names refers to their royal title, as they are related to the late king Si Savangtthana. They both now live in England, having fled after the revolution in fear of death. They are wonderfully generous people and I have spent many hours in Khamtoun's kitchen chatting and cooking, my favourite occupation.

This particular *laap* is unique to Luang Prabang. It has a soft texture and is eaten with a spoon. It has a sweet, aromatic flavour and is served with sour fish soup, which acts as a counterbalance. The fish is used raw, as is traditional, though most Westerners like it cooked. If you want to cook it you must mix the ingredients first and then dry-cook them in a pan for a few moments. In this recipe we use sea bass, but wild salmon could be used instead. Do not use farmed salmon or the flesh becomes sloppy when minced.

- 2 wild sea bass, about 675 g (1 ½ lb) each, scraped to produce 225 g (½ lb) raw flesh
- 225 g (½ lb) golfball-sized green/white aubergines, destalked and cut in half
- 3 spring onions, white part only
- 2 cloves garlic in their skins
- 3 dried red chillies
- 4 tablespoons or more *paa-dek*, English-style, or 1 tablespoon anchovy sauce
- 2.5 cm (1 inch) piece galangal – peeled and finely chopped
- 1 tablespoon roasted rice powder
- fish sauce to taste
- 1 small handful Thai coriander, finely chopped
- 5 springs mint, finely chopped
- 3 spring onions, green part only, finely chopped
- cooked fish skin, finely chopped

Fillet the fish from tail to head (you can get your fishmonger to do this, but it goes against the Lao ideal of ultimate freshness, so it is better to do it yourself). Then with a sharp broad knife hold the tail end of a fillet and scrape the flesh away from the skin into a pile. Do not chop it up or put it in a blender as this will ruin the texture of this particular type of *laap*. Repeat this for all four fillets.

Take the prepared aubergines, spring onions, garlic and chillies (pricked, or they will pop) and sear them on a gas ring until they are totally black (my friend Khamtoune uses a heat-diffuser mesh over

the flame and does them all at once). It is important that these ingredients are seared totally jet-black as it imparts a particular flavour.

Meanwhile make the *paa-dek* water (see p. 332).

Having made the *paa-dek* you can now begin to make the *laap*.
In a pestle and mortar, take the seared dried chilli and pound to a
paste. Add the galangal, pound again to a paste, then add the garlic and spring onion. Pound all this together and then add the
aubergine and continue to pound until it is a soft mash of the mixed
ingredients. This will take about 10 minutes.

Add a ladle of warm fish stock from the soup. Pound some more
and then add the raw fish. Add four tablespoons of English *paa-dek*
water. Now take a wooden spoon and beat the mixture as though it
were an omelette. The aim is to double the size of the mixture by beat-
ing it with warm stock. (If the stock is too hot or cold it will not work.)

Beat the mixture for another 10 minutes, tasting it continually,
and add four tablespoons of fish stock three times, plus several
squirts of fish sauce. (The smell of galangal and the seared chilli
and garlic is extremely aromatic and masks the smell of the fish.)
The aim is to create a light purée, almost like a mousse.

When you have attained the right consistency, add four tablespoons of roasted rice powder and fold it into the mixture. (At this
point, if you won't eat it raw you can cook it in a dry pan with no oil.)

Fold in the chopped coriander, mint and spring onion.

The *laap* should be like an aerated purée in texture, grey in
colour due to the scorched ingredients, and it should taste sweet,
salty and perfumed. In Laos it is served with salad leaves and bitter herb leaves. Here, it goes well with radicchio leaves, the sour
soup and sticky rice.

HOW TO COOK STICKY RICE

Buy a packet of glutinous rice from your Asian supermarket or mail
order (see suppliers, p. 337). Pour out as much as you would like to
serve, because it does not expand when cooked unlike fluffy rice.

Put into a bowl with plenty of water and soak overnight, changing the water a couple of times. If you forgot to soak it overnight then you can soak it for a minimum of two hours. Give the rice a final rinse and drain it.

Get a steamer (a conical bamboo one is best, available cheaply in Thai supermarkets or see p. 337, as it adds a certain perfume, but any steamer will do). If the holes in your steamer are large then line the bottom with greaseproof paper pierced with 20 holes so the grains don't fall through.

Fill the bottom with water, the top with your drained rice and steam for approximately 25 minutes without the lid, turning it over in one lump halfway through. If you are using a conical rice steamer, take it off the heat halfway through and toss it a bit. The rice should lift from the bottom and turn over in one lump. If you are using a flat steamer, use a spatula to turn it, or roll it around as it is steaming.

When ready, the rice should look opaque and firm. If it's gooey you've cooked it too long, if it's crunchy, not enough. (Laotians cook it perfectly every time. I, however, still sometimes get a gooey bit at the bottom of the conical basket. I've learnt to live with it.)

Take it out of the steamer and roll it around on the work surface to release a bit of water, then put it in a basket and serve. To eat, roll it into a ball in your hand and use to soak up things as you would with bread.

The great thing about sticky rice is that you can eat it for days – just shove it back in the steamer and give it a good blast and there's your lunch.

(N.B. Once cooked, don't store it in the fridge – it goes hard.)

ROASTED RICE POWDER

This can be bought in packets in Asian stores, but it does not smell the same so it is better to make your own on the day.

Place a couple of handfuls of sticky rice into a dry wok or skillet on a medium heat. Roast the rice, shaking the wok frequently and stirring with a wooden spoon to cook it evenly. The rice is done when it looks toasted and golden brown.

Transfer it to a bowl to cool. Grind the roasted rice in a coffee grinder or pound in a pestle and mortar to a fine powder. Store in a jar.

THE FAMOUS *PAA-DEK* OF LAOS

You can buy Thai and Philippino versions of *paa-dek* in jars [see suppliers on p. 336] which will give you the most authentic Lao flavour.

I have also found a good alternative in a bottled anchovy sauce available in most Asian supermarkets (see suppliers, p. 335), which you can just splash in to give a near-as-damn-it authentic flavour with the added bonus that it is easier to handle. Or use English bottled versions of anchovies and salt (*not* vinegar), or anchovy paste in a tube.

If none of these are available, you can make your own, as many British Laotions do in an emergency.

HOME-MADE ENGLISH *PAA-DEK* WATER

Place 400 ml (^{3}/$_4$ pint) of fish stock (or half a stock cube with ^{1}/$_2$ litre/ 1 pint of water) in a small saucepan with 10 tinned anchovy fillets (in oil). Bring to the boil and simmer for a few minutes until the anchovies have almost dissolved. Sieve out the lumps and boil vigorously for another few minutes to produce a salty, muddy brown liquid. Yum.

Desserts

Laotians don't eat dessert in the way we do in the West, as all the dishes come to the table at once rather than in courses. Instead, sweet things tend to be eaten as snacks between meals, on the run, as a picnic or sitting at a market stall. Rice, as usual, predominates, and simple sweetened rice pudding made from slow-cooked and stirred rice, water and sugar is the most common sweet dish, on a par with fresh fruit served peeled and chopped on a communal platter. Below I have listed a few things that could be made as dessert and served at the end of a meal if you so wished.

FRUIT IN ICED COCONUT MILK

Vandara makes a delicious version of this with her sweet home-grown papaya, but you could use mango or melon instead, or simply sliced bananas. The fruit should be perfectly ripe.

> 800 ml (1 ½ pints) fresh coconut milk, or two tins
> 2 tablespoons palm sugar or brown caster sugar
> 1 teaspoon salt
> 1 large papaya, *or* 3 mangoes, *or* 1 honeydew melon,
>   peeled and cut into 5 cm (2 inch) cubes

Warm the coconut milk in a saucepan and dissolve the palm sugar and the salt into the liquid. Bring the milk to the boil, remove from the heat immediately, leave to cool a little, then place in the fridge until really cold. Add the fruit chunks, and crushed ice if you like. Serve with a sprig of mint.

BANANA RICE BALLS

My favourite snack. In Laos they are made very sweet, but I use less sugar in my recipe because I like the contrast of the semi-sweet surround with the very sweet ripe banana centre. You may wish to add more.

> 1 tin coconut milk
> 300 g (12 oz) cooked sticky rice
> 5 tablespoons palm sugar or brown caster sugar
> ½ teaspoon salt
> 2 very ripe bananas, sliced, then cut in quarters

Heat the coconut milk in a pan until it reaches boiling point. Add the sticky rice, sugar and salt and stir constantly until all the liquid has been absorbed. Empty the contents of the pan on to a piece of foil or baking parchment and flatten it down with the back of a spoon to the thickness of 1 cm (1/3 inch).

When completely cool, peel off a rough circle of about 6 cm (2 ½ inches) across, flatten it in the cup of your hand, place a quarter of a slice of banana in the centre and mould the rice around it. Roll it into a firmer ball with your hands and then drop it into the bowl of desiccated coconut to coat it all over. Place on a serving dish.

They may be a bit lumpy at first, but you get better with prac- tice. If you find it easier you can make baton shapes instead. Repeat until you have run out of rice and then refrigerate for an hour to firm them up. Serve as a snack. Or eat them for breakfast, as I sometimes do.

STICKY RICE WITH MANGO

250 ml (½ pint) coconut milk
3–5 tablespoons palm sugar or brown caster sugar
½ teaspoon salt
250 g (10 oz) cooked sticky rice
2 ripe mangoes, peeled and sliced or diced

Heat the coconut milk in a pan until it reaches boiling point. Add the sugar and salt and stir constantly until the sugar has dissolved. Add the sticky rice and mix thoroughly. Place the sweetened rice in a clean bowl to cool.

When cool, remove from the bowl and flatten down on a serving platter or separate out on to several plates and serve with mango on top.

LAO INGREDIENTS AND SUPPLIERS

South-east Asian Supermarkets

This is by no means an exhaustive list, but I can recommend the following stores in various parts of the UK.

London
Amaranth Thai Supermarket, 346 Garratt Lane, SW18
Tel. 020 8871 3466

Talad Thai Supermarket, 320 Upper Richmond Road, SW15
Tel. 020 8789 8084

Tawana Supermarket, 18 Chepstow Road, W2
Tel. 020 7221 6316

Wing Tai Supermarket, 13 Electric Avenue, SW9
Tel. 020 7738 5898

Glasgow
China Town Groceries, 42–46 New City Road
Tel. 0141 353 2338

Manchester
Kim's Thai Food Store, 46 George Street
Tel. 0161 228 6263

Birmingham
Wing Yip Superstore, 375 Nechells Park Road
Tel. 0121 327 6618

Specialist Ingredients and Suppliers

Lao ingredients can be quite hard to track down, but here are a few suggestions:

Paa-dek:

Mam Ca Sak, or Pickled Gouramy Fish, made by Suree Pantai Oriental Foods and distributed in the UK by Manning Impex Ltd, Aldershot, GU12 4DL. Tel. 01252 350288.

Mam Nem or Asian Anchovy Sauce, and a British one, Geo Watkins Anchovy Sauce, should be available in good delicatessens.

GIA Anchovy Paste can often be found in the tinned fish section of supermarkets.

Fermented soya bean sauce

Hot Bean Sauce, made by Yeo's, is commonly found in Asian stores.

Chilli jaew

Chilli Paste with Sweet Basil Leaves is distributed by Thai Boy.
Tel. 0208 737 2727.
Email: *info@thaiboy-foods.com*

Coconut milk

Found in most supermarkets. Look at the ingredients label and check that it reads 'coconut milk/cream and water'. Some tins include corn starch and unnecessary chemical preservatives.

Frozen coconut water from young coconuts is sometimes available in the freezer section of Asian shops.

Lao River Algar Snacks (Kai Pen)

Available from *www.lotusfoods.com* tel: 00 1 866 972 6879

Lao coffee beans

Available from *www.jamesgourmetcoffee.com* tel: 0870 787 0233

Ant eggs

These are sometimes available, frozen, in specialist Asian supermarkets, but you have to ask around.

Canned eggs are available from *www.dcothal.com/food/insects/htm*

Smoked pheasant and smoked pigeon

Available from *info@oksmoke.co.uk*, tel: 0184 860 0298

Sticky rice, noodles, preserved herbs, coconut milk

Available from *www.thai-taste.com*, tel: 0870 241 1960

Frog's legs

Available from *www.simsonsfisheries.co.uk*

Lao conical bamboo rice steamer, basket and pot

You can purchase a steamer, basket and pot at many Thai supermarkets. I buy mine at a very low cost from Tawana Supermarket, 18 Chepstow Road, London W2, tel. 020 7221 6316.

ACKNOWLEDGEMENTS

My heartfelt thanks go to all those mentioned in the book who with typical Lao openness and charm helped me on my journey and generously shared their local knowledge and recipes. In particular, I owe my deepest gratitude to Vandara, Rachel and Somphan who treated me like one of the family. I would like to thank Khamtoune Sisophan, Soun Vannithone, Lay Sisophan, their families and the Lao Community Centre in Haggerston for their friendship, support and advice.

A special mention goes to Alan Davidson for advising me with a lightness of touch that only a wise man can give to an amateur enthusiast. His help has been invaluable and his friendship an honour. And, Juliet Munro, my chief sub, for reading everything as I wrote and advising me with such enthusiasm and kindness, thank you.

I would also like to thank: Elizabeth Zeschin for inspiring me, and for all her valuable and selfless help along the way – that goes for Ros Belford too; Kitty Bland, Janine Furness, Lizzy Pole, Christine Guerrier, Luke Freeman and Wendy Deaner for cheering me on; Davina Lilly for keeping me on the straight path; my agent, Lizzy Kremer at Ed Victor, for being a great agent and a friend; my publisher Katy Follain for her unwavering encouragement; and the Arvon Foundation course led by William Dalrymple, Katie Hickman and Rory Maclean – it made all the difference.

And last but not least, my mother, Patricia, and sister, Rebecca, without whom I would never have seen the world or had such fun in it.

My thanks, for their help via conversations and correspondence, also go to:

Bill Elliot, Cave Biologist, University of Texas; Oliver Bandmann, Ban Khilly, Luang Prabang; Ian Baird, Dr Ian Glover, Professor Emeritus Reader of South-east Asian Archaeology, University College, London; Dr Peter Bellwood, Professor of Archaeology, Australian National University; D.J. Jukes, Sandra Yuck, Joost Foppes, Isabel Souvanlasy, Tim Pfaff, Yannick Upravan, Sheena Sloane, Ruth Borthwick, Boualin Pitommasin, Andre Pilecki and Virginia Lagarde.

BAD TEMPERED DUCK IN A BASKET

SELECTED BIBLIOGRAPHY

Anderson, Edward F. *Plants and People of the Golden Triangle*, Dioscrides Press, Oregon, 1993

Bounyavong, Outhine. *Mother's Beloved, Stories from Laos*, Silkworm Books, Chiang Mai, 1999

Ciochon, Russel & Jamie, James. 'Laos Keeps Its Urns', *www.archaeology.about.com*, USA, 2002

Chazée, Laurent. *The People of Laos: Rural and Ethnic Diversity*, White Lotus Press, Bangkok, 1999

Chazée, Laurent. *Oiseaux Du Laos, Identification, Distribution et Chasse*, Laurent Chazée, Vientiane, 1994

Cranbrook, Earl of. *Mammals of South-East Asia*, Oxford University Press, 1991

Clendon, K.R. 'The role of forest food resources in village livelihood systems', NTFP Project Report I, March/April 1998, & II, September/October 1998: IUCN

Cummings, Joe. *Lonely Planet Guide: Laos*, Lonely Planet, London, 2002

Cummings, Joe. *Lao phrase book*, Lonely Planet, London, 1995

de Berval, Rene (in collaboration). 'Notes from the Kingdom of Laos, 1959', a special issue of the cultural monthly *France-Asie*, printed in France by A. Bontemps Co. LTD, Limoges, 1959

de Marini, G.F. *A New and Interesting Description of the Lao Kingdom*, White Lotus Press, Bangkok, 1998

Davidson, Alan. *Fish and Fish Dishes of Laos*, Prospect Books, Totnes, Devon, 1995 (reprinted 2003)

Engel, David H. & Suchart Phummai. *What's That TREE? A field guide to tropical plants of Asia*, Times Editions, Singapore, 2000

Evans, Grant. *The Politics of Ritual and Remembrance: Laos since 1975*, Silkworm Books, Chiang Mai, 2000

Evans, Grant *et al. Where China Meets Southeast Asia: Social and Cultural Change in the Border Regions*, White Lotus Press: Bangkok, 2000

Evans, Grant. *Xieng Khouang – A Guide*, booklet available from White Lotus Press, Bangkok

Francis, Charles M. *Mammals of Thailand & South-East Asia*, Asia Books, Bangkok, 2001

Grabowsky, Dr Volker & Walther Kasper-Sickerman. Essay on Muang Sing, 2002, *www.haw-hamburg.dej*

Gosling, Betty. *Old Luang Prabang*, Oxford University Press, 1996

Harmand, F.J. *Laos and the Hilltribes of IndoChina*, White Lotus Press, Bangkok, 1997

Hutton, Wendy. *Tropical Vegetables of Thailand*, Asia Books, Bangkok, 1997

IUCN Technical Report. 'Community Fisheries in Lao PDR – A survey of techniques and issues,' 1994

IUCN Status Report, Richard Salter. *Wildlife in Lao PDR*, 1993

Johnson, Curtis. *The Laos of North Siam*, White Lotus Press, Bangkok, 1998

Kremmer, Christopher. *Stalking the Elephant Kings*, Silkworm Books, Chaing Mai, 1997

Kuper, Jessica ed. *The Anthropologists' Cookbook*, Keegan Paul International, London, 1997

Lefevre, E. *Travels in Laos: The fate of Sip Song Pana and Muong Sing (1894–1896)*, White Lotus, Bangkok, 1995

Mansfield, Stephen. *Lao Hill Tribes*, Oxford University Press, 2000

Marcus, Russell. *English-Lao, Lao-English Dictionary*, (revised edn., Charles E. Tuttle Company, Singapore, 2001

Mixay, Somsanouk. *Treasures of Lao Literature*, Vientiane Times Publications, 2000

Motono, Akira & Noriko Negishi. *Butterflies of Laos*, Kirihara Shoten, Tokyo, 1989

Perazic, Elizabeth. 'Little Laos', *National Geographic*, USA, January 1960

Pourret, Jess G. *The Yao, The Mien and Mun Yao in China, Laos and Thailand*, Art Media Resources, Chicago, 2002

St Ruth, Diana & Richard. *Theravada Buddhism*, Global books, Kent, 1998

Sepul, Rene & Cic Olsson. *Luang Prabang*, Raintrees, Vientiane, 1998

Simms, Peter & Sanda. *The Kingdoms of Laos; Six Hundred Years of History*, Curzon, Surrey, 1999

Sing, Phia. *Traditional Recipes of Laos*, Prospect Books, Totnes, Devon, 1995

Storrs, Adrian & Jimmie. *Discovering Trees and Shrubs in Thailand and S.E. Asia*, Tecpress books, Thailand

Stuart-Fox, Martin. *A History of Laos*, Cambridge University Press, 1997

Vannaboupha, Douangchanh. *Let's Speak Lao*, Vientiane, 2000

Veevers-Carter, W. *The Garden of Eden*, Oxford University Press, 1986

Weiwen, Zhang & Qingnan Zeng: *In Search of China's Minorities*, New World Press, Beijing, 1993

Lao Websites: *www.global.lao.net*; *www.savannanet.com*; *www.theboatlanding.laopdr.com*; www.unesco.org; *www.laoworld.com*; *www.uxolao.org*; *www.lan-xang.com*; *www.vientianetimes.com*.